J. A. Jorge
N. M. Correia
H. Jones
M. B. Kamegai (eds.)

Multimedia 2001

Proceedings of the Eurographics Workshop
in Manchester, United Kingdom,
September 8 – 9, 2001

Eurographics

Springer-Verlag Wien GmbH

Professor Dr. Joaquim Jorge
Departamento de Engenharia Informática, IST/Technical University of Lisbon, Lisbon, Portugal

Professor Dr. Nuno Correia
Departamento de Informática, New University of Lisbon, FCT/UNL, Caparica, Portugal

Professor Dr. Huw Jones
Chair of Landsdown Centre for Electronic Arts, Middlesex University, Barnet, UK

Professor Dr. Meera Blattner Kamegai
Department of Applied Science, University of California, Davis, Las Vegas, USA

Typesetting: Camera-ready by authors

With 94 Figures

ISSN 0946-2767

ISBN 978-3-211-83769-6 ISBN 978-3-7091-6103-6 (eBook)
DOI 10.1007/978-3-7091-6103-6

Preface

This book presents the results of EG Multimedia'2001, the Sixth Eurographics Workshop on Multimedia, held in Manchester, UK, on the 8th and 9th of September, 2001. All six such workshops are successful examples of fruitful international cooperation under the auspices of the Eurographics working group on Multimedia. The workshop covered a wide range of subjects, from media production to content processing and delivery, with a special focus on issues related to interactive video environments. These included standards and approaches for interactive television, hypervideo, collaborative video, augmented reality, mobile multimedia, the integration of TV and the Web, content analysis, processing and presentation. The program consisted of two invited keynote presentations, eighteen technical papers and one demonstration, attracting a diverse world-wide group of thirty attendees. Technical papers were organized in six sessions spanning the two days: 3D in Multimedia, Multimedia Architectures and Authoring, Video and Coding, Content Based Retrieval and Security, Interactive Media and Interactive TV. The demonstration presented a multimedia system for aerobics and fitness training, exploring the combination of sound and interactive graphics in an effective manner. The keynote presentation by V. Michael Bove provided insights into new architectures for large scale pervasive computing. The second invited presentation by Glorianna Davenport discussed the relations between creativity and interactive movies as participatory art enabled by new media.

An international program committee of 27 specialist experts reviewed all submissions and their recommendations were used for selecting the final papers:

Ann Blandford, Middlesex Univ., UK
Meera B. Kamegai, CommunityVision inc., USA
V. Michael Bove, MIT Media Lab, USA
John F. Buford, Verizon, USA
Teresa Chambel, FC/UL, Portugal
Nuno Correia, UNL, Portugal
Roger Dannenberg, CMU, USA
Glorianna Davenport, MIT Media Lab, USA
Marc Davis, amova.com, USA
David De Roure, Univ. of Southampton, UK
David Duce, Oxford Brookes Univ., UK
Pedro Faria Lopes, ISCTE, Portugal
Ephraim Glinert, NSF, USA
Nuno Guimarães, FC/UL, Portugal
W. Herzner, Aust. Rsch. Ctr. Seibersdorf, Austria
Nicholas Higgett, de Montfort Univ., UK
Gareth Jones, University of Exeter, UK
Huw Jones, Middlesex Univ., UK
Joaquim Jorge, INESC, Portugal
Rainer Lienhart, Intel, USA
Jonatas Manzolli, Univ. of Campinas, Brazil
Pietro Marchisio, CSELT, Italy
Ryohei Nakatsu, ATR MIC Rsch. Labs, Japan
M. Noelle, Aust. Rsch. Ctr. Seibersdorf, Austria
Mario Rui Gomes, IST/UTL, Portugal
Matthew Turk, UCSB, USA
Hong Jiang Zhang, Microsoft, USA

We thank all authors and presenters for the quality of their contributions and the Program Committee Members for their support and cooperation. Thanks go also to Roger Hubbold and Nigel John from University of Manchester for their help with the overall organization, Janet Adnams and Mary McDerby from MCC for their help with registration and local arrangements. Paula Centeno was exceedingly helpful with all secretarial details and pre-workshop proceedings. We would also like to thank the Institute for International Scientific Cooperation of the Portuguese Ministry for Science and Technology and the British Council for their financial support.

Nuno Correia, New University of Lisbon, Portugal
Huw Jones, Middlesex University, UK
Workshop Chairs

Meera Blattner Kamegai, CommunityVision Inc., USA
Joaquim A Jorge, INESC and Technical University of Lisbon, Portugal
Program Chairs

September 2001

List of Contributors

Abreu, Jorge
Akanksha
Allison, Colin
Almeida, Pedro
Alves, Renata Sofia
Ar, Sigal
Bateman, Martin
Batista, Thais V.
Boyd Davis, Stephen
Branco, Vasco
Câmara, António S.
Chang, E.-C.
Cohen-Or, Daniel
Demartini, C.
Elad, Michael
Fellner, Dieter
Fels, Sidney
Guan, X.
Hauser, Juergen
Huang, Z.
Jones, Huw
Kankanhalli, Mohan
Leite, Luís Eduardo
Löffler, Jobst
Lohse, Marco
Mallinder, Hugh
Manzolli, Jonatas
Montrucchio, Bartolomeo
Montuschi, P.
Morsdorf, Felix
Nobre, Edmundo
Noimark, Yuval
Prabhakaran, B.
Quaglia, Davide
Ruddle, Alan
Ruiz, Jr, C. R.
Sanna, A.
Slusallek, Philipp
Sousa Filho, Guido
Tal, Ayellet
Tian, Jing
Volmer, Stephan
Wambach, Patrick
Wu, Y.
Zvi, Tali

Contents

Content Based Retrieval and Security

Interactive Media

Interactive TV

Demonstration

Self-Organizing Multimedia and Extremely Distributed Architectures (Keynote Presentation)

William Butera and V. Michael Bove, Jr.

MIT Media Laboratory, Cambridge MA USA
{bill, vmb}@media.mit.edu, http://www.media.mit.edu/~vmb/obmg.html

Abstract. The Object-Based Media Group at the MIT Media Laboratory is developing robust, self-organizing programming models for dense ensembles of ultra-miniaturized computing nodes which are deployed by the thousands in bulk fashion, *e.g.* embedded into building materials. While such systems potentially offer almost unlimited computation for multimedia purposes, the individual devices contain tiny amounts of memory, lack explicit addresses, have wireless communication ranges only in the range of millimeters to centimeters, and are expected to fail at high rates. An unorthodox approach to handling of multimedia data is required in order to achieve useful, reliable work in such an environment. We describe the hardware and software strategies, and demonstrate several examples showing the processing of images and sound in such a system.

1 Introduction

We begin by observing that semiconductor process technology will shortly arrive at the point where autonomous computing elements – possibly coupled with sensing or actuating devices – can be scaled to the size of large sand grains and sold at bulk prices. It then will become possible to move computing out of the sort of packaging in which it is currently housed and make it part of the built environment, embedding processors in rboards, and into everyday objects such as furniture, clothing and random surfaces. As a representative embodiment, consider the architecture advanced by Sussman, Abelson and Knight [1]: ultra-miniaturized computing nodes each fitted with an on board microprocessor, 50K of memory and a wireless transceiver, all shrunk down to the size of a pin head and powered parasitically.

In the domain of interest, these nodes would be embedded in a 2D surface (such as the plywood in a table top) with a density on the order of tens of thousands per square meter. Positioning would be pseudo-random, with no local restrictions on density or regularity. Once exposed to power, they should boot and self organize their local address space. External I/O would be via physical proximity with an object fitted with a transceiver whose protocols are identical to the transceivers on the chips.

In our research we adopt a hardware reference model constructed around a single IC with dimensions 2 mm x 2 mm. Onboard subsystems include a block for power harvesting, a full featured microprocessor, a wireless transceiver for inter-particle communication within a radius of at most a few centimeters, a 50 MHz internal clock, a ROM for the operating system, and approximately 50K RAM for program and data space. More detail on the hardware characteristics of the proposed system can be found in [2] and [3].

2 Software Model

Such an ensemble of processing nodes, running asynchronously (and perhaps intermittently) and communicating locally via an ad hoc network places unusual demands on the programming model. Worst among these are:

- *Asynchrony:* Clock level synchrony is out of the question. Two neighboring particles cannot be guaranteed to have the same clock rate, let alone phase lock. Event level synchrony also seems beyond reach. In an unknown topology with sporadic unit failures, there is no way for a process on one particle to predict what processes will be running on a neighboring particle. Code running on one particle should never explicitly synchronize to events generated on another particle.
- *Extreme Fault Tolerance:* Allied with the inherent asynchrony is the propensity of individual particles to fail completely, whether because of lack of power, hardware problems, interference with communications, or physical damage (*e.g.* hammering a nail into a surface filled with these processors may disable one or more.)
- *Network Locality:* Particles can communicate directly only with other particles in the immediate spatial vicinity. While the size of the neighborhood can vary substantially, current experiments run on neighborhood sizes ranging from 8 to 20 particles.
- *Adaptive Topology:* Any ensemble of embedded particles will have final topology which is unknown at the time that much of the application code is written. While it will always be possible to recover an approximate coordinate system at run-time, no application code should rely on a particular spatial layout of the processors.
- *Code Compactness:* On-particle memory is very limited, inter-particle bandwidth is slow compared to processor speed, and there is no external support for virtual memory. Functions running on a given particle should therefore be self-contained and sized to fit completely in a single particle.
- *Shared Data:* Nevertheless, the utility of a single particle's computation will often go up if it has access to results from local computations on neighboring particles. With the caveat that no process can predict what processes are running in the neighborhood, tagged data passed within the neighborhood should be available to processes running on a given particle.
- *Mobility:* Inter-particle migration of code segments will increase both the functionality of the individual particles and the adaptability of the overall

system. The restriction here is that exact trajectory of the migrating code cannot be pre-ordained.

Programs running on a particle's microprocessor reside in the particle's RAM space. Most of the RAM is available for use as program, data, and scratch space for these programs. However, a section of the RAM is reserved for what we refer to as the I/O space – an area which is at least readable by any program running on the particle's microprocessor. A subset of the I/O space is called the HomePage. The HomePage is an area where programs can both read and write tagged data. Any program local to the particle can post to the HomePage, and posts to the HomePage are readable by all local programs.

The remainder of the I/O space is subdivided into mirrored instances of the HomePages of neighboring particles. When a program on a given particle posts a piece of tagged data to the particle's HomePage, copies of that post appear at the mirror sites of all the neighboring particles. The caveat is that the latency in the mirroring operation is unconstrained.

Collectively, the I/O space functions as a public bulletin board, where the HomePage portion is writable and the entire I/O space is readable.

At run-time, code segments migrate nomadically looking for particles on which to install themselves. In those particles where entry into the program RAM is successful, the code segments will set up shop and begin searching for relevant data in the I/O space. The side effect of the code segment's activities is additional posts to the HomePage. Often, the number of code segments seeking entry will exceed the particle's capacity. The allocation of program space is regulated by the operating system (OS) in response to competition among the code segments. Each code segment must draw its competitive advantage from the I/O space and therefore, indirectly from the activity of other code segments. The competition is arbitrated by the particle's OS. And when a particular code segment loses out, it is de-installed and passed to the output port to migrate further via diffusion.

As a platform for application development, we have developed a simulator modeled after the Gunk simulator [4]. Code segments are written as Java objects with the functions for communicating with the OS implemented as public methods. Each segment is archived individually as a serialized Java object. I/O portals, capable of mimicking the networking behavior of the particles, can be arbitrarily positioned to diffuse the code segments into the particle ensemble. Ilustrations to follow are snapshots taken from the simulator environment.

How does a particle in one location get data to particles more distant than its direct communications radius, given that there is no explicit addressing? A method that we have found useful is to diffuse a code segment that generates a gradient field tagged with a label identifying the source (Figs. 1,2). It is then possible for code segments in remote locations to "ride the gradient uphill" to communicate with the source, or indeed to migrate back in that direction. More details can be found in reference [2].

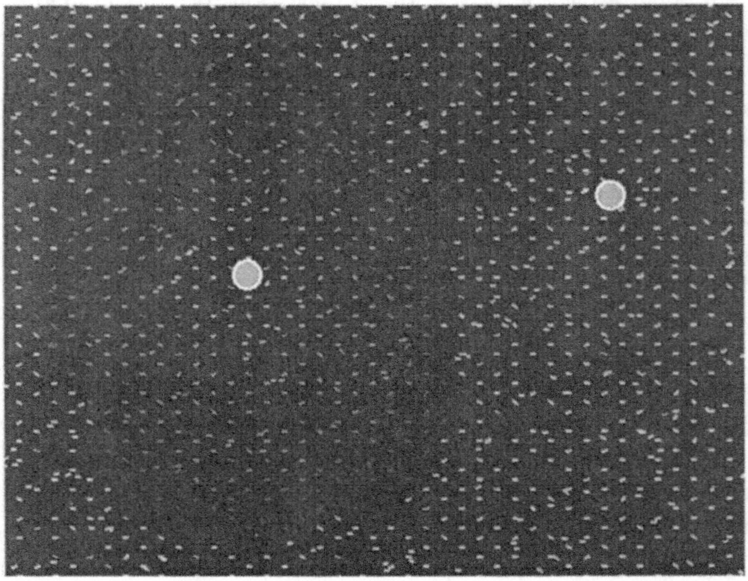

Fig. 1. Snapshot of the simulator, showing code diffusing outwardly from the source on the left.

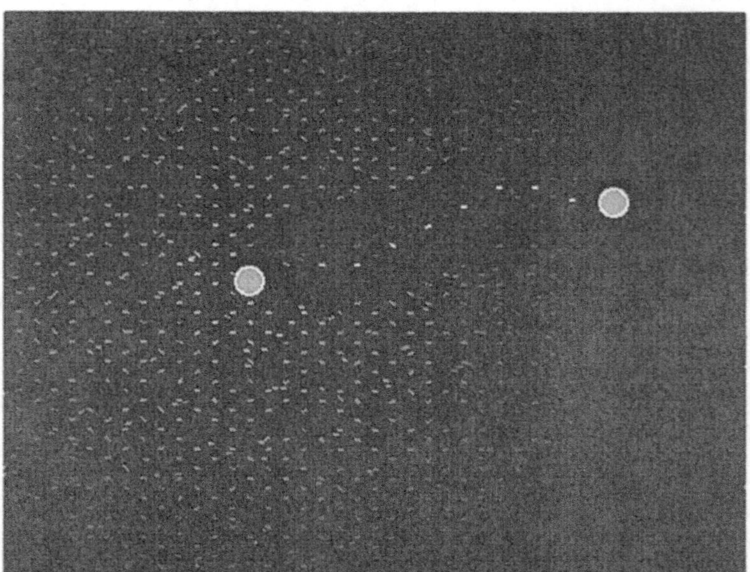

Fig. 2. The portal on the right can now route information to the portal on the left by following the gradient.

3 Multimedia Applications

The use of such a system for storage or processing of streaming multimedia data is complicated by the lack of explicit addressing. Data packets must therefore themselves know where to go and to make this decision dynamically in response to the topology of the particle ensemble.

An example application we have implemented on the simulator stores packetized audio data in the memory of a particle ensemble. Data is exchanged with the particle ensemble via streaming through arbitrarily positioned I/O portals. On input, the audio packets should diffuse outward, quickly distancing themselves from the input portal. Once the input streaming is complete, the packets should uniformly distribute themselves throughout the ensemble's collective memory. In the process, they should also randomize their position, effectively decorrelating the time codes of the packets from their spatial position. Finally, on output, the packets should reestablish their original sequential ordering prior to streaming out through an output portal.

During pre-processing, audio is packetized and each packet is embedded into a code segment called a Carrier. The Carriers also record a stream-relative time code for the packet. Once the Carriers are streamed into the particle ensemble, the transport behavior of the audio packets is defined by the migration strategy of the Carrier. At the start of every execution cycle, the Carriers determine whether they are diffusing through the ensemble or being retrieved for playback. In the diffusion mode, the Carriers migrate randomly, yielding a quasi-uniform distribution of the Carriers over the entire particle ensemble, and a spatial shuffling of the Carriers. This is the default mode and is active during storage. Carriers enter their call-back mode when they see a gradient radiating from an output portal. The posts from this gradient field list estimates of the distance back to the output portal, an ID for the requested audio stream, and range of time codes which are active and should soon be queued for playback. When a Carrier sees the post from the CallBackGradient, it does one of three things: if its time code falls within the range of active time codes, it proceeds directly toward the output portal; else if it is too close to the portal, it moves away from the gradient source, thus increasing the bandwidth efficiency in the vicinity of the portal; otherwise, it builds a local average of time codes, and adjusts its position relative to this average using the gradient field for orientation.

Using a similar diffusive strategy, one can use this system to store images. If the images are subjected to a hierarchical wavelet decomposition and the more important coefficients are replicated in multiple packets, even relatively small subsets of the particle ensemble can yield usable (if imperfect) reconstructions of the images.

4 Acknowledgments

The authors wish to thank numerous co-workers from the faculty, staff, and student body at the MIT Media Laboratory and the MIT Laboratory for Computer

Science. Particular thanks to Joshua Lifton, Stefan Agamanolis, Chris Hanson, and James McBride. This work has been supported by the Digital Life Consortium and by a fellowship from Intel corporation.

References

1. H. Abelson, D. Allen, D. Coore, C. Hanson, G. Homsy, T. Knight, R. Nagpal, E. Rauch, G. J. Sussman, and R. Weiss: Embedding the Internet: amorphous computing. Communications of the ACM **43(5)**, (2000).
2. W. Butera: Programming a Paintable Computer. PhD thesis, Massachusetts Institute of Technology, Cambridge MA USA, (2001).
3. W. Butera and V. M. Bove, Jr.: Literally Embedded Processors. Proc. SPIE Media Processors **4313**, Society of Photo-Optical Instrumentation Engineers, Bellingham WA USA, (2001).
4. S. Adams: A high level simulator for Gunk. Technical report, Massachusetts Institute of Technology AI Lab, Cambridge MA USA, (1997).

Story Networks: "The medium is the message"; The content, your souvenir
(Keynote Presentation)

Glorianna Davenport

MIT Media Lab, USA and MediaLabEurope,
Dublin, Ireland

Abstract. Storytelling -- a fundamental mode of human communication -- has adapted in form, content, and technique as new expressive technologies have appeared and evolved. The past century has witnessed the growth of storytelling tools, electronic media channels, and the mass media one-to-many "broadcast" model. Today -- as we transition to digital media, ubiquitous networking, audience-sensing devices, and computer-aided content delivery -- new models of media storytelling are emerging. These forms may be designed to find you (as opposed to your finding them); to be tradable (in a peer to peer fashion) and modifiable; to be highly distributed in the space/time; to interconnect and invite browsable exploration by crowds and/or to be aggregated over time by one or more participant authors. This talk considers the form, content and technologies associated with customizable, personalizable stories of the future.

Adaptive Visualization of Distributed 3D Documents Using Image Streaming Techniques

Jobst Löffler[1] and Dieter W. Fellner[2]

[1] Fraunhofer Institute for Media Communication, Schloss Birlinghoven, D-53754 Sankt Augustin, Germany
jobst.loeffler@imk.fhg.de
[2] Institute of Computer Graphics, Technical University of Braunschweig, Rebenring 18, D-38106 Braunschweig, Germany
d.fellner@tu-bs.de

Abstract. With the emergence of open information spaces such as digital libraries, advanced techniques for interactive visualization of complex and protected 3D documents are needed. This paper presents a new visualization concept which deals with the problems of complexity and security of digital 3D documents in open information spaces. A dynamic combination of remote and local 3D rendering is used to allow scaling of the information quantity on the client side. The software architecture SCA3D (3D Scalable Scenes Architecture), which provides functionality for adaptive visualization and protection of intellectual property rights, is presented.

1 Introduction

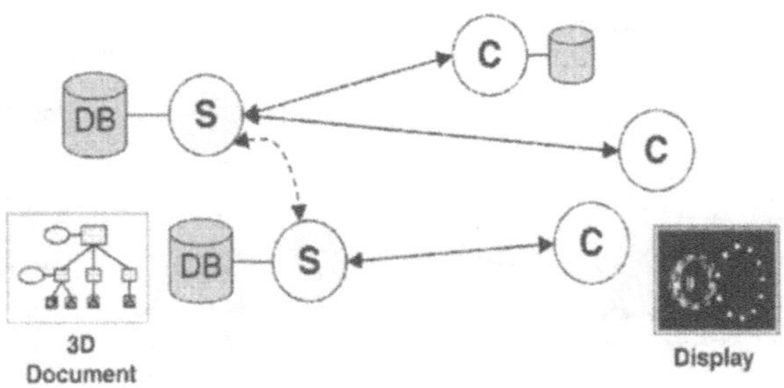

Fig. 1. 3D Visualization in open information spaces.

Distributed work involving 3D scenes as part of multimedia documents within networked information systems needs technical support for retrieval, interactive visualization and communication. A networked information system is called an open information space if access to documents and services is not restricted to a predetermined area such as to groups of previously known users and information servers. Homogeneous conditions for work with digital objects and interfaces to other information spaces are characteristics of an open information space which comprises several information servers, document databases, multiple clients and telecommunication networks between them. Figure 1 shows an open information space built up of two information servers (S) with document databases (DB), a number of users (C), who can also use additional local databases, and an interface between the information servers.

Documents of a digital library used by a group of students and a tutor working on a research project which involves 3D models (for example an architectural construction project) is a practical example. A digital library allows users to explore already existing 3D documents, generate and add new documents as a result of project work and discuss results. A digital library system should also allow visual cut-and-paste, indexing and extending 3D documents. Protection of the original document and management of document copies are important issues which need to be considered during system development. In order to exploit the full potential of the open information space, both work at the central facility on a LAN using specialized equipment and work at home using standard PCs and low-bandwidth connections should be equally possible. In this paper a visualization architecture is introduced which deals with these issues of complexity and security by using a combined approach of remote and local 3D rendering and an object-oriented document model for 3D scenes. A document-request-broker approach is presented which allows access to objects of distributed 3D documents via proxy objects with a varying level-of-information called object representations.

The remainder of the paper is organized as follows. In section 2 background information is discussed. In section 3 the software architecture SCA3D is presented, while in section 4 its adaptive behavior is evaluated. Finally, in section 5 conclusions are drawn.

2 Visualization of 3D Documents using Hybrid 2D/3D Scenes on Client Side

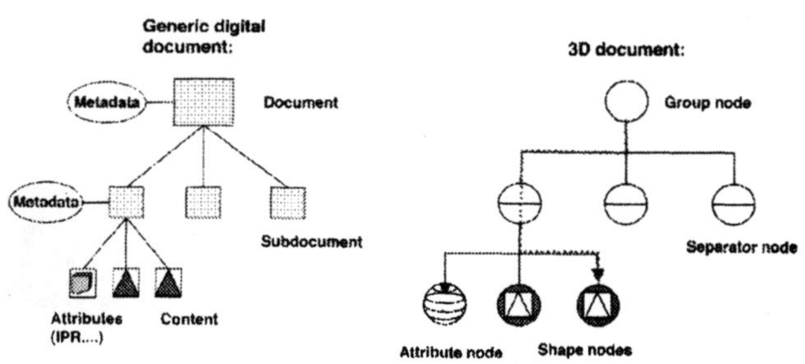

Fig. 2. Generic digital document and 3D document.

Considering 3D scenes as ordinary documents emphasizes that 3D scenes can be handled in the same way and can have similar features, such as cut-and-paste, support of retrieval, indexing or extensibility. They are subject to the same constraints with regard to security or complexity as generalized digital documents in distributed information spaces (see also [6]). 3D scenes can be seen as digital documents because both have a common composition, which comprises a structure plus the actual content (see also [10]). In Figure 2 the assembly of a generic digital document and a 3D document with path information is shown. 3D documents include structure information, which can be mapped onto an internal document model commonly known as the scene graph, and contain geometric objects as content, which are represented as shape nodes in the scene graph. Today's rendering systems, like OpenInventor [14] and Java3D, use this scene graph concept to enable interactive visualization.

The scene graph concept corresponds to an object-oriented document model, as described for example by the W3C DOM (Document Object Model) [2]. This model defines a document and its components in an object-oriented way: objects are distinguishable, they are arranged following a certain hierarchy (scene graph structure), object data and state are encapsulated and only accessible via a well-defined interface. Using the OpenInventor scene graph model, interactive visualization of 3D scenes is performed by applying actions, such as *render* or *pick*, to the scene graph and thereby changing the state of the objects. Applying a render action generates image data showing the results of a lighting simulation. Other methods of the object interface are used to construct a 3D scene by generating new objects, copying object data or removing objects from the scene graph. Object manipulation can be done using methods which change the internal state of the object, for example by calling the method *setValue(float r)* of the radius field of a sphere. Meta-data like node names or information concerning security issues, typically access rights or copyright data, can be integrated into a 3D document by filling the data fields of attribute nodes.

2.1 Combining Remote and Local 3D Visualization

Visualization of distributed 3D documents can be done by copying the data to the client's computer and using a local rendering pipeline or alternatively by rendering the data on a server machine and distributing the rendered image data. Local 3D visualization, where the entire visualization pipeline is performed on the same machine, takes advantage of available hardware acceleration for geometry processing and display. On the other hand in open information spaces there are important reasons not to distribute all geometry information without control, because security, bandwidth and performance requirements must be taken into account. Examples using local 3D visualization with data replication are presented in [1], [5] and [8]. Many of these systems are used to support cooperation with distributed 3D visualization. Alternatively, remote 3D visualization as a service can be used to let users interactively visualize 3D scenes. On the client side of a network connection a visualization application reads the images transmitted from the server and displays them using an interactive image viewer. A user interacts with a 3D scene by sending back the performed actions over a reliable connection to the server where they are applied. The advantages of such a system are that it can deal with complexity and security requirements because the original data can remain on the server. But using remote visualization also brings some disadvantages: image generation on the server side and the transmission of images with high resolution cause a delay in the interaction loop which can disturb the interactive impression. The approach of remote 3D visualization and control of distributed 3D worlds over image streams is discussed in [7], [3] and [9]. This work indicates that interactive frame rates for remote visualization are hard to reach with today's systems.

A solution that combines the advantages of both approaches and minimizes the disadvantages would combine remote and local 3D visualization and synchronize both processes in a uniting software architecture. There are still relatively few references that discuss a combination of remote and local 3D visualization One example [4] introduces a concept and system for distributed 3D visualization of volume data for medical applications. A solution that minimizes delay in remotely controlled 3D environments by selective pixel transmission and mapping onto a basis of local geometry is presented in [11].

2.2 Object Representations with Varying Level-of-Information

Geometry-based content is commonly described either as an exact representation through parametric curves and surfaces or as polygonal 3D meshes such as triangle meshes. But working with distributed and complex 3D scenes does not imply that a user needs or wants the full geometric information of 3D objects from the beginning.

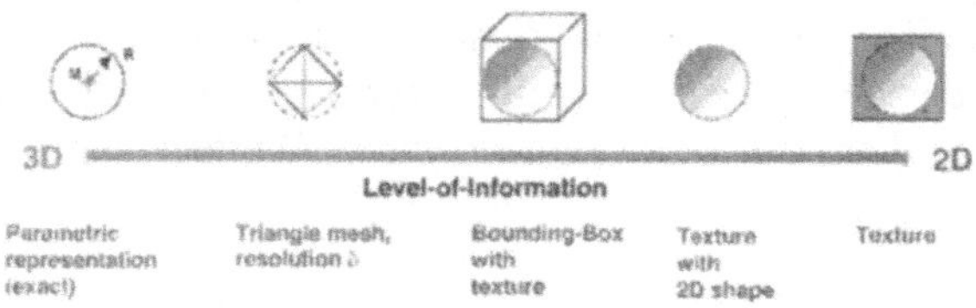

Fig. 3. Object with increasing level-of-information.

A client who just wants to get an overview of a virtual world or to navigate in it can work with representations that have a low level of complexity, like images or texture plus bounding box information. A full 3D representation needs to be transmitted in 3D mesh or parametric model form only when a request for high-level local interaction with objects is made. Figure 3 illustrates the idea of representing 3D objects with increasing level-of-information. The Level-of-Information approach presented here is based on dynamic control of the distribution process of object representations which best fit the connection and local performance conditions of a client. The following object representations for 3D objects are supported by the SCA3D architecture: *parametric models*, *polygonal mesh models with adaptable resolution*, *bounding box plus texture*, *texture plus 2D shape* and *plane texture*. The level-of-information is connected to the accessible object information of a representation.

In Figure 4, object representations are plotted into a bandwidth-vs.-performance diagram to illustrate how the configuration of a client scene can be adjusted to the connection bandwidth and the local CPU-Power of a client. Four different scenarios are classified with regard to bandwidth and power of a client: **(A)** a personal computer in a local area network (PC in a LAN), **(B)** a notebook computer with ISDN connection, **(C)** a personal digital assistant connected to a LAN (PDA in a LAN) and **(D)** a personal digital assistant with mobile connection

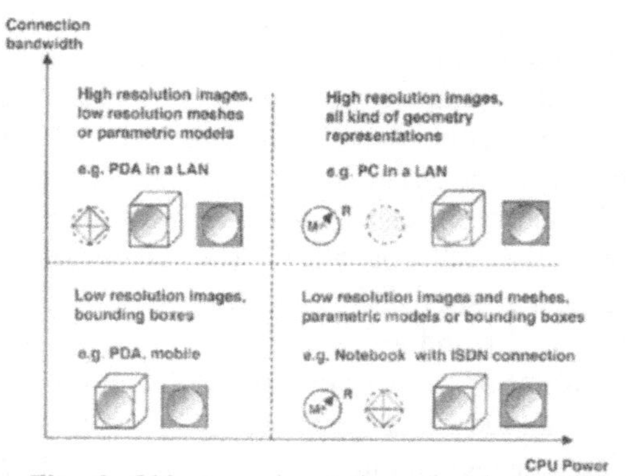

Fig. 4. Object representations forming a client scene under different conditions.

(PDA mobile). In case **(A)** representing a client with high bandwidth and very good CPU-Power all object representations can be used to build a client scene. For instance, such a client can use remote rendering in connection with high resolution images for navigation in a document collection and can be allowed the necessary permission to obtain the original data and then download all objects as full resolution geometry. A client who is represented by case **(D)** cannot download large amounts of geometry data over a small bandwidth connection and would not be able to process the geometry data locally. For such a client working on a 3D document, object representations like low resolution images and bounding boxes would be a good choice. In case **(B)** and **(C)** other representations such as meshes with varying resolution are suitable to fit the described conditions.

3 A Distributed Software Architecture for Adaptive 3D Visualization

The Scalable Scenes concept combines remote and local 3D visualization to maximize the advantages and minimize the disadvantages of the two approaches. Integrating both approaches into a common concept allows the realization of a system that enables interactive frame rates on the client side for local objects and security and complexity management for remote objects. Synchronization of the visualization pipeline on the server side with the client's visualization pipeline allows the user to navigate in remote 3D documents and to interact with objects of the same document located as copies on his computer. The concept distinguishes a remote navigation space on the server side and a local interaction space on the client side. A level-of-information slider provided by the client application controls which object representations can be transmitted to a client on a selection event. The positions of the LoI-slider range between 2D image objects and 3D original objects. Certain positions can be locked to prevent a user from transmitting protected objects. Locking is indicated by a hatched area of the slider of client 1 in Figure 5 which shows the concept of Scalable Scenes in an overview. Three states of an object are distinguished.

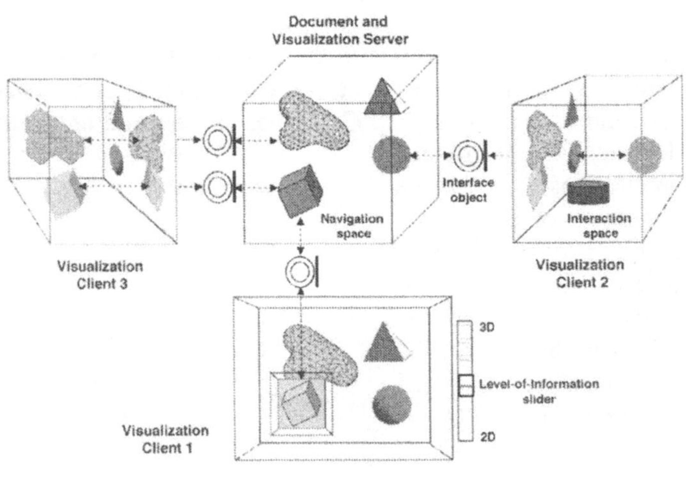

Fig. 5. The combined concept of Scalable Scenes.

An *inactive server-side object* is only present in the navigation space and can therefore be visualized remotely. An object which is selected by a user is in the state of an *active object*. An active object is present in the navigation space and represented on the client side by a suitable object representation which is connected to the server-side object via an interface object. The interface object provides a method of interface to the user which is accessible over the local object representation. Finally, an object can be in the state of an *inactive client-side object* indicating that this object was transmitted as original from server to client.

The SCA3D architecture is built to support multi-client collaboration. Every client with a connection to the SCA3D server is provided with a uniquely registered ID, so that its remotely callable methods are individually addressed. The collaboration model of SCA3D uses unique client IDs to maintain individual object references for every client. A multi-client image server is used to distribute image streams over socket connections to any number of clients. The software architecture comprises four layers (see Figure 6): a WWW layer, a visualization layer using the OpenInventor API, a document control layer using a CORBA implementation, and finally, an image layer used for image coding, transmission and decoding. The document control layer and the image layer are discussed in more detail in the following sections.

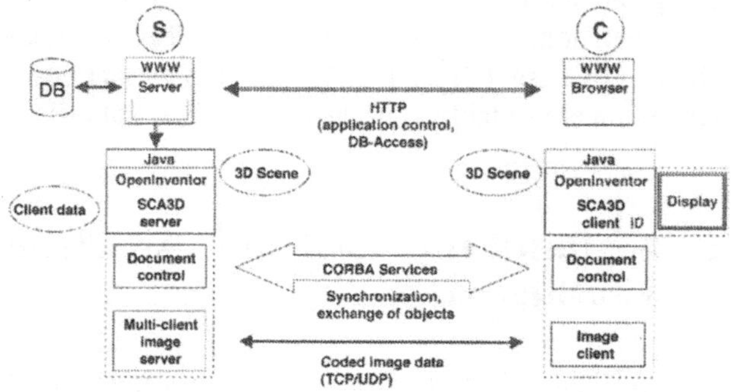

Fig. 6. Layer model of the SCA3D architecture.

3.1 A Document-Request-Broker Approach

Access to document objects in the distributed system is managed using a technique which is similar to an object-oriented middleware concept based on remote-procedure-calls (RPC) [13]. Generally, the standard architecture CORBA is used to develop distributed applications where remote objects are accessed via local proxy objects. On the server, method implementations provided by so called skeleton objects are used to apply the RPC. A similar approach, which we term *document-request-broker* (DRB), is integrated into the Scalable Scenes concept. The document-request-broker uses interface objects on the server side and local object representations on the client side

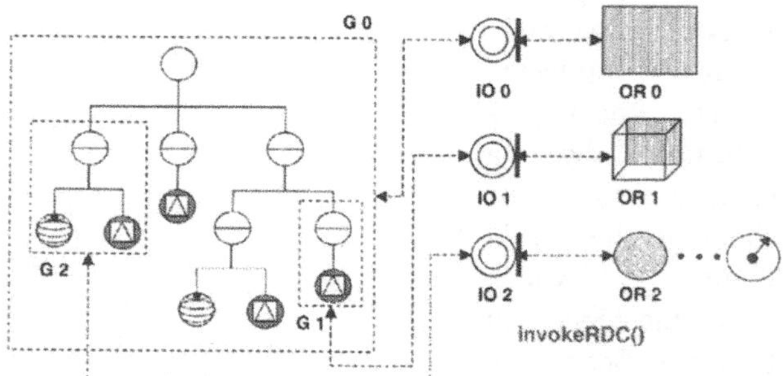

Fig. 7. Access to documents using proxy objects.

to support visual access to remote 3D documents. The object-oriented document model of a scene graph supports this approach very well.

The DRB-concept is shown in Figure 7. The document itself is equivalent to the group *G0* of the document-request-broker. It is represented on the client side by the object representation *OR0*, which is the remotely rendered image of the 3D scene. The original document and the client's object representation are connected by an interface object *IO0*. The client can now apply actions on the document by invoking methods provided by the object representation, such as *pickObject* or *getCopyrightInformation*. These *remote-document-calls* (RDC) are applied by the document-request-broker to the original document using the interface object's methods. In the next steps, further objects can be activated and interface objects together with object representations for subgroups of the document are generated and connected. All object representations mentioned above can be used to work with server-side document objects and therefore the information quantity can be scaled dynamically. For these purposes transformations between graphical representations of objects are performed on server side, e.g. by surface sampling of parametric surfaces and tessellation using an additional complexity node in the scene graph or by bounding box calculation. The position of the client-side level-of-information slider is used to control these transformation processes.

3.2 Organization of the Image Streaming Layer

Images are distributed in the software architecture to support object representations which use remotely rendered images. The basic configuration of the client scene requires that an image representation of the whole 3D document is generated on the server side with a certain server frame rate (**SFR**), transmitted to the client and mapped onto the client's projection plane with a certain texture mapping rate (**TMR**). To adjust the rate of an image stream to a client's condition, a mechanism for rate control is implemented in the image layer. The rate control technique applied here is also used in image streaming environments to prevent network congestion (see [12]).

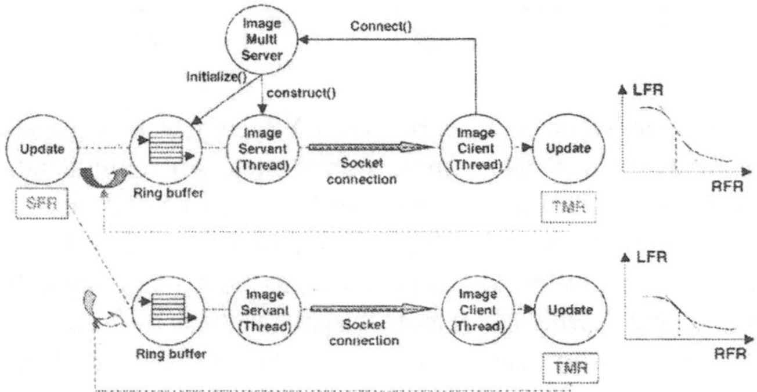

Fig. 8. The SCA3D image layer for multi-client support.

The SCA3D image layer uses server-side image buffering with a feedback from receiver and sender to control the filling rate of the image ring buffer. The rate with which the ring buffer is filled depends on the ratio of the fixed server frame rate and the individual texture mapping rate of each client. An image servant thread on the server side reads the image data from the ring buffer and writes them to a connected image client thread over a socket connection previously provided by an image multi server. On the client side, the images are mapped onto the projection plane with the adjusted texture mapping rate. The setup of the image layer with its Java classes is shown in Figure 8.

To find the appropriate ratio of server frame rate and texture mapping rate for each client, a performance measurement step must be performed. For this purpose the local frame rate (**LFR**) and remote frame rate (**RFR**) are measured and their dependency is evaluated. In Figure 8 the characteristic LFR-vs.-RFR diagram for both clients connected to the server is shown on the right side. To produce the dependency curve, the remote image frame rate was stepwise increased from a minimum value to a maximum value by changing server frame rate and texture mapping rate accordingly.

4 Adaptive Behavior by Control of Frame Rates and Local Geometry Load

The software architecture SCA3D implements an adaptive behavior with regard to local and remote frame rates. When a client connects to a server, the optimal ratio between local and remote frame rates will be adjusted in order to minimize delays for local and remote actions using a performance evaluation process which is performed at fixed intervals. The remote frame rate is influenced by three factors: the delay caused by image generation, by data transmission over the network and by texture mapping on the client side. The reciprocal value of the overall delay is used here to approximate the RFR value (see Equation 1(left)). The local frame rate is estimated as the reciprocal of the local delay of an action (see Equation 1(right)). It depends mainly on the amount of geometry information to be rendered, on the adjusted texture mapping rate and on the resolution of texture images.

$$RFR \cong \frac{1}{Tgen + Tnet + Tmap}, \qquad LFR \cong \frac{1}{Tlocal} \qquad (1)$$

In order to support work on a distributed 3D document it is necessary to find the optimal ratio between local and remote frame rates. An optimal ratio of local and remote frame rates enables fluent local work on 3D objects and a remote visual feedback with a small delay reflecting the state of the server-side document. In the upper right corner of Figure 9 (a) this is demonstrated by showing a 3D object that is moved locally together with the remote visual feedback reflecting the state of the original document. The difference of local and remote delay results in an impression that the remote object is connected to the local object representation with an elastic band.

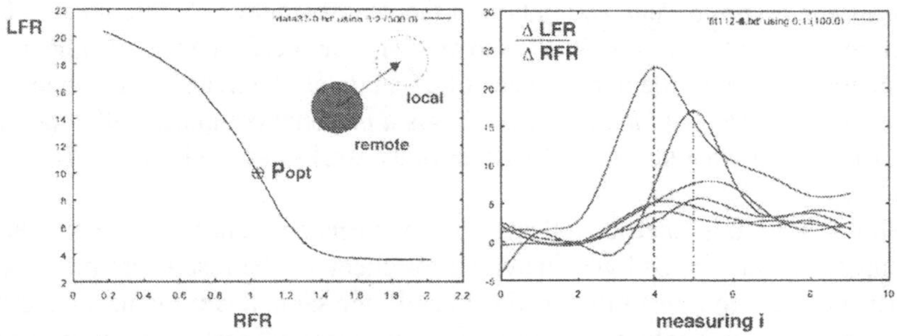

Fig. 9. Estimation of the optimal ratio: (a) LFR vs. RFR (left), (b) slope of LFR-vs.-RFR curve for varying geometry (right).

Figure 9 (a) shows the experimental results of a performance test for one client as an LFR-vs.-RFR curve with the optimal ratio *Popt*. This point is estimated by evaluating the slope of the curve. The characteristic curve of a client application, which is busy with texture mapping and with local rendering, shows a point of maximum slope indicating the optimal ratio of local and remote frame rates. This point is used to adjust the local texture mapping rate and the server-side push rate of the image ring buffer. Diagram 9(b) shows the changing slopes resulting from performance evaluation of the same client for a varying geometry load. The client's behavior changes under varying conditions and performance evaluation must be repeated from time to time.

To minimize the overall delay, the optimal ratio of local and remote frame rates of every client has to be adjusted individually using the rate control mechanism described above. The server frame rate, which is proportional to the maximum texture mapping rate demanded in the environment, and the texture mapping rate of a client are used to control the push rate of the image buffer. The delay factor for filling the image buffer is estimated as the reciprocal of the ratio $\omega i = SFR/TMRi$ between the server frame rate and the individual texture mapping rate. By multiplying the server frame rate with the delay factor, image streams at optimal frame rate can be delivered to every client.

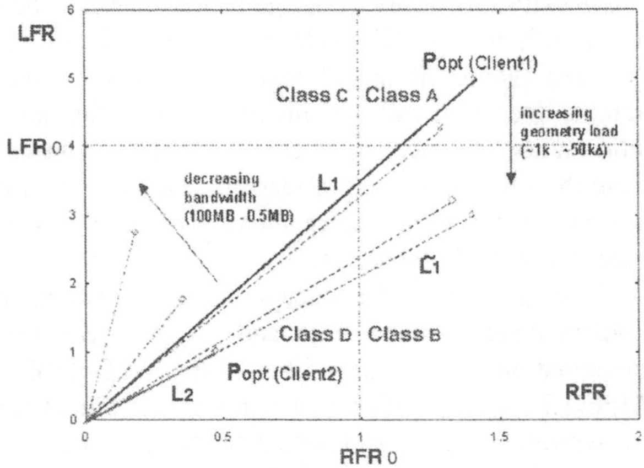

Fig. 10. Performance comparison of two clients.

In order to compare clients, a performance metric is needed which reflects the differences in processor power and bandwidth. The metric is then used to control the level-of-information slider and to provide a client with object representations best fitting the individual local conditions. Figure 10 shows the comparison of two clients with help of the LFR-vs.-RFR diagram. The performance of client 1 is better than that of client 2, which is expressed by the difference of the length L of the vector from the origin to *Popt*. Evaluation of the vector length of both clients in LFR-RFR space as $L = \sqrt{LFR^2 + RFR^2}$ shows that the performance of client 1 is approximately five times the performance of client 2. Both clients were connected to the server over a LAN (*10 Mbit/s*). Client 1 was a personal computer with a powerful processor ($L1=5.2$) whereas client 2 was an older workstation with less CPU-power ($L2=1.1$).

To show how this metric reflects the performance changes under varying conditions, the geometry load was increased for client 1. The results are presented in Figure 10. The remote frame rate remained nearly the same under the new conditions whereas the local frame rate was decreased in indirectly proportion to the number of triangles in the client scene. The performance value changed from $L1=5.2$ to $\tilde{L}1=3.4$ as a response to a change of the triangle number from *1000* triangles to *50000* triangles. The distance ΔL between the clients changed from $\Delta L=4.1$ to $\Delta\tilde{L}=2.3$. Also the behavior of client 2 under changing bandwidth conditions between server and client is shown in Figure 10. The bandwidth was decreased stepwise during the tests from *100 Mbit/s* to *0.5 Mbit/s* and the optimal ratio of the frame rates was re-evaluated after each step.

Using this performance metric, clients represented by the classification scheme shown in Figure 4 can now work together on a 3D document because the system adjusts the level-of-information on the client side. To achieve this goal performance, classes are defined using threshold values (*LFR0* and *RFR0*) for local and remote frame rates as shown in Figure 10. Correlation of performance classes with the geometry load caused by accessible object representations allows control of the level-of-information on the client side.

5 Conclusions

The starting point of this paper was distributed work on 3D documents in open information spaces. The software architecture SCA3D presented here is a solution for interactive visualization of distributed 3D documents with integrated techniques for complexity and security management. The basic concept of the architecture combines local with remote 3D rendering and uses hybrid 2D/3D client scenes. An object-oriented document model together with a document-request-broker approach for remote-document-calls is integrated into the concept to enable scaling of the information quantity on the client side. The adaptive behavior of the architecture was described by introducing a technique for rate control known from image streaming systems and a performance metric which allows a comparison of clients working together on a 3D document.

Generalization of the concept to support distributed work on documents which also contain image, video, audio and text data will be explored in future stages. The combination of standards like XML, W3C DOM (document object model) and MPEG-7 together with a document-request-broker approach is seen as very promising to support retrieval and visualization of generic documents in open information spaces.

References

1. Carlsson, C., Hagsand, O.: DIVE- A Platform for Multi-User Virtual Environments. Computer & Graphics, Vol. 7(6) (1993) 663-669
2. DOM (W3C): Document Object Model (DOM) Core Specification. W3C (2000)
3. Engel, K., Sommer, O. and Ertl, T.: A Framework for Interactive Hardware Accelerated Remote 3D-Visualization. EG/IEEE VisSym '00 (2000), 167-177
4. Engel, K., Hastreiter, P., Tomandl, B., Eberhardt, K. and Ertl, T.: Combining Local and Remote Visualization Techniques for Interactive Volume Rendering in Medical Applications. IEEE Visualization '00 (2000), 6-10
5. Fellner, D.W., Hopp, A.: MRT-VR Multi-User Virtual Environment. AAA'97 (1997)
6. Fellner, D.W., Havemann, S., Müller, G.: Modeling of and Navigation in complex 3D Documents. Computer & Graphics, Vol.22(6) (1998), 647-653
7. Haulsen, I., Jung, T., Tuchtenhagen, D: Remote Control of Virtual Environments Using Image Streams. Second IMA Conference on Image Processing (1998)
8. Hesina, G. et al.: Distributed Open Inventor: A Practical Approach to Distributed 3D Graphics, ACM Virtual Reality Software & Technology '99 (1999), 74-81
9. Löffler, J.: Object-based Image Coding for Cooperative 3D Visualization. International Conference on Computer Graphics WSCG (2000), 197-203
10. Löffler, J.: Content-based Retrieval of 3D Models in Distributed Web Databases by Visual Shape Information. IEEE Information Visualization IV'00 (2000), 82-87
11. Mann, Y., Cohen-Or, D.: Selective Pixel Transmission for Navigating in Remote Virtual Environments. Eurographics Conference EG'97, Vol.16(3) (1997)
12. Riley, M., Richardson, I.: Digital video communications. Artech House, ISBN 0-89006-890-9 (1997)
13. Siegel, J.: CORBA: fundamentals and programming. Wiley, ISBN 0-471-12148-7 (1996)
14. Wernecke, J.: The Inventor Mentor - Programming Object-Oriented 3D Graphics with Open Inventor. Addisson Wesley, ISBN 0-201-62495-8 (1998)

Reusing Motions and Models in Animations

Akanksha, Z. Huang, B. Prabhakaran, and C. R. Ruiz, Jr.

School of Computing
National University of Singapore
{akanksha, huangzy, prabha, conradod}@comp.nus.edu.sg

Abstract. Computer animated 3D models have been increasingly used in multimedia presentations because they can be viewed and manipulated directly in 3D. In this paper, we propose a database approach for this problem. Our main objective is to help authors create multimedia presentations by reusing existing animations. In our approach, animations are stored in databases. We define a set of metadata that describe the animations. Authors can search on these databases by issuing queries. A set of motion editing operations are defined and used to manipulate the query results to create new ones according to the requirements of the presentations. We have developed an animation toolkit implementing the approach and the results are promising.

Keywords: Multimedia presentations, animation, database, reuse, metadata

1 Introduction

Computer animated 3D models have been used increasingly in multimedia presentations. One main reason for this is that the computer animated 3D models can be viewed and manipulated directly in 3D.

However, users who require animations in the presentations may find it difficult to produce the desired motion sequences. Creating animations of good quality needs considerable effort of skilled animators, actors, and engineers. Thus, reusing the existing animations to create new ones becomes an appealing problem.

The major idea of reusing animations is to adjust the existing motion sequences for the new requirements while at the same time, retain the flavor of the original motion. One method was proposed by Bruderlin and Williams [3], who treated motions as signals and applied techniques of signal processing to adapt them. A variant of their method, motion-displacement mapping, was introduced by Popovic and Witkin [10]. Other works include Gleicher [4], Hodgins [5], and Monzani et al.[9]. All these methods address the reuse for a specific type of animation and manipulate on low level kinematic or dynamic structures of geometric models.

Using database in computer animation is not a new concept. Thalmann et al. [12] presented an *Informed Environment* that creates a database dedicated to urban life simulation. Using a set of manipulation tools, the database permits integration of the urban knowledge in order to simulate more realistic behaviors. Ayadin et al. [1] used databases to guide the grasp movement of virtual actors. Their approach creates a database based on divisions of the reachable space of a virtual actor. Kakizaki [7] proposed a multimedia presentation framework using animation databases. It uses a scene graph and an animated agent in multimedia presentations. The motion of the agent is categorized into three classes: pointing, moving, and gesturing. The reuse of animation has not been addressed in any of these three database methods.

Our Approach: We propose a database approach for using animations in multimedia presentations. The major contributions include the following technical aspects:

- Augmented scene graphs (with the incorporation of Interpolator Nodes) as data structure for representing animations of 3D models.
- A set of metadata for describing the animations.
- Similarity measures for computing the relevance factor of an animation to resolve queries on the databases.
- A set of operations applied on the query results that help in reusing animations.
- An animation toolkit implementing the approach.

A specific area, where animations can be applied in a multimedia presentation, is a document produced for the hearing impaired. The toolkit can be used to generate animations of sign language. The sign language can be translated from the audio clips.

We will focus on the database aspects of the approach without the details of specific animation techniques such as inverse kinematics [6, 13]. We will present them separately. The remaining part of the paper is organized as follows:

Section 2 describes the storage of animations as databases. Section 3 discusses the operations the user can invoke to retrieve, insert, and adjust geometric models and motion, to create an animation. Section 4 shows, by means of examples, the different ways in which the query results can be manipulated. Section 5 briefly describes the implementation. Section 6 provides a conclusion of the work done and discusses possibilities for future work.

2 The Animation Databases

Now, we describe how we organize animations as databases. The major idea is to use the *augmented scene graphs.* A standard scene graph is a hierarchical structure to describe geometric models. We augment it in order to represent motion sequences of the geometric models by introducing a new node for the motion. We specify a set of metadata to describe motion sequences and geometric models that are associated with the augmented scene graph model. The metadata is then organized together with animations as a relational database. We provide a set of operations that can be used to query the animation databases. Finally, the query results can be adjusted in temporal and spatial domains according to the new specifications of the query metadata.

2.1 The Scene Graph

The scene graph was originally designed for real-time 3D graphics system Performer [11]. The Performer scene graph is a tree structure. The nodes in the tree have different types. Typically, leaves in the scene graph represent geometric models and interior nodes represent transformation objects. It also contains data about the geometric models in a scene, such as their shape, size, color and position. Each piece of information is stored as a node in the scene graph.

An animation object consists of two fundamental elements: geometric models and their motion sequences. A geometric model is a mathematical representation of 3D scenes in the world. It can be as complex as a human body model comprising sophisticated shapes with hundreds of degrees of freedom (DOFs). The motion sequences represent the kinematic information of the geometric models. A typical representation is keyframe.

To represent a motion sequence of a specific geometric model we incorporate the motion node: *Interpolator.* An *Interpolator* node is associated with a geometric model of multiple DOFs. In an Interpolator node, keyframes are defined for all DOFs: {key $[k_1, k_2, ..., k_i, ..., k_m]$, keyvalue $[v_1, v_2, ..., v_i, ..., v_m]$}, where k_i is the *key frame number* or *key frame time.* v_i is a vector in the motion configuration space: $v_i = [u_{i,1}, u_{i,2}, ..., u_{i,j}, ..., u_{i,n}]$, where $u_{i,j}$ is a *key value* of DOF j (in displacement for translational DOFs and angle value for rotational DOFs) at k_i, and n is the number of DOFs of the model. The key and keyvalue together form one motion sequence for a model.

In our implementation, the scene graph is represented in VRML format. VRML is a text-based language used to model virtual environments [14]. One VRML file can be decomposed into many smaller VRML Text Descriptions which represent individual geometric models and motion sequences. These *Text Descriptions* are then stored in the VRMLText table of the database. The animation objects are linked to the VRMLText table by a Has-A relationship. In the case of geometric models the table stores the prototypes and nodes which are used, where as, for motion sequences it contains the Interpolator nodes and Event Routing.

One simple example of a scene graph representing an animated blue cube is shown in Figure 1 whose VRML description is given below.

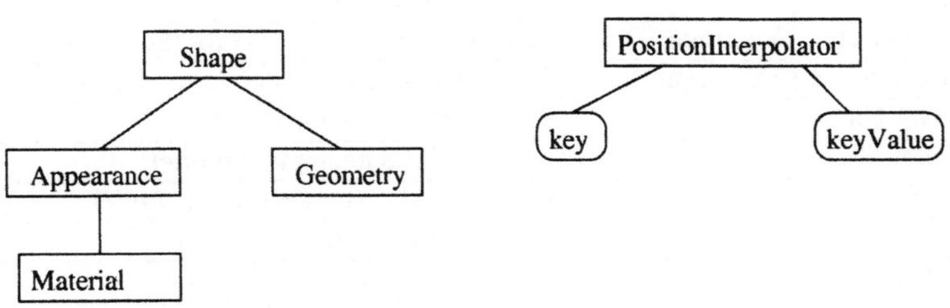

Fig. 1. An example of the scene graph of an animated blue cube. Three key frames are defined in the PositionInterpolator node.

```
Shape{
   geometry Box { size 1 2 3 }
   appearance Appearance { material Material { diffuseColor 0 0 1 } }
}
PositionInterpolator {
   key [ 0.0 0.5 1.0 ]
   keyValue [ 2.0 0.5 2.0, 2.0 0.5 3.0, 2.0 0.5 3.0] }
```

2.2 Animation Metadata and Database Organization

Metadata is widely used in the query of multimedia databases [2]. We have defined content-descriptive metadata for geometric models and their motion sequences. Their storage and querying are dealt with in a similar manner. The queries are performed based on the metadata and result in animation object(s) best matching the user requirements. We consider the following types of animation metadata.

- Metadata describing the geometric models: Type, Size, Position, Color, and Orientation.
- Metadata describing motion information: Motion Type, Motion Speed, Start Time, End Time, and Style.

For database organization, we use a relational database management system, *MS Access*, to store the animation databases. Scene graphs are stored and indexed. The metadata are stored in the fields of the database. (In the current implementation, the metadata for each animation object are manually added to the scene graph). By doing it in this manner, we can use SQL-like queries to retrieve animation objects. The fields of the database for the geometric models and the motion sequences are shown in Table 1 and Table 2, respectively. The geometric models and motion sequences of each animation object are stored in two separate tables of the database and are linked by the Object ID being the primary key.

Table 1. Database fields for a geometric model.

Field Name	Description
Object ID	A unique ID for the geometric model and its motion sequences
Category ID	A unique ID of the category the geometric model belongs to
Model Name	The name of the geometric model
Model Type	The type of the geometric model
Size	The scaling factor of the geometric model
Position	The location of the geometric model
Color	The color of the geometric model
Model TextID	The unique ID linking to the VRML Text Description
Proto TextID	The unique ID linking to the VRML Prototype

Table 2. Database fields for the motion sequence.

Field Name	Description
Object ID	A unique ID for the geometric model and its motion sequences
Motion Name	The name of the motion sequence
Motion Type	The type of the motion sequence
Motion Speed	The speed of the motion sequence
Start Time	Motion starting time sequence
End Time	Motion ending time sequence
Style	Motion style, e.g., brisk
Motion TextID	The unique ID linking to the VRML Text Description

Besides the geometric model table and the motion sequence table, the scene also has its table in the database, which is linked to the geometric model table by a Has-A relationship. Models are also linked to a Model_Component table which links records on the model table to other models if it is a complex model. A complex model is made up of simple models (or atomic models). Here also there exists a Has-A relationship. We also have a category class and each model belongs to a certain category. In our database the model table is linked by an Is-A relationship to the category table. Generally relational databases are designed based on an Entity-Relation (ER) diagram. The ER diagram of our framework is given in Figure 2.

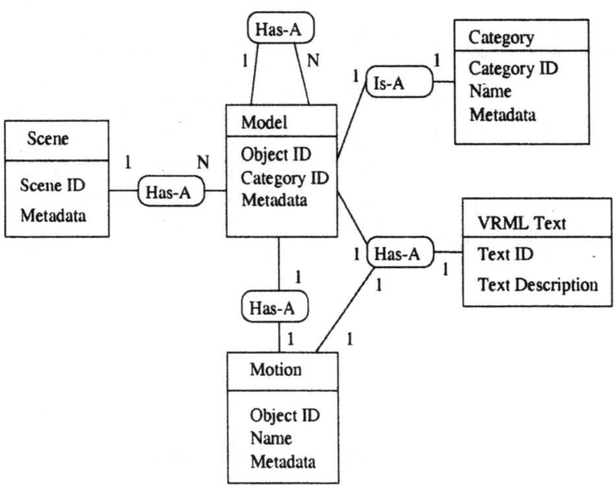

Fig. 2. The ER diagram of RDBS for the scene graph.

Using this design we can index the database by propagating the metadata of the animation objects upward, thus a scene would have all the metadata for its child animation objects. The searching would first be conducted at the higher levels of the scene graph and will descend to lower levels only if a match is found. An alternative is by using categories as indexes, where animation objects or scenes are also assigned categories.

A query on the animation database is resolved by making use of a generic multi-attribute equation to compute the relevance of each motion sequence. A record satisfies the query on the condition that the relevance is equal to or higher than a predefined threshold.

Similarity measures are specified for the Motion Type, Style, Interval, Speed, etc. as well as metadata of the Geometric Models. Conceptually, a similarity measure $SIM(i,q,k)$ (normalized) is the similarity of an animation A_i, with query q, based on metadata k. It will be 0 if k does not occur in the metadata of A_i. The higher the occurrence rate and the closer the values are, the higher the similarity measure.

The overall similarity measure is the weighted sum of the individual similarity measures. The weights have a significant effect on the outcome of a query. For an animation, default weights are assigned based on the relative difficulty of readjustment of the metadata, such that the summation of weights is 1. The user has an option to change the weights if required.

Table 3 depicts an example of query results when a user performs the following query: Motion Type: running; Motion Style: normal; Motion Interval: 0-5; Motion Speed: 5. Given a threshold value of 0.5, only the top three records will be retrieved.

Table 3. The relevance scoring for a multiple result query.

Rank	Type	Style	Start Time	End Time	Speed	ID	Score
1	Run	fast	15	25	5	Nancy	0.60
2	Run	happily	0	20	2.5	Girl	0.50
3	Run	merrily	0	5	2.5	Nancy	0.65
4	Walk	normal	0	10	10	Andy	0.45
5	Wave	normal	6	18	15	Andy	0.42
6	Walk	sluggish	5	10	12	Man	0.24

3 Operations for Reusing Animations

This section discusses the operations a user can invoke to retrieve, insert, and adjust animation objects to scene graphs in order to create a new motion sequence. These operations are performed on the output of a user query. The metadata are used to adjust the queried results for a new animation. The operations can be divided into three categories: spatial operations, temporal operations, and motion adjustment operations.

3.1 Spatial Operations

Spatial operations on motion sequences involve changing the position, size, and orientation of geometric models. The operations used to query and manipulate the spatial attributes of an animation, are as follows:

1. *Insert Operation:* this operation inserts a geometric model into a scene under specified conditions. The user can include the new x, y, z coordinates of the model, and/or the time frame when the model will be shown.
2. *Delete Operation:* this operation deletes a geometric model from a scene. This can help the user eliminate unnecessary models from a retrieved result.
3. *Extract Operation:* this operation extracts a geometric model from a scene. It could also be used to extract an atomic geometric model from a complex model.
4. *Edit Operation:* this operation edits the metadata of a geometric model. The user can edit the position, size, and orientation of the model.

3.2 Temporal Operations

Motion is an integral part of any animations. Temporal operations help in retargeting motion for new characters and scenes. The operations for manipulating motion are use, get, and disregard.

1. *Use Operation:* this operation utilizes a motion to a character. We have adapted the motion-mapping approach to re-use existing motion to other models. The user maps the interpolator points of the motion to the joints of the geometric model to be applied to.
2. *Get Operation:* this operation extracts motion from a character. In a scene graph, motion is defined by keyframe animation and by the nodes: OrientationInterpolator and PositionInterpolator, among others. We simply search for the interpolators that are linked to the specified model and copy the keyframes.
3. *Disregard Motion:* this operation deletes the motion of a geometric model. This can be done by searching for the keyframes that are used on the model and by deleting them, including the timer node that was used.
4. *Project Operation:* this operation projects a specific time interval from a motion sequence based on the user's specified conditions. For example, if the user queried and found an animation matching all the requirements, except for time constraints, the user may opt to project a portion of the animation.
5. *Join Operation:* the operation allows the user to join two key frame sequences together. This provides the user with the ability to generate more complex motion from standard motion. The time base will be automatically adjusted.

3.3 Motion Adjustment Operations

In most cases, when a motion of a geometric model is reused by another one, it is necessary to adjust the motion to the new scene. Motion is usually very specific and hence we propose a set of operations to help the user adjust the motion to the new scene.

1. *Crop Motion:* operation cuts the motion into a smaller motion sequence by deleting the keyframes and calculating the appropriate substitutions.
   The crop operation edits all the Interpolator nodes (described in Subsection 2.1) for a particular motion, based on the crop value α. If α falls between two consequent keyframes k_i and k_{i+1}, the key frames from k_{i+1} to k_m will be deleted. The new ending key value k'_m can be computed using the key frame interpolation if it is not an existing one.
2. *Duplicate Motion:* operation duplicates the key frames to expand the duration of the motion. This helps if the user requires the same animation as what is retrieved but with a longer period.
   The duplicate operation adjusts all the Interpolator nodes for a particular motion, based on the duplicate value α. The old key frames will be duplicated α times.
3. *Change Speed:* operation changes the speed of the motion. It is implemented by scaling the key time base, i.e., the period represented in {key $[k_1, ..., k_m]$} of a PositionInterpolator node. So the duration of the motion will be changed. In order to keep the same duration, the new motion can be used in conjunction with the previous two operations.
4. *Retarget:* operation allows the user to adapt an existing motion sequence to meet the new constraints. Our current implementation uses inverse kinematics [6, 13] for articulated 3D models. The position and orientation of the end effectors are specified automatically by the new constraints or interactively by users. The inverse kinematic algorithm can compute the new position and orientation values of other internal joints automatically in real time.

To facilitate ease in using the system, a series of operations is automatically generated, depending on the specifications of user in the Animation Toolkit. The series is then applied to the query results to meet the requirements. The users do not need to know the operation syntax. They interact with the system, via the toolkit.

4 Examples of Manipulating the Query Results

Now, we present examples of using the operations described in Section 3 to manipulate the query results for reusing animations. Using the operations, three different types of reuse are possible: adjusting the motion sequence of a model (Subsection 4.1), applying motion to a different model with a similar structure (Subsection 4.2), and generating complex motion sequences for a model (Subsection 4.3). Using our database approach, the resulting motion will take the flavor of the original ones. Together with the operations defined in Section 3, the following clauses are also used.

FROM : used to specify the file in which motion/model is present
TO : used when applying a motion to a model or inserting a geometric model in a scene
WHERE : used to specify the condition of the query
WHEN : used to specify the duration in which the model is presented

4.1 Adjusting Motion of a Model

In this type of motion reuse, the motion needs to be modified. For example, the user can change the speed of motion and the duration. The modified motion is applied to the same geometric model that the motion was applied to previously. In a more general manner, the user can adjust motion to meet the new constraints. For example, the user wants to adjust an existing wiping motion to fit the new table in the scene. The following operations can be applied: EXTRACT woman FROM scene; GET wiping FROM woman; EXTRACT table FROM scene; INSERT table; EDIT table translation(10,5,8); USE wiping TO woman; RETARGET wiping. The result is shown as a snapshot in Figure 3.

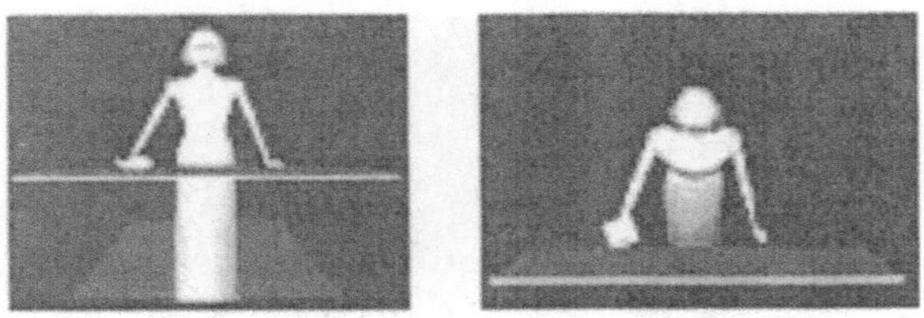

(a) (b)

Fig. 3. Retargeting an existing motion to the new geometric model in the scene: (a) wiping a table; (b) bending to wipe a lower table.

4.2 Applying Motion to a Different Model

This type of reuse is needed in the case when the motion and model required, in the presentation, are not available in the same scene of the database.

For example, the user intends to create an animation of a man walking in a room. The query results are a room, a walking woman, and a model of man from three scenes respectively (Figure 4).

To generate the animation, according to the requirements, from the query results, the following steps will be conducted: (1) INSERT the model of man into the room, (2) EDIT to make the model of man well scaled and located in the room, (3) EXTRACT the walking motion sequence from the walking woman, and finally (4) USE the motion sequence to the model of man (Figure 5).

The motion mapping technique we use is based on the work of Lee et al. [8] and Gleicher [4], without the restriction that the two models should have the same structures. Since the interpolator nodes of one model can be connected by the user, using the GUI, to another model it offers much more versatility. For example, the walking woman described in the previous example can be remapped to an animal such as a cow. Since the scene graph provides a hierarchical

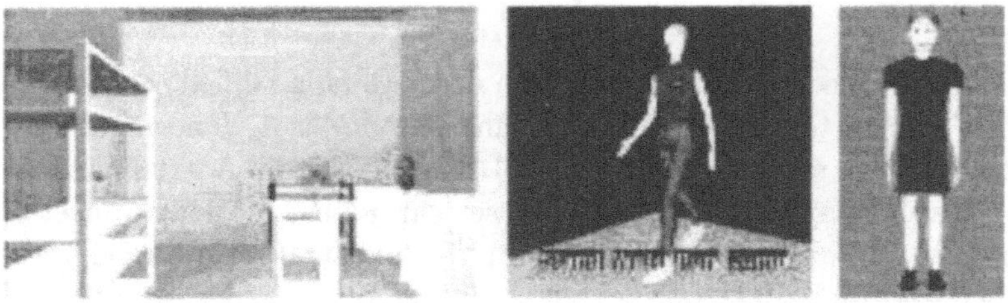

(a) (b) (c)

Fig. 4. Query results from three scenes: (a) a room; (b) a walking woman; (c) a man.

Fig. 5. Applying a walking sequence of a woman to man.

structure of both the human and the cow, the user can connect the respective segments of the cow with the interpolator nodes of the walking woman (Figure 6).

4.3 Generating Complex Motion Sequences

Complex motion can be derived by combining two or more motion sequences into a single sequence. The motion sequences may be from a single model or multiple models. The resulting complex motion may be applied to one of the original models or to a different model. An example of complex motion could be a man "walking" (lower body) and "waving" his hand (upper body) at the same time. In Figure 7, the snapshots show the individual motion sequences and the new motion sequence created. The following operations are applied to reuse the animations: GET walking FROM Andy; GET waving FROM Andy; JOIN Andy.walking WITH Andy.waving.

5 Implementation

We have developed an animation toolkit based on the proposed database approach using Visual Basic 6.0 (VB). Access 97 was used as the primary database

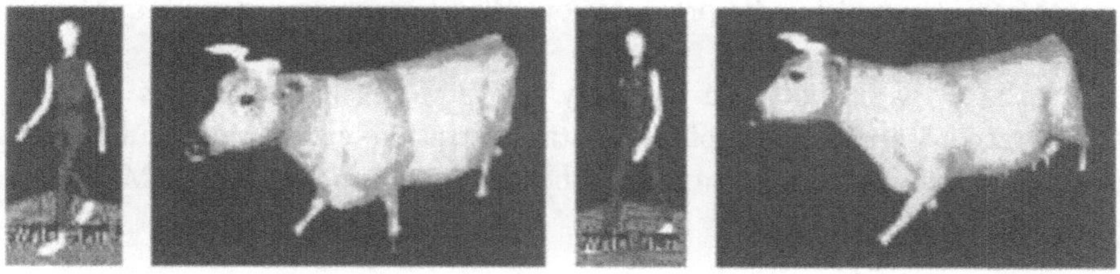

(a) (b) (c) (d)

Fig. 6. Mapping the motion of a walking woman to a cow: (a) frame 1 of woman; (b) frame 1 of cow; (c) frame 2 of woman; (d) frame 2 of cow.

Fig. 7. An animation reuse example combining two sequences.

for the storage of the animations represented in scene graph. The scene graph can be rendered by Open GL Optimizer, IRIS Performer, and VRML browser. To parse and browse the animations we used the ActiveX object Web Browser, which invokes the default web browser of the system with the installed VRML browser, such as Cosmo Player or MS VRML viewer.

The GUI of the system uses a Multiple Document Interface with menus and toolbars. The major GUI components are the Query, Scene Graph, VRML Text Document, and VRML Browser windows. The user can create a new animation by choosing the new operations through the menu or the toolbar.

6 Conclusion and Future Work

Using animations of 3D models has been receiving more interest in multimedia presentations. In this paper, we have addressed this problem by a database approach. We have implemented an authoring toolkit using the approach and our experimental results are promising.

We are still working on a unified multimedia presentation system to integrate the animation toolkit with those of other types of media to support authoring a more complex multimedia presentation. We are considering more applications for usability study.

Presently the toolkit is in the early stages of development. It is possible to incorporate a standard form of metadata description, e.g., XML at a later stage. We also will do the comparison study between our framework and MPEG-4.

7 Acknowledgments

The 3D models of the woman, the man, and the barmaid are available from http://www.ballreich.net, http://www.seamless-solutions.com, and http://www.geometrek.com respectively. We thank the anonymous EGMM 2001 reviewers for the suggestions to improve the paper.

References

1. Ayadin, Y., Takahashi, H. and Nakajima, M. Database Guided Animation of Grasp Movement for Virtual Actors. *Proc. Multimedia Modeling '97.* (1997) 213-225
2. Bohm, K. and Rawok. T. C. Metadata for Multimedia Documents. *SIGMOD-Record Special Issue on Metadata for Digital Media.* Vol. 23, No. 4, Dec. 1994.
3. Bruderlin, A. and Williams, L. Motion Signal Processing. *Proc. ACM SIGGRAPH '95.* (1995) 97-104.
4. Gleicher, M. Retargeting Motion for New Characters. *Proc. ACM SIGGRAPH '98.* (1998) 33-42.
5. Hodgins, J. and Pollard, N. Adapting Simulated Behaviors For New Characters. *Proc. ACM SIGGRAPH '97.* Los Angeles, CA. (1997) 153-162.
6. Huang Z., Boulic R., Magnenat-Thalmann N., and Thalmann D. A multi-sensor approach for grasping and 3D interaction. *Proc. CGI '95.* Leeds, UK. (1995) 235-254.
7. Kakizaki, K. Generating the Animation of a 3D Agent from Explanatory Text. *Proc. ACM MM '98.* (1998) 139-144.
8. Lee, W.M. and Lee M.G. An Animation Toolkit Based on Motion Mapping. *IEEE Computer Graphics International.* (2000) 11-17.
9. Monzani J. S., Baerlocher P., Boulic R., and Thalmann D. Using an Intermediate Skeleton and Inverse Kinematics for Motion Retargeting. *Proc. Eurographics 2000.*
10. Popovic, Z. and Witkin, A. Physically Based Motion Transformation. *Proc. ACM SIGGRAPH '99.* (1999) 11-19 .
11. Rohlf J. and Helman J. IRIS Performer: A High Performance Multiprocessing Toolkit for Real-Time 3D Graphics. *Proc. ACM SIGGRAPH '95.* 550-557.
12. Thalmann D., Farenc N., and Boulic R. Virtual Human Life Simulation and Database: Why and How. *Proc.International Symposium on Database Applications in Non-Traditional Environments (DANTE'99).* IEEE CS Press, 1999.
13. D. Tolani, A. Goswami, and N. Badler. Real-time inverse kinematics techniques for anthropomorphic limbs. *Graphical Models* 62(5), Sept. 2000, 353-388.
14. The VRML Consortium Incorporated. The Virtual Reality Modeling Language. *http://www.vrml.org/Specifications/VRML97/.* International Standard ISO/IEC 14772-1: 1997.

3D-dvshop: a 3D Dynamic Virtual Shop

A. Sanna, B. Montrucchio, P. Montuschi, and C. Demartini

Politecnico di Torino, Dip. di Automatica e Informatica, C.so Duca degli Abruzzi 24,
I-10129, Torino, Italy
{sanna,montru,montuschi,demartini}@polito.it,
WWW home page: http://www.polito.it/~{sanna,montru,montuschi,demartini}

Abstract. In recent years, virtual reality has shown all its potential in a large spectrum of applications: training, simulation, CAD, and so on. Although existing technologies allow the creation of immersive virtual reality browsing experiences, little has been devoted to applying this new tool to electronic commerce (e-commerce) since almost all e-commerce web sites present products in a 2D on-line catalog. In this paper we present 3D-dvshop, a dynamic 3D virtual shop: a user can build his or her own shop, choosing a set of products that will be dynamically placed in a collection of specially created "rooms". The use of technologies such as VRML and Java allows full 3D interaction with products. In this way, the browsing experience can be more natural, attractive, realistic, and fun.

1 Introduction

E-commerce allows a new kind of business since enterprises can promote their products without temporal and physical constraints: users can consult, at any time, on-line catalogs and purchase objects otherwise not accessible. Although e-commerce is growing alongside the expansion of the Internet, some problems remain concerning the human/machine interface. Almost all e-commerce web sites offer the user a "simple" 2D on-line catalog where object characteristics are often restricted to 2D pictures.

This kind of approach is different from that experienced when we go shopping. People like and want to interact with the objects to *discover* them and the experience of shopping, involving meeting other people, looking windows and so on, is absolutely natural and fun. However, most common user interfaces are flat and cannot completely satisfy a consumer; a traditional e-commerce web site (using HTML) can be suitable for some products such as books, but not for objects with which a user may want to interact.

Although virtual reality (VR) has been widely used in some applications (for instance training, simulation, medicine, and entertainment) there have been few attempts to create more exciting virtual reality browsing e-commerce experiences. A real 3D interface could allow consumers to immerse themselves in a virtual shop where it is possible to interact with products, to meet other people (represented by their avatars), to hear sounds, and so on; in this way, people could experience perceptions similar to the real ones.

Three main reasons have inhibited the development of 3D commerce on the web:

- performance: only recently have PCs are being able to manage interactively realistic 3D objects/environments, and modem connections for downloading large and complex 3D scenes can take a very long time,
- navigation: although our perceptions are tuned to operate in 3D worlds, it could be difficult for a customers to navigate and orient themselves in order to find objects of interest in a virtual shop,
- technology: the description of text and hyper-text on the web has been standardized by the HTML language but only the definition of VRML 2.0 [1] (published on August 1996) has provided web designers with a standard tool for designing 3D interactive and animated virtual worlds. Concurrent with VRML, a set of proprietary technologies has been developed, but they often only allow insertion of 3D interactive objects into HTML pages.

The proposed project 3D-dvshop (3D-dynamic virtual shop) attempts to tackle these issues in order to dynamically generate a virtual shop ad hoc for each user; in this way, only products of interest are placed into the virtual world that can be organized according to a customer's choices. The option of retrieving only selected information from the database allows both reduction of the amount of data composing a scene (lower connection latency times) and greater ease of navigation for the user. The technology used for developing 3D-dvshop is as much as possible standard since VRML and Java have been used to describe and create both the rooms of the shop and the interactive and animated objects. Moreover, a set of interfaces allows the web site administrator to easily manage the product database.

The paper is organized as follows: Section 2 reviews the main examples of 3D technologies devoted to 3D e-commerce and introduces the concept of user interface metaphor, while a detailed description of the proposed project is presented in Section 3. Finally, remarks and evaluations can be found in Section 4.

2 Background

2.1 Technologies for 3D e-commerce

Cult3D [2] is an interactive 3D solution allowing designers to build and display high-quality interactive 3D graphics for web sites, Microsoft Office and Adobe Acrobat. It is targeted toward product visualization, e-commerce, distance learning, gaming and entertainment applications. A Cult3D object is designed in three steps: creation of the model in 3D Studio Max, export of the object by Cult3D Exporter, and addition of animation and interaction effects by means of Cult3D Designer. Although Cult3D objects look very realistic (effects such as: bump and environment mapping, bilinear filtering, transparency, high resolution texture, stereoscopic 3D are supported) the web implementation is not a real 3D environment but a collection of traditional HTML pages including some 3D objects.

3DAnywhere [3] enables web site authors to present three dimensional objects over the Internet and allows the viewer to rotate and control object size and shape. 3DAnywhere is entirely written in Java, so it will run on any Java-enabled system; this means that no platform- or browser-specific plug-in is required.

Shout3D [4] is an approach to online visualization and immersion that lets any standard web browser display interactive 3D graphics without needing extra plug-ins; in fact, Shout3D starts from models described in a slightly modified VRML language and converts them into Shout3D applets that can be inserted in HTML pages as JavaScripts. Shout3D objects can look very realistic since sophisticated graphic effects as well as integrated sound are supported.

Superscape e-Visualizer (SeV) [5] is a technology specifically designed for the web that allows designers to integrate photo realistic interactive 3D objects with the 2D components on their web pages. The main advantage of SeV is the reduced size of the file to be transmitted; even systems with slow modem connections can take advantage of this kind of solution. 3D objects are regenerated on the client machine by means of a subdivision surface algorithm. The subdivision surface consists of a control mesh, which is the original polygon model, and a set of instructions that generate new polygons based on the positions of the vertices on this starting shape.

Blaxxun3D technology [6] is based on Extensible 3D (X3D - a subset of the existing standard VRML97), a project coordinated by the Web3D Consortium [7]. Blaxxun3D characteristics can be summarized as follows:

- compact standard Java applet (approximately 55KB),
- no plug-in and therefore no extra download or installation required,
- simple integration with existing home pages,
- platform-independent (PC, Mac, Linux),
- compatible with VRML/X3D,
- supports 3D objects and interactivity,
- extensible with built-in API interfaces.

Janet3D [8] is another Java-based technology for creating interactive 3D applications on the web; the two base components of Janet3D are netMarker and 3Dcatalog. The former is a 3D communication system supporting the design process within a CAD environment, the latter a 3D catalogue.

Anfy3D [9] claims to be the fastest interactive 3D renderer today with shading available in Java technology; Anfy3D API is the Anfy3D engine for the Java language.

On the other hand, Kaon technology [10] allows conversion of several 2D digital images of a product into 3D models. The result of a conversion is a fully 3D polygonal model with photographic surface images. Surface textures come in both low resolution for quick downloading and high resolution for detailed viewing.

It is worth stressing how all these technologies produce realistic and interactive 3D objects and can add animations to models, but do not provide the user a 3D environment where avatars can walk and move around the objects.

A completely different approach is used by PanoramIX [11] where a set of photos is used to generate a virtual environment where the user can move and follow links.

Like PanoramIX, Photovista [12] can produce extremely compact files, often a third to a quarter the size of QuickTime VR [13] files and typically less than 100KB. Photovista does not require any plug-in and generated panoramas can be directly browsed by Internet Explorer 4.01 or higher, or Netscape Navigator 4.07.

QuickTime VR [13] (QTVR) encompasses three basically distinct technologies:

- panoramas overview: the view from a single point in space out to a surrounding environment,
- objects overview: the view from multiple points in space onto a single point, or object,
- scenes overview: QTVR scenes are a collection of one or more QTVR panoramas and/or object movies linked together via as set of links called: hot spots. In QTVR scenes, users can navigate from panorama to panorama, panorama to object, object to panorama, or object to object as they move about in the scene.

A plug-in is necessary to display QTVR panoramas/objects/scenes.

In these cases, the user is surrounded by the environment but cannot interact with objects since this is not a real 3D technology.

With respect to previously presented solutions, VRML [1] is a free, open and standard technology designed for 3D rendering on the web that describes a scene by means of a text file that has to be interpreted by a VRML browser. VRML 2.0 allows the description of dynamic worlds and scripting capabilities can be associated with the objects. VRML and Java have been used in the project VRCommerce [14] in order to carry out an immersive 3D solution for e-commerce. VRCommerce consists of an editor for creating 3D malls and stores and has some tools to provide an easy and smooth navigation within them.

The Java 3D [15] application programming interface provides a set of object-oriented interfaces that support a simple, high-level programming model. Three basic characteristics are the strength of Java 3D:

- the Java 3D API's scene-graph model allows creators to focus on object and scene composition,
- the Java 3D API incorporates geometry compression as part of its specification, which allows very large 3D objects to be quickly downloaded over the network for remote viewing and manipulation,
- the "write once, run anywhere" model has reduced the complexity and the cost normally associated with producing software on and for multiple distinct hardware platforms.

2.2 User Interface Metaphor

A major problem for users of modern information systems is the retrieval of new and previously viewed information from the system. Typical "WWW worlds" are often a collection of heavily interlinked and structured information and appropriate navigation metaphors can help to make the structure easier to understand, and therefore, easier to use [16].

The information space structure can be communicated to the user through a graphical representation of the space and the elements in it. Examples of such visualizations are the Information Visualizer [17], the Navigational View Builder [18], the Narcissus system [19], Chalmers landscape metaphore [20], the visualizations for the Hyperwave system [21] and Celentano's work for generating VR interfaces from XML and DTD documents describing the web site structure [22].

Recently, Russo et al. in [23] have defined the concept of *metaphor-aware navigation*, that is, the navigation is tightly bound to the visual metaphor used and the way the user moves in the virtual world is determined by the metaphor that the same world is based upon.

In the e-commerce contest an effective navigation metaphor should allow the user to retrieve, as fast as possible, the desired products; this can be a very difficult task when users navigate virtual malls comprising several shops and corridors. The proposed project 3D-dvshop (3D-dynamic virtual shop) tackles this problem by dynamically generating a shop where only the selected objects are placed; a set of rooms, connected by enter/exit doors, contains the objects that are arranged on shelves.

3 3D-dvshop Architecture Description

3D-dvshop is a system composed by three entities: database server, web server, and clients. Database and web servers can be on the same machine, but logically they are two separate entities. The database engine is Oracle 8i Enterprise 8.1.6 running on Linux. The choice of Oracle mainly depends on its capability to manage "objects" called BLOB (Binary Large Object) that allows insertion into the database of files containing text, images, sounds and so on as binary streams. Apache web server has been chosen and an engine for the dynamic generation of the virtual shop (entirely written in Java by means of Servlet technology) has been developed; the engine extends the functionalities of the web server and is executed by the Apache Servlet Engine. Finally, a client can be any VRML browser supporting VRML 2.0 specifications. VRML allows both egocentric (moving a viewpoint through the world) and exocentric (moving the world in front of a point of view) navigation.

3.1 Database

Each product belongs to a specific category and can be obtained as a composition of more objects; moreover, each product can be represented by more than one

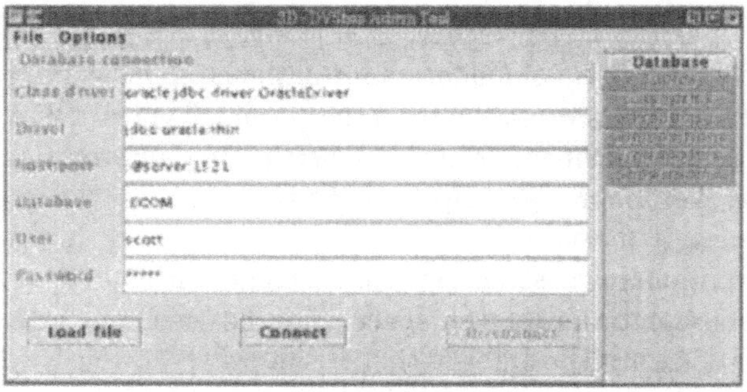

Fig. 1. The Administrator Tool interface

VRML model. In general, a VRML model is a collection of heterogeneous files: VRML code, textures, JavaScripts, Java code, metadata and so on, and it must be referred to an interface. Each VRML model is related to a bounding box that completely encapsulates it; bounding boxes are used to place products over shelves without collisions. In the same way as products, rooms are represented by VRML models.

Table generation can be performed in two different ways: by means of SQL commands or by using a program of administration expressly developed for 3D-dvshop. The Administrator Tool (AT) (Fig. 1) has been entirely developed in Java and it employs JFC for the graphic interface and JDBC for database connections. At the start of a connection the Database Panel is the only active panel, allowing database connection/disconnection operations; the following parameters are required for a connection: class driver, driver, host:port, database name, user, and password. Connection parameters can be also inserted by file. The second panel of AT (Tables Panel) allows table operations (creation, visualization, deletion, emptying) and presents the user a hierarchical structure where state information (for instance the number of records) is reported for each table.

The Categories Panel manages product categories providing insertion, update, and deletion operations. A category is specified by a unique code and by a name.

The Products Panel allows product management; in particular, the administrator can assign a product to a category. For each product a name, description, trade-mark, price, size and weight may be indicated.

The Compositions Panel describes how a product can be composed of a set of objects, while VRML Model and Show Room Panels manage object and room VRML models, respectively.

A bounding box size must be specified for each object and start points and sizes have to be indicated for shelves in room models. It is important to note how complex VRML models containing sounds, scripts, metadata (such as MPEG) and so on are also managed as BLOBs and loaded as binary streams; in this way, an object is seen as easily manageable within a hierarchical structure. Therefore, an object is a directory containing all files of the arbitrary hierarchical structure and a file having `.proto` extension representing the model prototype (see VRML specifications about prototype definition). Moreover, each object is given a standard initial position representing its orientation on a shelf.

3.2 Engine for Shop Generation

A virtual shop is built by means of two "components": a set of VRML models representing products and one or more rooms where products are placed. Each room is a VRML model in the same way as a product, while the prototype file `room.proto` contains the following parameters:

- room: environment prototype,
- exit: defines the enter/exit door placed in the first room of the virtual shop,
- nextRoom: defines a door for the access to the next room of the shop (if it exists),
- previousRoom: defines a door for the access to the previous room of the shop.

Exit, NextRoom, and PreviousRoom have been described as doors, but they could be any other enter/exit system.

3D-dvshop generates a virtual shop by a servlet called `SceneServer` that receives a user query for a search in the database; a query is performed by a form managed by the `ServForm` servlet.

A product search can be performed according to a set of fields; the first three text fields can be left blank or filled to match the *Name*, *Description*, and *Trade-Mark* that the objects have in the database. Other fields allow searching by category, use of Boolean operators (AND/OR), and selection of the type of room in which objects will be placed. The compiled form is sent to the `SceneServer` servlet that finds objects satisfying the search keys in the database and builds a virtual shop.

The user sees a page split into two frames: on the right the 3D scene and on the left the list of the objects found. For instance, searching for category and selecting "Notebook", a shop containing two objects will be displayed as shown in Fig. 2. When the user approaches an object, all information about the product will appear in the left frame (see Fig. 3). Moreover, users can interact with objects by rotating and moving them and, if defined, can activate any animations associated with the objects themselves. In the second example the search has been performed on *all categories* and only the kind of room has been specified; in this case, seven objects have been retrieved from the database, and since it is impossible to place all them within just one room, two environments linked by a door are automatically generated. Fig. 4 shows four products placed in the first room and the connection door labeled by *NEXT*.

Object orientation depends on shelf position, as a shelf is described in the database by: a starting point, an orientation angle, and a bounding box. The orientation angle allows rooms of arbitrary shape to be generated, making the virtual shop more realistic. A movie of 3D-dvshop can be found in EG digital library.

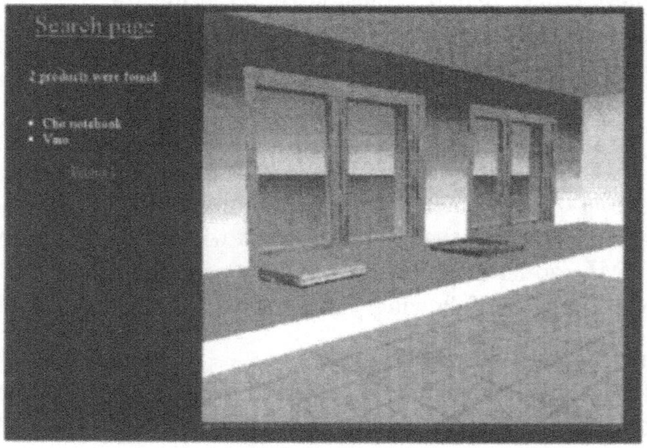

Fig. 2. Result of a search for category

4 Remarks and Evaluations

Evaluating the complexity involved in building a shop or a product is a very difficult task; it mainly depends on the appearance the "object" must have; if it has to appear as realistic as possible, a long time has to be spent in the design phase. However, almost all recent 3D modelers (for instance, 3D Studio Max) provide easy and intuitive tools for creating extremely realistic 3D models that can be successively exported into VRML.

On the other hand, database management is a straightforward task, since all database operations (adding and deleting products, modifying object properties, inserting new kinds of room, organizing products for categories) can be performed by the Administration Tool described in Section 3.1.

From the user point of view, the system evaluation mainly concerns the usability. Environments and the objects are created on the fly according to the user requests; in this way, only the products of interest, instead of the entire database, are presented. This has two main advantages: reduced size of the VRML model (i.e. lower connection and rendering times) and displaying to the user only specified objects of interest. Objects are placed in one or more rooms according to search results; rooms are sequentially connected by doors to minimise the chance of a customer missing a product of interest. Moreover, some VRML browsers (for instance CosmoPlayer [24]) can receive compressed textures, further reducing download latency times, and navigation can take advantage of accelerated graphic boards now available at low cost.

5 Conclusion

3D-dvshop is a tool for 3D e-commerce browsing experiences and the whole system is entirely written in Java and VRML, two standard and free technologies.

Fig. 3. Approaching an object and interacting with it

It provides realistic appearance since both the environments and the products are fully 3D, interactive, and possibly animated. VRML and Java allow description of very realistic objects both in appearance and behavior; moreover, the database's capability to manage binary streams allows easy inclusion of metadata.

A customer can move inside the virtual shop; at the moment 3D-dvshop implements a WoW (Window on World Systems) paradigm (also called Desktop Virtual Reality System) where the scene is displayed on a monitor, but this only concerns the human/machine interface and does not involve the system architecture. Visualizing products into separate windows could be another choice, but this would not allow the same feeling of immersion.

Acknowledgments

This work is supported by The National Research Council (CNR) in the frame of the project *Strumenti e Tecniche per la Realizzazione di Negozi Virtuali Distribuiti*.

We thank Ing. Giampiero Alberelli for his support in developing 3D-dvshop.

References

1. The Virtual Reality Modeling Language International Standard ISO/IEC 14772-1:1997, http://www.vrml.org/Specifications/VRML97
2. Cycore Cult3D, http://www.cult3d.com
3. 3DAnywhere, http://www.3danywhere.com
4. Shout3D, http://www.shout3d.com
5. Superscape, http://www.superscape.com
6. Blaxxun3D, http://www.blaxxun.com

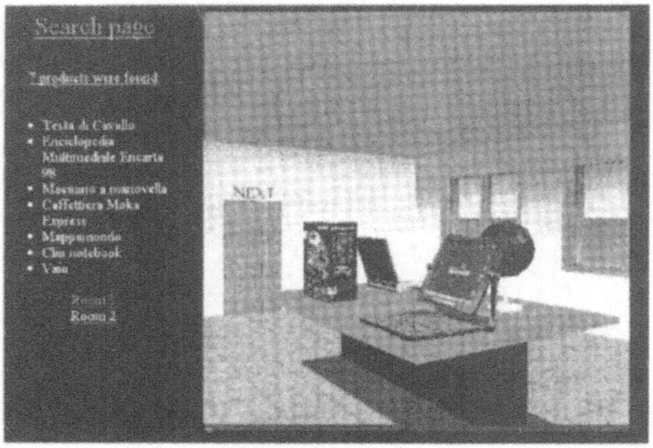

Fig. 4. Two rooms are automatically generated

7. Web3D Consortium, http://www.web3d.org
8. Janet3D, http://www.janet.de
9. Anfy3D, http://www.anfy3d.com
10. Kaon technology, http://www.kaon.com
11. PanoramIX, http://www.ibm.com
12. Photovista, http://www.mgisoft.com/webtools/photovista/pvmain.asp
13. Quicktime VR, http://www.apple.com/quicktime/qtvr
14. Mass Y. and Harzberg A.: VRCommerce - Electronic Commerce in Virtual Reality. ACM Conference on Electronic Commerce (1999)
15. Sun Microsystem, http://java.sun.com/
16. Dieberger, A., and Frank, A.U.: A City Metaphor to Support Navigation in Complex Information Spaces. Journal of Visual Languages and Computing **9** 6 (1998) 597-622
17. Card, S.K., Robertson, G.G., Mackinley, J.D.: The Information Visualizer: An Information Workspace. CHI'91 (1991) 181-188
18. Mukherjea, S., Foley, J.D.: Visualizing the World-Wide Web with the Navigational View Builder. GVU report GVU-TR 95-09 (1995) accessible at ftp://ftp.gvu.gatech.edu/pub/gvu/tech-reports/95-09.ps.Z
19. Hendley, R.J., et. al: Narcissus: Visualizing Information. InfoVis'95 IEEE Press (1995) 90-96
20. Chalmers, M.: Using a Landscape Metaphor to Represent a Corpus of Documents. COSIT'93 Springer (1993) 377-390
21. Andrews, K., Pichler, M., Wolf, P.: Towards Rich Information Landscapes for Visualising Structured Web Spaces. Proc. of 2nd IEEE Symposium on Information Visualization (InfoVis'96), San Francisco CA (1996) 62-63
22. Celentano, A.: Virtual worlds as metaphors for Web sites exploration: are they effective? IEEE Symposium on Visual Languages (1999) 204 -205
23. Russo dos Santos, C., Gros, P., Abel, P., Loisel, D., Trichaud, N., Paris, J.P.: Metaphor-aware 3D navigation. IEEE Symposium on Information Visualization (InfoVis'00) (2000) 155-165
24. CosmoPlayer VRML browser, http://www.cai.com/cosmo

Realising Real Time Multimedia Groupware on the Web

Colin Allison, Martin Bateman, Alan Ruddle

University of St Andrews
St Andrews, KY16 9SS
{ca,mb,alanr}@dcs.st-andrews.ac.uk

Abstract. Real-time audio and video conferencing has not yet been satisfactorily integrated into web-based groupware environments. Conferencing tools are at best only loosely linked to other parts of a shared working environment. This is mainly due to the special Quality of Service (QoS) requirements that these types of resources demand. This paper describes an approach to overcoming this problem by integrating the management of video and audio conferences into the resource allocation mechanism of an existing web-based groupware framework. The issue of adaptation is discussed and a means of initialising multimedia session parameters based on predicted QoS is described. In addition to linking audio and video media rendering quality to the predicted network QoS, the use of models to reduce bandwidth is also explored, replacing video content with control data. Component technologies utilised include the TAGS groupware framework, the Java Media Framework, a Conference Control Architecture and VRML-based avatars that can intermix with real actors.

1 Introduction

Web-oriented component technologies adhere to the 'anytime anywhere' requirements of distributed groupware and are largely platform neutral. The growth of the web as the preferred medium for group work has meant that, while the underlying principles of distributed groupware remain, there is now a clearly preferred means for its implementation and deployment. Systems which involve audio and video conferencing channels in addition to shared objects are referred to as real-time distributed groupware (RDG). Although a significant amount of groupware has been developed as embedded web applications, audio and video conferencing is still very much a bolt-on, and not at all satisfactorily integrated, or even possible to integrate. So, pre-web RDG exemplars such as the Warp shared spreadsheet [1] are particularly difficult to realise on the web[1].

[1] The Warp-based RDG exemplar was a multi-user, distributed, non-blocking shared spreadsheet object augmented with multicast audio and video channels. It used X-windows, IP Multicast, and RPC2, and is therefore an example of pre-web groupware. It was also a

The TAGS framework for groupware [2,3] differs from Warp in that it is completely web-oriented. It is currently used to support the development of groupware in the form of collaborative multi-user resources for teaching and learning. It has however proved difficult to incorporate real-time audio and video conferences into the system. Efforts to date have resorted to starting applications such as vic [4] and rat [5] either totally independently or from a browser script. This is not satisfactory as it means that (i) the session is not integrated in any useful way with the groupware resource allocation mechanisms, and (ii) a degree of technical expertise beyond that found in typical web users is required. This paper describes an approach to tackling this problem by using TAGS in conjunction with the Java Media Framework, a Conference Control Architecture and VRML-based Avatars that can intermix with real actors. The following sections describe the TAGS resource allocation mechanism, the Java Media Framework (JMF), QoS issues, adaptation strategies, a Conference Control Architecture and the role of Avatars in QoS-aware groupware environments.

2 Groupware Resource Allocation

TAGS, the Tutors and Groups Support scheme, is a project that researches, develops and deploys distributed learning environments. In TAGS groups form the basis of (i) privileges and access control, (ii) information dissemination and event awareness and (iii) allocation of shared resources. A home page, or portal, is generated dynamically for each TAGS user, and presents access via hyperlinks to all the resources allocated to all the groups that that an individual belongs to. TAGS provides three main abstractions for tutors: users, groups and resources. Each user is a member of one or more groups and each group is allocated zero or more resources. The concept of a resource is deliberately loose. It can be a simple timetable, an automated assessment exercise or an interactive multi-user simulation.

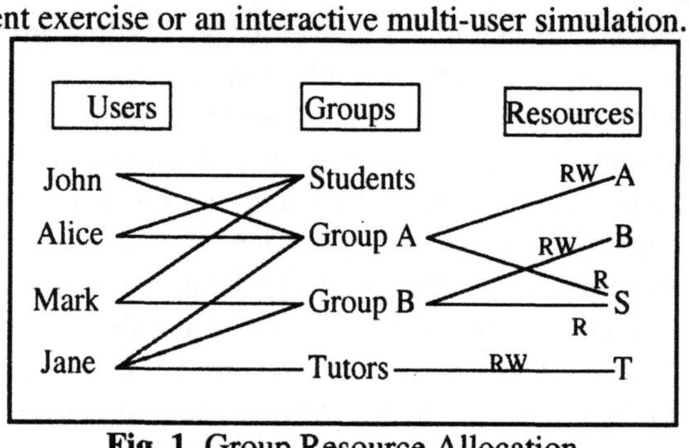

Fig. 1. Group Resource Allocation

In practical terms, tutors construct a collaborative learning environment by using the Users, Groups and Resources management tool. This sets up arbitrary relationships between users and resources, using groups as the basis for the mapping. Users and groups are unique by name; resources are unique by name and type. Access

system that required a significant degree of technical expertise to install and use, in strong contrast to the ease of use and deployment associated with web-based approaches.

rights can be specified when a resource is allocated to a group. A resource may simply be distinguished as Read-only or Read-Write, or it may export a more subtle set of access methods. This allows a particular resource instance to be allocated with different access methods to different users. Figure 1 illustrates an example set of relationships between users, groups and resources. John, Alice and Mark are members of the Students group. There are no resources shown allocated to the Students group. Jane is a Tutor and has created Groups A and B. John, Alice and Jane are in Group A and have resources A and S allocated. S is allocated to group A on a Read-only basis, whereas A is Read-Write. Mark and Jane are in Group B, which can access resource B as Read-Write and resource S as Read-only.

Could this allocation model be used to manage video conferences, as shared resources? The IP Real Time Protocol [6] (RTP) supports multicast *sessions* and participants, where a session is a short-lived entity which consists of members consisting of IP hosts specified by a mixture of multicast and unicast addresses and port numbers. In order to interoperate with the TAGS framework, there must be functionality to allocate the sessions to groups from within TAGS. This would mean that multimedia sessions are easy to setup and join, since the complexity of multicast addresses and port numbers is abstracted away from the user. The traditional method of joining multimedia conferencing session on the MBone [7] is via the Session Directory protocol, implemented by the `sdr` tool. SDR displays a list of sessions which are either scheduled to take place or which are currently underway. The entries consist of a multicast IP address, a port number, the multicast scope in the form of a Time To Live (TTL) value, the RTP payload type and some textual information about the session. From this information any session advertised by sdr may be joined. The mechanism we propose replaces the need to use `sdr` when joining a multicast session from within the TAGS framework, although it does not eliminate the need for the session directory protocol.

3 The Java Media Framework

The Java Media Framework (JMF) [8] is a collection of APIs which aim to provide a method for handling time based multimedia within Java. It does this by allowing the capture, transmission, storage and displaying of various formats of audio and video. There are two main distributions for the JMF, a pure Java implementation and a native library version. The pure Java implementation is limited in that it is unable to capture or transmit video/audio. It can however, render audio/video streams that it receives. In the native version the majority of the processing is performed by platform specific code. This has significant performance advantages over a pure Java implementation and offers greater capabilities for the programmer and user. A simple JMF application has three main parts. There is (i) a DataSource, which receives multimedia data from devices such as video capture cards or sounds cards; (ii) a Processor that can be used to change the format, frame rate, image depth or bitrate of the multimedia data - for example, video could be encoded to H.263 at 23 fps 120Kbps; (iii) a DataSink which is used when sending the data to its final destination - this could be to the screen, to a file, or the network.

JMF supports various network protocols for the transmission of multimedia. The most interesting of these from this projects point of view is multicast RTP[6] which can be used to disseminate realtime multimedia to a group of users. JMF's major advantage when compared to other video conferencing technologies is that since it is Java based, it can be incorporated into applets that can then be integrated into a web environment. There are several ways in which the bandwidth used within a conferencing session can be varied. These include, video frame rate, video size, image resolution, image depth, audio resolution, audio sample rate, changing codec and changing media. Table 1 shows the RTP payload types that are supported by the default installation of the JMF. Additional multiplexers, demultiplexers, filters and codecs can be added to the JMF via means of a plug-in architecture. Plug-ins must be registered on the host machine before they can be used.

A/V	Media Encoding	Cross Platform	Native Library	Bit Rate (sample)
A	G.711 (U-law) 8Khz, 8 bits mono	Rcv/Tx	Rcv/Tx	64 kb/s,
A	G.723 mono	Rcv	Rcv/Tx	6.5 kb/s
A	4-bit mono DVI, 8 Khz	Rcv/Tx	Rcv/Tx	32 kb/s
A	4-bit mono DVI 11.025 Khz	Rcv/Tx	Rcv/Tx	44 kb/s
A	4-bit mono DVI 22.05 Khz	Rcv/Tx	Rcv/Tx	Varies 0.0 -100 kb/s
A	MPEG Layer I 48 Khz @ 16 bits per sample, mono,			64 kb/s
A	MPEG Layer II 22 Khz @ 16 bits per sample, mono,			32 kb/s
A	MPEG Layer III 44 Khz @ 16 bits per sample mono	Rcv/Tx	Rcv/Tx	64 kb/s
V	JPEG (411, 422, 111) *	Rcv	Rcv/Tx	1.5Mb/s @ 320x200 @ 19fps
V	H.261	-	Rcv	-
V	H.263 **	Mode A Only	Rcv/Tx	120kb/s @ 176x144 @ 25fps
V	MPEG-I ***	Tx	Rcv/Tx	Depends on encoded media

* *Video dimensions must be multiples of 8 pixels*
** *Can only be transmitted as one of 128x96, 176x144, 352x288*
*** *Only from pre-encoded media e.g. mpeg encoded file.*

Table 1. JMF Supported Multicast RTP payloads

The primary channel of communication in a video conference is the audio channel, with the video link providing additional information, such as the expression of the other person. This generally aids in communication by providing telepresence and leads to fewer misunderstandings, even when the bit rate used for audio is low. The default native H.263 video codec has a relatively low bit rate and high picture quality.

4 Quality of Service Issues

An important distinction between different types of traffic is whether timeliness is more important than reliability. For example, a multi-way video-conference can tolerate the loss of some data in transit, but will run into severe difficulties if packets are not delivered within a given time frame. The reference application for the work described in this paper is to support synchronous communication between small groups of people using a variety of media. For example, in a tutorial session consisting of a tutor and half a dozen students the allocated resources would include synchronous duplex video and audio channels, and shared objects. Shared objects typically require full data integrity rather than very low latency and high bandwidth. On the web this usually means employing HTTP/TCP.

Groupware Environment *multiple resources with different QoS requirements*	
shared objects, usually server based	peer-to-peer multicast media flows
Hyper Text Transfer Protocol (HTTP)	Real Time Protocol (RTP) *a time-aware protocol*
Transmission Control Protocol (TCP) *two-party completely reliable data exchange, no time guarantees*	User Datagram Protocol (UDP) *adds port numbers to IP datagrams, the basis for best effort IP multicast*
Internet Protocol (IP) *unreliable, best effort*	

Table 2. Network protocols and the QoS they provide

Table 2 summarises the network protocols involved in supporting web-based groupware that includes real-time multimedia. A video connection using the JMF H.263 video codec at 176x144 and 24 f/s requires 120Kb/s and an audio connection using LPC encoding at 8 Khz mono requires 5.6Kb/s. per second. Putting these together means that a reasonable quality audio/video conference requires a total of 125.6Kb/s per sender. Multicast networking avoids the $2*n^2$ connection problem, where n is the number of participants. So, where a tutorial group consists of 6 students and one tutor, the overall bandwidth required is about 879.2Kb/s. The networks used to facilitate communication may have different characteristics for different groups. Postgraduates may engage in a small symposium, whilst being connected directly to 100Mb/s ethernet switches. An undergraduate tutorial might involve a shared connection to a 10Mb/s hub for participants connecting from student residences. The need may arise for cross-institutional conferences during which data must traverse each institution's connection to a wide area network, at which point competing traffic may severely constrain bandwidth availability and increase jitter. Some participants may participate from a home computer. Here the technology used in the "last mile" will constrain bandwidth. ADSL allows up to 256 Kb/s upload, ISDN-2 128 Kb/s and a V90 modem 56 Kb/s. In the scenario where bandwidth is plentiful, the system should be able to make full use of the available resources, thereby ensuring a good QoS for the participants. On the other hand, when bandwidth is scarce, a solution is required that does not waste the constrained resource or act unfairly in relation to competing traffic.

4.1 Case Study: The Finesse Groupware Environment

Finesse [9] is a TAGS-based learning environment used to teach fund management to Business and Finance students. At its core is a Portfolio Management Facility [10] which uses real time data[2] from the London Stock Exchange. Groups of students are allocated a Portfolio with a starting balance of £100 million. They can inspect changes and historic data in a range of companies, buy and sell shares, look at their portfolio profit and loss, and follow links to other sources of market information. Money left unused is credited with interest based on rates that are downloaded daily. Each group is also allocated a Notebook facility, to communicate with each other and their tutor concerning their investment decisions. The QoS for the share data is interesting in that it has to be both timely *and* reliable. Ideally, teams would also be allocated video conferencing sessions to further increase the real world dimension of the learning environment.

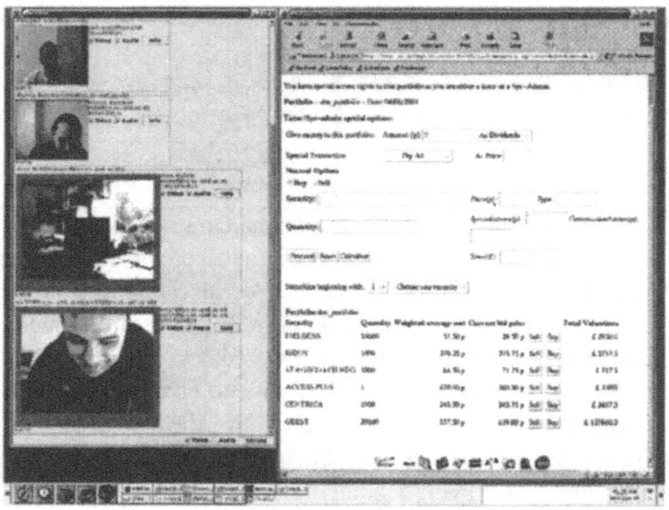

Fig. 2: A Finesse Session

An early attempt to do so using the Mbone tools co-located on the same machine as the web browser suffered from the same problems as the Warp-based shared spreadsheet. JMF-based applets makes it possible to allocate conference sessions to groups, in the same way that they are allocated Portfolios and Notebooks. Fig. 2 shows the Finesse environment (the transaction page is showing) expanded to include an allocated conference resource.

5 Adaptation Strategy

Research [11] has shown that consistency of quality is often more important to users than the actual quality of service achieved. For example, if during the lifetime of a video session, the achievable frame rate varies between two bounds, it is arguably

[2] The data source used is free, is 20 minutes old and is sampled every 5 minutes.

better to present using the lower bound throughout the session rather than try to dynamically optimise the quality. Given that it is desirable to avoid adaptation to network conditions during the lifetime of a session, it follows that a long period of probing from a low starting point for an appropriate operating point is undesirable. Previously, it has been envisaged that this problem could be addressed by combining admission control with resource reservation [12] to provide a guaranteed QoS for the duration of a session. Assuming (realistically) that such facilities are unavailable, what can be achieved in their absence?

The approach under investigation involves collecting statistics of the conditions experienced by past sessions in a common repository and then making predictions at the start of a conference about the conditions that are likely to prevail during its lifetime. This approach is similar to that adopted for a Location Information Server [13]. These predictions can be used to initialise relevant parameters, so that a QoS appropriate to the available network resources can be achieved at the start of, and maintained for the duration of, the conference. Furthermore this can be achieved without expert user intervention, which is an important consideration where the participants in a conference may not be expert users.

6 QoS Aware Conference Control

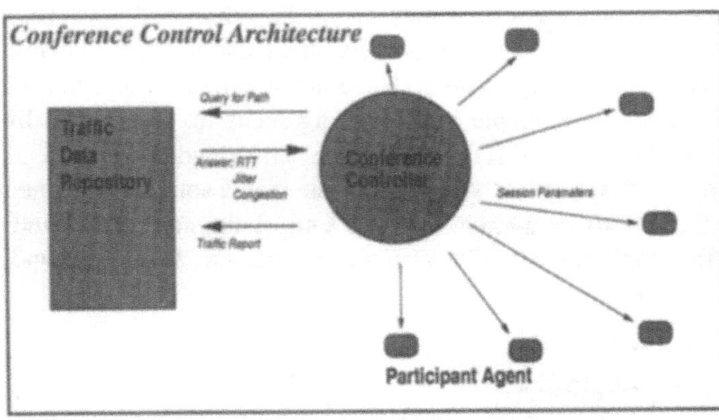

Fig. 3. Conference Control Architecture

There are three main components of the system shown in Fig.3; a Traffic Data Repository (TDR), a Conference Controller (CC) and Participant Agents (PAs). These components build upon the services provided by the Real Time Protocol (RTP) and the Real Time Control Protocol (RTCP).

RTP provides end-to-end network transport functions suitable for applications transmitting real-time data, such as audio, video or simulation data, over multicast or unicast network services. RTP does not address resource reservation and does not guarantee quality-of-service for real-time services. The data transport is augmented by a control protocol (RTCP) to allow monitoring of the data delivery in a manner scalable to large multicast networks, and to provide minimal control and identification functionality. An RTP session provides the association between a set of participants that are communicating using RTP. For each of the participants the session is defined by a network address and two ports. One port is for data and the other for control traffic. In a multimedia conference, each medium is carried in a separate RTP session with is own control packets. Thus in the scenario of a conference utilising video, voice, chat, a whiteboard and a presentation application there would be five RTP sessions. The session is also the granularity at which information about the state of the network is collected and disseminated to participants. In a session there may be multiple senders and receivers of data. RTCP Sender Reports contain a Synchronisation Source identifier (SSI), which is unique within the scope of a session. Associated with each SSI are a number of traffic statistics. These include timestamps to facilitate the calculation of Round Trip Times (RTTs), counts of the total packets sent and the total number of packets lost during the session, and the proportion of packets lost since the last report. There is also an estimate of the inter-arrival jitter.

6.1 Participant Agent

A PA is located on the server running the web environment. At start up it receives a description of the path to each participant from the conference controller and the sessions available in the conference. Based upon the bandwidth information the agent decides which sessions to subscribe to and, based upon the jitter description, it configures the size of the play out buffers for the subscribed sessions. The play-out buffers must be either set to an appropriately small size in order to maintain the real-time interactive nature of the system. There are situations where the play-out buffer could be increased, for example in a lecturing scenario. During the lifetime of the conference the PA receives RTCP Receivers and Senders reports. These reports contain estimates of packet loss and jitter for the media sources. The agent maps these statistics from SSIs to IP numbers. At the end of the conference and periodically throughout the conference traffic statistic reports are generated and sent to the conference controller.

6.2 Conference Controller

The CC is located on a central machine. At the initiation of the conference it queries the TDR for predictions of traffic conditions on the paths between conference participants. Based upon this information, it determines which media to use in the conference and the total bandwidth available on each path. From this information it uses a policy to partition the bandwidth between the available media and determines appropriate frame rates, resolutions and sampling rates. These policies can also take the relative importance of the users into consideration. For example, in a tutorial session the tutor's media could be given higher bandwidth allocations and therefore higher quality. For the duration of the conference, the CC monitors the entry and exit of participants and receives reports from PAs of the network conditions. In the case of a strong mismatch between expected and experienced conditions, it may be necessary to adjust bandwidth allocation and other parameters. When this happens, update instructions are sent to each PA, using the Lightweight Reliable Multicast Protocol. At the end of the conference, the CC generates a report to the TDR of the network conditions and traffic characteristics between each of the participants. This report allows the repository to determine the accuracy of its predictions and to update the data held on the utilised paths.

6.3 Traffic Data Repository

The TDR provides a central repository for information about network paths. Consequently, information gathered from one conference can be made available to future conferences. The age of the data held in the repository is also maintained. This enables a CC to make a judgement about the reliability of the data. The TDR provides an interface that allows it to be remotely queried by a CC or other application about the expected traffic characteristics for a path. The TDR will also receive reports from the CC about the network conditions experienced during a session.

6.4 Collecting the Path Characteristics

In the above architecture it is the responsibility of the Participant Agent to monitor RTCP reports and generate reports to be utilised by the CC. This involves two functions: determining the end point IP addresses of sources and receivers and extracting meaningful traffic statistics from RTCP Sender and Receiver Reports. These statistics are then aggregated into reports for the CC. The CC is then able to take any necessary control actions and generate its own reports to the TDR. RTCP packets contain reports for synchronisation sources and receivers. It is necessary to establish a mapping from the SSI to unicast IP addresses, because the SSI may change between sessions. This can be achieved by observing the IP address of the source. The IP address of the report originator can also be determined from the source IP address on the reports. With these addresses established statistics generated by RTCP can be associated with the path between the two unicast IP addresses. Traffic statistics need to be extracted from the data streams.

There are three main statistics of interest. The proportion of packets lost (congestion), the round trip time and the inter-arrival jitter.

- Congestion: Each receiver's report contains the fraction of packets lost since the previous report. The receiver calculates this fraction by dividing, the number of packets it received by the number of packets expected, since the last report.
- Round Trip Time Estimation: It is necessary to determine the RTT to facilitate mapping between fair window sizes and fair rates. Each sender's report contains an NTP time stamp for the time that the report was generated. This is used with receiver's reports to facilitate the calculation of RTTs.
- Jitter: It is necessary to determine the amount of jitter to configure the play-out buffer for real-time media. Too large a buffer will increase delay, too small a buffer will result in packets arriving too late to be of use. A measurement of inter-arrival jitter is included in receiver's reports. This is an estimate of the statistical variance of the RTP data packet inter-arrival time.

7 A Role for Avatars in Adaptation?

When advice from the CC suggests realtime video is not easily sustainable a model-based approach may prove useful in order to maintain telepresence. If a model of a participant is already present on each participant's machine then relatively low bandwidth control data can be multicast to animate that model. The need for a video stream is removed while the illusion of video conferencing still remains. From another perspective, if the quality of the video is likely to be very poor then an avatar may perform as well, or better, and use considerably less bandwidth.

Avatars may be created on the web by using the virtual reality modelling language (VRML) [14], the current standard being VRML97 [15], with X3D [16] currently being specified. A VRML viewer is used to view an avatar. These come in a number of different forms, applets/browser plug-ins, standalone applications and graphical components that can be embedded into other applications. A VRML viewer which conforms to the External Authoring Interface (EAI) [17] allows other applications to control what is happening within a virtual world. This is useful for conferencing as it allows the avatar to be synchronised with the audio channel (lip movements for example). This mechanism also provides a method of animating the avatar so that it moves like a desktop video conference participant, for example blinking and moving, instead of staying in the same place all the time.

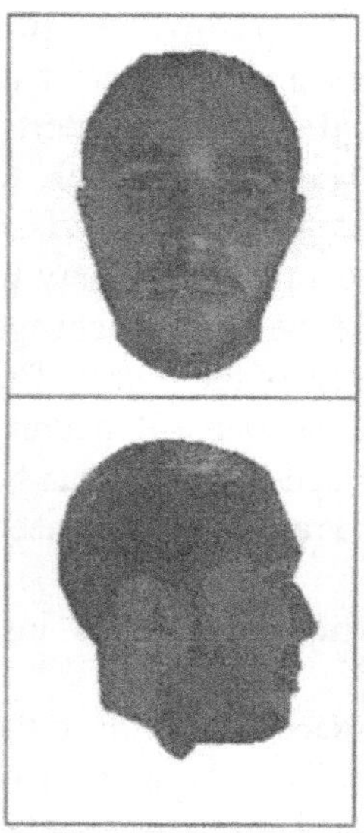

Fig.4a. The basis for a simple avatar

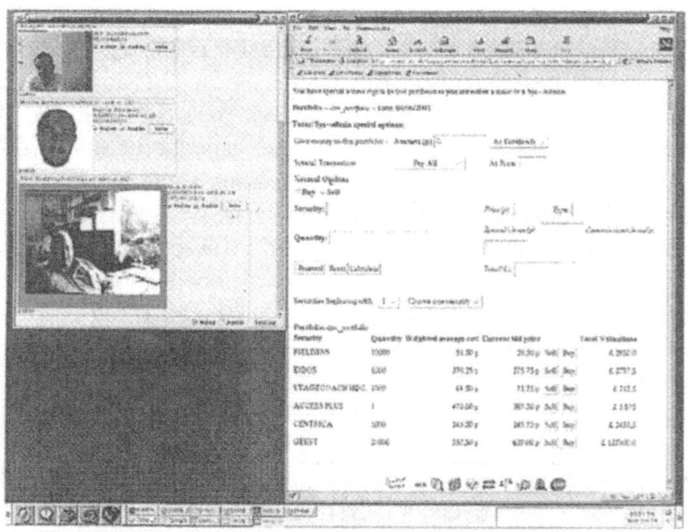

Fig.4b. The avatar in a conference with real actors

A simple avatar can be constructed from two perspectives and is around 80KB (Fig. 4a). This must be initially downloaded to each participant agent. In the case of the tutorial, with 6 students and 1 tutor this would require 560KB of avatar data to represent all participants. With the use of silence suppression and avatars the bandwidth required to participate in a conference could be reduced from 880Kb/s per second to 6.Kb/s, (the bandwidth required for a single audio channel), assuming that only one person talks at a time. Figure 4b shows the avatar appearing in a video conference.

7.1 Face Tracking

Face tracking techniques [18] based on the position and direction of a participants head can be derived and used to control their avatar, thus returning some of the feedback that a standard video channel provides. A face tracking avatar requires 5 pieces of control information: the x, y, z positions in space and the horizontal and vertical roll. With this information the face can be placed in 3 dimensional space and the direction it is facing controlled. Control information is 75 bytes per message (assuming 16 bit number for each element), which at 16 frames per second is around 1K per second per person within the multimedia conferencing session. So, in the example tutorial session, this is only 7Kb/s per second for all the members of the session. However, facial tracking and image manipulation are potentially difficult to implement well and further work is necessary to evaluate the feasibility of this approach.

8 Conclusion

Although video conferencing is seen as an essential part of distributed groupware there is still little sign of its presence in the growing number of web-based groupware environments. When it is present it is not integrated with the web and is typically difficult to install and use. The JMF, which supports RTP, offers the possibility of creating video conferencing session applets which can be allocated using the same high-level mechanisms as other shared resources. An approach based on the use of TAGS groupware resource allocation system to incorporate RTP sessions implemented as JMF applets looks promising.

Inevitably, as with all time-sensitive media, QoS issues surface. It was noted that consistency throughout a session is preferable to chopping and changing with the prevailing network conditions. This raises the problem of finding an appropriate set of QoS initialisation parameters that can be realistically supported for the duration of a session. A Conference Control Architecture has been described that addresses this problem through the maintenance and use of a Traffic Data Repository to store and predict network conditions. The CCA also allows for different QoS initialisations for heterogenous connections. In much video conferencing the most important dimension is the audio, with the video providing realism through telepresence. An approach using the web-oriented VRML to create simple models of participant's faces - avatars - is being investigated as it has the potential to dramatically reduce bandwidth requirements for situations where that resource is scarce.

The systems described in this paper represent a novel and promising approach to realising real time multimedia groupware on the web. Further work will concentrate on their continued development and evaluation.

9 References

1. Allison, C., F. Huang, and M.J. Livesey, *Object Coherence in Distributed Interaction*, in *Multimedia'99*, N. Correia, T. Chambel, and G. Davenport, Editors. 1999, Springer-Verlag: New York. p. 123-132.
2. Allison, C., M. Bramley, R. Michaelson, and J. Serrano. *An Integrated Framework for Distributed Learning Environments*. in *"Advances in Concurrent Engineering", 6th ISPE International Conference on Concurrent Engineering*. 1999. Bath.
3. Allison, C., D. McKechan, A. Ruddle, and R. Michaelson. *A Group Based System for Group Based Learning*. in *European Perspectives on Computer-supported Collaborative Learning, the proceedings of Euro CSCL 2001*. 2001. Maastricht: Maastricht McLuhan Institute.
4. McCanne, S. and V. Jacobson. *VIC: A Flexible Framework for Packet Video*. in *ACM Multimedia*. 1995. San Francisco.
5. Perkins, C.S., O. Hodson, and V. Hardman, *A Survey of Packet-Loss Recovery Techniques for Streaming Audio*. IEEE Network, 1998.
6. Schulzrinne, H. and e. al., *IETF RFC 1889 RTP: a transport protocol for real time applications*. 1996.
7. Jacobson, V., *et al. A Reliable Multicast Framework for Lightweight Sessions and Application-Level Framing*. in *ACM SIGComm 95*. 1995.
8. Sun Microsystems. *JMF: The Java Media Framework*. 2001.
9. Helliar, C.V., R. Michaelson, D.M. Power, and C.D. Sinclair, *Using a Portfolio Management Game (FINESSE) to Teach Finance*. Accounting Education, 2000. **9**(1): p. 37-51.
10. Power, D.M., R. Michaelson, and C. Allison. *The Finesse Portfolio Management Facility*. in *9th CTI-AFM Conference*. 1998. York: CTI-AFM.
11. Bouch, A. and M.A. Sasse. *The Case for Predictable Network Service*. in *MMCN'2000*. 2000. San Jose: ACM.
12. Braden, B., D. Zhang, S. Estrin, and S. Jamin, *Resource ReSerVation Protocol (RSVP) -Version 1 Functional Specification*. 1996: IETF Working Document.
13. Ruddle, A. *A Location Information Server for the Internet*. in *International Conference on Communications and Computer Networks*. 2000. Las Vegas.
14. Web3D_Consortium, *VRML: The Virtual Reality Modeling Language*, in *http://www.vrml.org/*. 2000.
15. VRML_Consortium_Inc., *Part 1: Functional specification and UTF-8 encoding, International Standard ISO/IEC 14772-1*. 1997.
16. Web3D_Consortium, *X3D, http://www.web3d.org/TaskGroups/x3d/index.html*.
17. VRML_Consortium_Inc., *The virtual Reality Modeling Language (VRML) -- Part 2: External authoring interface, International Standard ISO/IEC FDIS 14772-2*. 2001.
18. Jie, R.S., U. Meier, and A. Waibel. *Real-time face and facial feature tracking and applications*. in *AVSP'98*. 1998. Terrigal, Australia.

Abstractions in Multimedia Authoring: The MAVA Approach

Jürgen Hauser, Jing Tian

Institute of Parallel and Distributed High-Performance Systems (IPVR)
University of Stuttgart, Breitwiesenstr. 20-22, D - 70565 Stuttgart, Germany
{juergen.hauser, jing.tian}@informatik.uni-stuttgart.de

Abstract. The support of abstractions in authoring systems increases the efficiency of the specification of multimedia documents. Authoring based on a very low abstraction, for example script programming, is very complex and time consuming. In addition, authoring systems supporting a high abstraction are so far restricted to one specific application area. This paper presents an extensible approach that supports abstractions in different application areas (such as computer-based training or a travel guide).
In this approach a meta document model and the corresponding presentation and authoring system are developed. During conception of the authoring system, different concepts (e.g. templates or application specific views) have been realized to introduce further abstractions.

1. Introduction

Although different multimedia document standards [1, 5], research approaches [3, 2, 6] and commercial products [14] have been proposed, the specification of multimedia documents and multimedia authoring are still very complex tasks. An investigation of existing approaches shows that so far multimedia authoring concentrates mainly on the support of the temporal and spatial layout of multimedia documents. Starting with interaction, things tend to become difficult and sometimes the use of scripting languages cannot be avoided [4].

Multimedia documents in different application areas differ in the way users interact with them and how documents react to this interaction. For example, a question in a computer-based training system can be answered either right or wrong. Depending on the answer a different reaction is expected. In case of a right answer, the user gets a compliment, while in case of a wrong answer he or she gets an explanation of the correct answer.

A tourist guide as another example is a multimedia presentation that provides information about particular places of interest. In a tourist guide, the current physical position of the tourist (e.g. in a city or on an island) determines what has to be presented. A change of position is an interaction with a multimedia presentation, so if the user moves into the proximity of a place of interest, the presentation of the corresponding part will be started.

To simplify authoring, an authoring tool has to provide abstractions for particular application areas. These abstractions simplify authoring and thus save time. A second requirement is that it should be possible to use the same authoring tool independently of the application area. And last but not least, it should be possible to add support for new application areas. The last two requirements cannot be satisfied by providing a particular authoring system for each application area (such as Macromedia Authorware).

In this paper an approach that supports authoring in different application areas is presented. Therefore the approach introduces a meta document language that has concrete instances for each application area. The meta language is based on an operator approach where relations between media items are expressed through operators. Application specific operators are a first step in providing a higher abstraction level for multimedia authoring.

A major aspect of an authoring tool is the design of a user interface that is used for authoring documents. It is very important that only a few interaction steps are required during authoring. A specification language on a high abstraction level keeps the authoring process simple in contrast to approaches with a low abstraction level (e.g. script programming). Abstractions and concepts of the authoring tool, for example a template mechanism, further simplify the authoring process.

The MAVA approach relies on the availability of abstractions (in terms of a language or a model) for an application area. If an abstraction is not available, it has to be realized by a MAVA expert, who has programming skills and knowledge about the MAVA presentation system. In practice, however, this is not a big disadvantage of the approach, because reuse of previously developed extensions is expected. Hence, the more extensions have been developed, the less development of new ones is required.

This paper gives an overview of the implementation of the MAVA presentation system and MAVA authoring tool. The realization of the MAVA system is based on Java and the Java Media Framework (JMF).

The results presented in this paper are achieved through the research project MAVA (*M*ultimedi*a* Document *V*ersatile *A*rchitecture), which is supported by a research initiative of the German Research Foundation (DFG) called "Distributed Processing and Exchange of Digital Documents (V3D2)" [13].

The paper is organized as follows. Related work is discussed in section 2. Section 3 introduces the meta document model used in the MAVA approach. In section 4 an authoring tool based on the meta model is presented. Section 5 discusses abstractions based on the model that were integrated into the authoring tool to support authors during specification. In section 6 the architectures of the presentation system and the authoring tool are presented together with details of the implementation. Section 7 summarizes this paper.

2. Related Work

There are two major alternatives for the specification of multimedia documents. The first is to provide a generic language which increases the effort for specification. Another alternative is to provide a specific presentation system for each application area.

A generic system provides a programming or scripting language for the specification of application specific functionality. In such a scripting language there is no support or model for any application area. Examples for presentation systems that provide a scripting language are MHGE5+MEHG6 [5] or Macromedia Director and its scripting language Lingo [14]. An application specific model provides a higher abstraction and therefore reduces the effort needed to specify a presentation. The realization of the semantics is encapsulated in components. Components are reused by the specification language model. Hence, the realization of the semantics and the descriptive specification are separated. Additional concepts, such as a library for scripts, simplify script programming, but they do not provide an application specific model which supports authors during specification.

In contrast, the MAVA approach hides how semantics are realized from authors. Authors just want to specify what the document should look like and not how its semantics are realized, as it is the case if script programming is used.

Another approach is the development of individual presentation systems for each application area. This approach leads to a big overhead for users and content providers because they have to know these systems in detail for content creation and support of users of these systems. Additionally, there is a big effort if each presentation and authoring system has to be developed from scratch. Examples for such an approach are Macromedia Authorware or Question Mark Designer. Also all approaches which provide a fixed language belong to this category (e.g. SMIL 2.0 [1], TIEMPO [3] or Madeus [2]). Their use is limited to the application area defined by their language concepts. For example it is impossible to specify a multiple choice question in SMIL 2.0 that gives the user a certain amount of time so that the user can alter his or her answer within that time. The reason is that the SMIL 2.0 language does not cover such an application area.

In [6] an approach is presented which allows the mapping different temporal concepts on a generic internal representation for temporal concepts. This is a first step towards enlarging the applicability of a system. But not all concepts are time dependent and therefore different models are reasonable. For example, the current position of a user determined by GPS (Global Positioning System) as another way to interact with a presentation leads to a model which depends on the spatial position of the user but not on time. Such a concept can be used in multimedia travel guides as described in the introduction.

3. A Meta Document Model Supporting Abstractions

Instead of using a generic language like a script language, the MAVA approach uses an operator-based language on a high abstraction level. In an operator-based approach, operators are used to specify relations between media items. A document consists of a set of media items and relations between them. A presentation system ensures that relations specified by authors are maintained during presentation. In that sense authoring is the selection of media items and the specification of relations between them.

Apart from the two basic document elements, media items and operators, there is an additional element, a so-called container element. A container is an element that contains operators and media items. Hence, a container is a further abstraction in the specification process. Logical parts of the document specification are grouped together and replaced by a container element. For example, the specification of a question in a computer-based training application can be placed into a container. The next example makes use of a container, namely a *question* container.

For an application area the meta document model has to be instantiated. This means that there are concrete media items, operators and containers for an application area. Fig. 1 shows two sample specifications for the examples mentioned in the introduction section where each example uses a different language.

In Fig. 1 operators are represented by rectangles containing the operator name. Containers are represented by a rectangle that has a shadow. Fig. 1a represents the computer-based training application. In this example a question is related with two scene containers. One represents the congratulation scene and the other one is the explanation scene. The specification has two relations which are represented by a *correct* operator and a *false* operator. The *correct* operator is used to specify which scene has to be presented when the answers is right, the *false* operator specifies which scene has to be presented when the answer is wrong. It is important to distinguish between source and destination media items because the *question* container is presented before the *congrats* or *explanation* scene. Hence, the *question* container is the source media item and the *congrats* scene the destination media. The question is also specified in a descriptive language (not shown in Figure 1). The specification is on a high abstraction level because the author does not need to specify how it is determined whether the answer is right or not.

Fig. 1b shows the example of a tourist guide. A document has always a root container. In case of a tourist guide this is a *LocationArea* container. The container type is denoted in angel brackets '<' and '>'. A *LocationArea* container includes *Location* containers wherein the presentation for particular places of interest is specified. In the example, the *LocationArea* contains one *Location* and a *setLocation* and *circle* operator. With the *setLocation* operator the presentation of the place of interest is situated on a map. The *circle* operator determines the maximum distance between the user and the place of interest to allow the presentation of the *Location* to begin. The exact distance is given by a parameter of the *circle* operator.

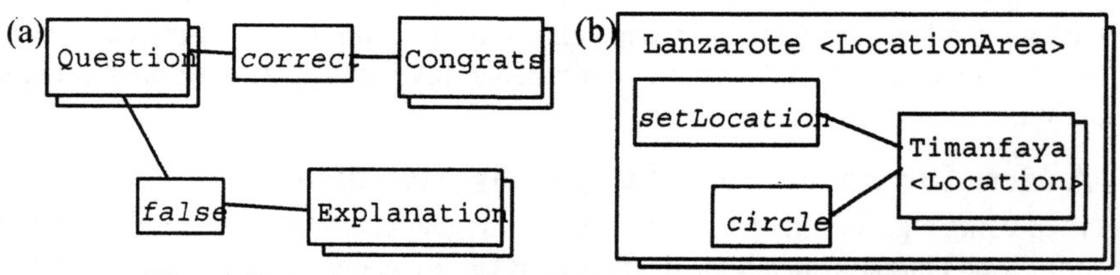

Fig. 1 ***Examples for specifications in two different application areas***

The realization of the semantics of the document model is very important. For the realization of semantics so-called managers have been introduced. A manager is responsible for the realization of the semantics of a set of operators. Corresponding media and container components realize the semantics of media items and containers. For details about the realization of the semantics please refer to [10, 11].

4. An Authoring Tool

The *MA*VA *Ed*itor (called MED) is an authoring system for MAVA documents. It visualizes the meta document model presented in the previous section and the necessary interaction steps for authoring MAVA documents. The graphical user interface makes use of the properties of the meta document model that are independent of the application area.

Fig. 2 gives an impression what the user interface of MED looks like. During authoring the author works with different windows. The most important window is the so-called icon view window. An icon view window represents one single container of the document. The window in the center of Fig. 2 (with the title "Timanfaya <Location>") shows the mapping of the abstract document model on. icons. The *Location* container comprises two media items and two operators. The *center* operator specifies that the video is centered in the presentation area, whereas the *while* operator [3] specifies that the video and the audio are presented in parallel.

To the left of the document window there are two windows for the selection of media items (top left) and operators (bottom left).

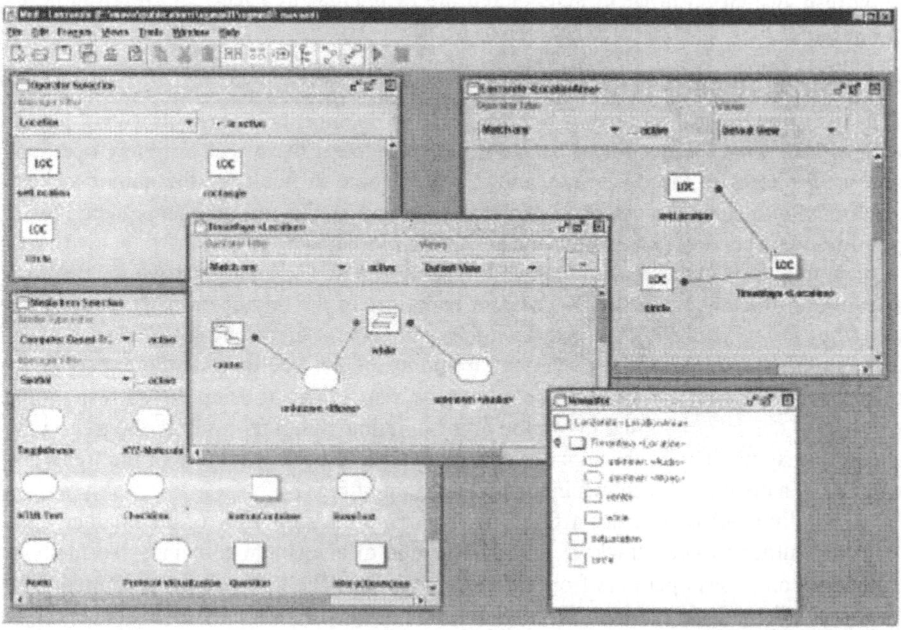

Fig. 2 A screenshot from MED

A document is specified by adding operators and media items and connecting operators to media items. MED provides all available operators, media items and containers in two windows (operator selection window and media item selection window). These windows provide filtering mechanisms to mask out operators which do not belong to a certain concept (e.g. temporal operators).

To add an operator to the document, an operator icon is dragged from the operator selection window and dropped into an icon view window. Media items are added in the same way. Parameters of media items and operators can be specified by so-called properties sheets which are invoked with the right mouse button.

A relation between media items is established by the connection of source and destination media items with an operator. To the left and the right of the operator there is a bullet as a user interface element to enable the connection of operators with media items. The bullet to the left is used for connections with source media, and the bullet to the right is connected to destination media. To connect a media item to an operator the author presses the mouse button on a bullet, moves the mouse pointer to the media icon and then releases the mouse button.

There are also operators which require only destination media items, for example the *center* operator which determines that a media item is spatially centered in the presentation area. Operators without source media just have a bullet to the right for the connection to destination media.

5. Abstractions in the Authoring Tool

Abstraction can be found not only in the meta document model, but also in the authoring system, in order to make authoring of documents easier and more intuitive for authors.

5.1 Navigation

For small multimedia documents, the structure of documents is straightforward for the author. But when the document becomes more complex, there will be many operators and media items in the document, and it will become difficult for the author to keep track of the document's structure. To make the navigation in documents clear, MED provides two concepts: a tree view and a filtering mechanism.

The tree view presents the document in form of a tree as an alternative for the visualization of documents in MED. The root container of the document is the root of the tree, the tree structure is obtained from the containment hierarchy introduced by containers. All containers of the document are nodes of the tree that can be expanded or collapsed. An author can open the icon view of a container or bring the corresponding window to the front by clicking on the corresponding container node in the tree view, allowing easy navigation through the document structure. An example of the tree view window of a document is shown in the bottom right of Fig. 2.

In addition, MED provides a filter mechanism in the icon view of a container. This helps an author to keep track of the specification of one single container. Normally, a container comprises operators from different concepts. The goal of operator filters is to mask out operators in the icon view, which do not belong to a particular concept. For example, if an author processes the temporal aspect of a document, he or she can mask out all operators that do not belong to the temporal concept. Hence, the author can concentrate on the temporal specification.

5.2 Templates

Templates are modules or patterns for regular reuse. The goal of templates in multimedia authoring is to improve reusability in multimedia document design. Compared to the systematic reuse in the field of software engineering [7], many authors still have to build multimedia documents from scratch [9]. To help authors, MED supports document templates as well.

Templates in MED not only improve reusability of authoring work, they also enable authors to design a document at a high level of abstraction. A part of the document, for example a multiple-choice question, can be saved as a template for later reuse. Since multiple-choice questions basically have the same structure, authors reuse a template each time. Hence, they no longer have to build the structure from scratch.

Some authoring systems such as Macromedia Flash, IBM Hotmedia and Tribeworks iShell do not support templates, which makes reuse of multimedia authoring very difficult. Although some authoring systems do support templates, e.g. Macromedia Authorware and ToolBook, there are still some common deficiencies in the template support of these authoring systems. On the one hand, the creation of sophisticated templates in these authoring systems still demands fundamental programming knowledge for script languages like Lingo and OpenScript. Since authors are not expected to be programmers, this requirement for programming knowledge has to be avoided. On the other hand, if the structural information is not visible and not clearly separated from the media information of the document, efficient reuse of parts of the document as templates is prevented.

The two problems described above can be avoided in templates provided by MED. Benefiting from the operator approach; the structural information in MAVA documents is visible and clearly separated from the media information of the document. The process of specifying templates in MED is the same as in normal documents. Any part of the document can be saved as a template for later reuse.

5.3 Application Specific Views

Further abstractions to simplify authoring are application specific views. Such a view makes an abstraction from the operators of a language and provides a graphical user interface.

For example, suppose there is the need to describe the spatial layout of a document in absolute coordinates. The required operators are *setPosition* and *setSize*. The specification of the spatial layout consists of several operators and attributes that have to be added step by step, but the spatial layout can be specified in a WYSIWYG view. A graphical visualization of the presentation area enables interactive positioning and resizing of media items. Dragging a media item to a new position determines the attributes for a *setPosition* operator. Hence, such an application specific view will create operators and alter attributes of operators automatically.

It is not possible to provide such views for all concepts. For example for temporal interval operators [5], such a view cannot be provided. It is also difficult to provide such a view for the relative spatial positioning of media items.

When possible, an additional view should be provided for all required specifications. This is not a must because documents can be specified on operator level anyway.

6. Implementation

Architectures for both the MAVA presentation system and the MAVA editor make use of similarities of the specification language in form of the meta document model. The meta document model leads to an implementation of the MAVA approach as a framework that can be extended by components. Components are used to realize the semantics of concrete specification languages (e.g. a manager for a set of operators).

6.1 MAVA Presentation System

Fig. 3 shows the architecture of the MAVA presentation system as it is implemented in the prototype. The core of the presentation system is the MAVA engine, which includes all functionality that is independent of the application area of a document. Examples for such functionality are document loading and class loading. The class manager loads all components that are required for the presentation of a document and caches them for optimization reasons if the extension is used in another document.

The MAVA presentation system provides a framework which is extended by different components loaded by the class manager. These components comprise operators and managers for the realization of a set of operators in a particular application area.

Media items are realized by media objects and media viewers. Media viewers are responsible for the presentation of a media item (e.g. a MPEG renderer) and media objects are responsible for the logical functionality of a media item. A multiple-choice question uses a check box button that has a state. The state describes whether the check box is selected or not. The state and the behavior of the check box are its logical functionality.

The MAVA presentation system is an extensible multimedia presentation system because all required media items, operators and managers for the presentation of a document are dynamically loaded prior to the presentation.

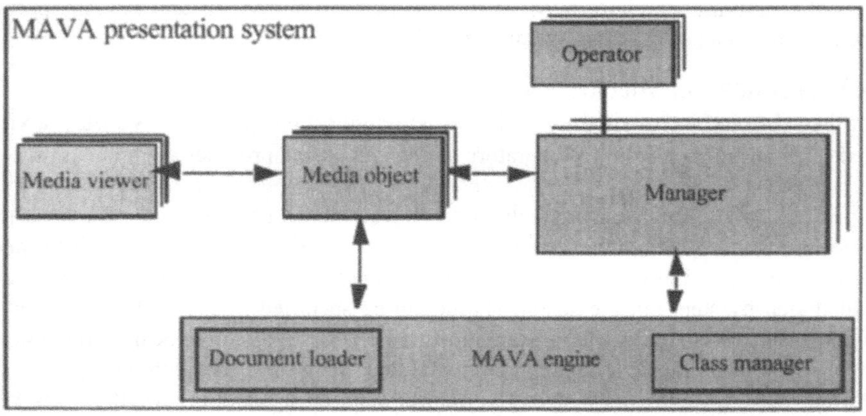

Fig. 3 Architecture of the MAVA presentation system

6.2 MAVA Editor

The core of the MAVA document Editor Architecture is the DEVR (document elements and views repository) and the editor document model (Fig. 4). The editor document model includes all functionality for an internal representation of a document. A document specification is a graph where media items and operators are vertices and connections of operators with media items are edges. For operators the functionality includes handling of references to media items, for containers the management of adding and removing of elements and for all elements the handling of their attributes.

The DEVR holds information on which specification languages can be used currently. Based on the DEVR, the type of actual document elements that are represented as vertices in the document graph are managed. For example the vertex of a media item has a reference to the type description (e.g. an audio medium) in the DEVR. The description from the DEVR describes which attributes are available, like the URL of the media data or the volume during play-out of an audio. The operator description also indicates to which types of media items an operator can be connected.

Based on the editor document model there are three different models that are part of a model-view-controller construct [8]. These models provide different views on the original editor document model. For example the XML model describes the mapping of the document model onto XML. The current implementation uses a graph representation and not a tree-based XML representation for reasons of simplicity (i.e. the document is a graph). Using an XML representation would make the XML model unnecessary but would complicate other modules. Hence, the graph is mapped only for storage in XML. A detailed description of the XML format used for storing and transferring MAVA documents can be found in [12].

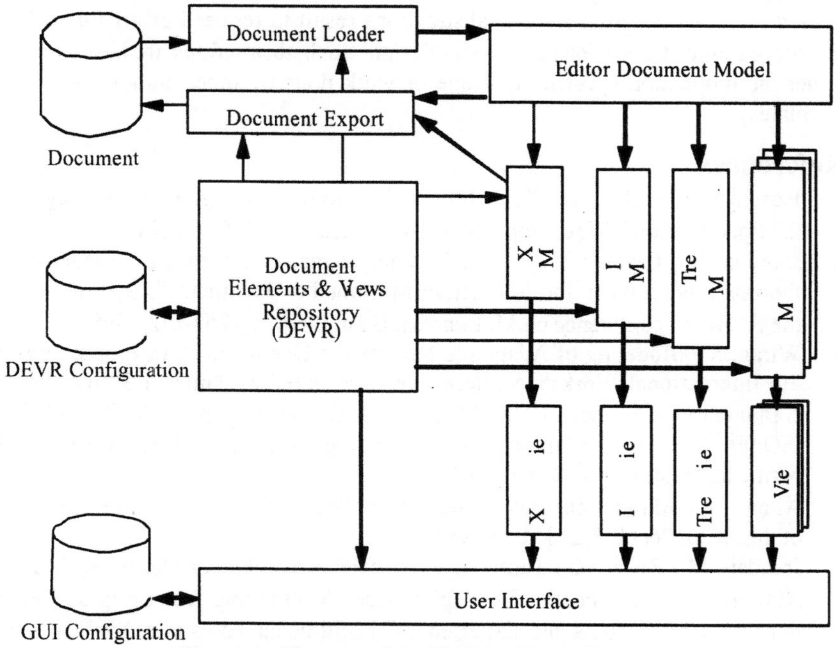

Fig. 4 ***Architecture of the MAVA editor (MED)***

The icon model describes all properties of the document model for the icon view in which an author uses drag and drop for editing a document. The tree model provides the model used for the tree view that supports navigation. For all these models there is also a view component that is responsible for the view and control of the corresponding model. It is also possible to integrate application specific views as described in section 5.3. The availability of application specific views is described by the DEVR. All views are integrated in the graphical user interface.

The last two important modules are the document loader and the document export. The document export module stores the XML model in a file. The document loader realizes the creation of the editor document model based on an XML file that represents a MAVA document.

The current configuration of MED is stored in two configuration files. The DEVR configuration stores the content of the DEVR and the GUI configuration stores the configuration of the graphical user interface, such as window size and working directory.

7. Summary

This paper presents an operator based approach for multimedia authoring. The main goal of the MAVA approach is to support extensibility of the multimedia system with specification languages for different application areas. This is achieved by application specific models (e.g. a computer based training or a travel guide) that provide a high level of abstraction. For authoring, these models are represented by operators. Operators are a mechanism to reuse application specific functionality and templates are used to reuse parts of existing documents in other documents.

An authoring tool that allows interactive document specification is also presented. Throughout the paper different levels of abstraction of the approach are shown and discussed. In practice, high level of abstractions result in reduced effort for authors and therefore reduced costs for multimedia design. Such abstractions are based on reuse of either an application specific language or work done by other authors (e.g. reuse of templates).

References

1. Hoschka, P. et al. (Eds.) "Synchronized Multimedia Integration Language (SMIL) 2.0 Specification". W3C Proposed Recommendation. W3C. 6/2001.
2. Jourdan, M., Layaida N., Roisin, C., Sabry-Ismail, L., Tardif, L. "Madeus, An Authoring Environment for Interactive Multimedia Documents". In Proceedings of the ACM int. conference on Multimedia, Bristol, UK, pp 267-272, 1998.
3. Wirag, S. "Modeling of Adaptable Multimedia Documents". In Proceedings of the 4th International Workshop Interactive Distributed Multimedia Systems and Telecommunication Services, (IDMS'97), Darmstadt, Germany, pp. 220-230,9/1997.
4. ISO/IEC DIS 13522-5."Information Technology - Coding of Multimedia and Hypermedia Information - Part 5". 1995.
5. Allen, J.F. "Maintaining Knowledge about Temporal Intervals". In Communication of the ACM, 26(11):832-843, 11/1983.
6. Jourdan, M., Roisin, C., Tardif, L. "A scalable Toolkit for Designing Multimedia Authoring Environments". In special issue "Multimedia Authoring and Presentation: Strategies, Tools and Experiences" Multimedia Tools and Applications Journal. Kluwer Academic Publishers, 2/3(12):257-279. 1999.
7. Gamma, R. Helm, R. Johnson and J. Vissides: "Design Patterns: Elements of reusable object-oriented software", Addison Wesley, 1995.
8. Goldberg, A. "Smalltalk-80: The Interactive Programming Environment". Addison-Wesley Reading, 1984.
9. Marc Nanard, Jocelyne Nanard and Paul Kahn; "Pushing Reuse in Hypermedia Design: Golden Rules, Design Patterns and Constructive Templates", In Proceedings of the ninth ACM conference on Hypertext and Hypermedia, pp. 11-20, 6/1998.
10. Hauser, J. "Realization of an Extensible Multimedia Document Model", In Proceedings of Eurographics Multimedia '99". Milan, Italy, pp. 113-120, 9/1999.
11. Hauser, J. and Rothermel, K. "Specification and Implementation of an Extensible Multimedia System. In Proceedings of IDMS 2000, LNCS 1905, pp 241-253, Springer, 10/2000.
12. Hauser, J. "A Component-based Extensible Multimedia System" in Proceedings of the International Conference on Parallel and Distributed Processing Techniques and Applications PDPTA'01, pp. 1243-1249, 6/2001.
13. German Research Foundation (DFG). "Distributed Processing and Exchange of Digital Documents (V3D2)". URL: http://www.cg.cs.tu-bs.de/dfgspp.VVVDD.
14. "Director version 8.5". URL: http://www.macromedia.com/products/director. Macromedia. 2001.

Extended Format Definition and Quality-driven Format Negotiation in Multimedia Systems

Marco Lohse, Philipp Slusallek, Patrick Wambach

Computer Graphics Lab, Saarland University,
P.O. Box 15 11 50, 66041 Saarbrücken, Germany
{mlohse, slusallek, wambi}@graphics.cs.uni-sb.de

Abstract. Multimedia middleware needs to support a wide variety of devices together with their respective data formats. This becomes increasingly relevant and difficult in a distributed environment where new devices and formats can become available at any time and must be taken into account when deciding how to set up a flowgraph of distributed multimedia components.
In this paper we present an automatic algorithm for configuring and connecting a high-level flowgraph of multimedia components. Given this abstract flowgraph of participating devices and key components, the algorithm automatically selects necessary additional components, chooses suitable formats, and connects the flowgraph, while trying to achieve the best possible quality.

1 Introduction

Traditional multimedia middleware such as DirectShow from Microsoft [1] or Apple's Quicktime [2] provides access only to multimedia devices directly connected to the same PC an application is running on. The network is supported as a source of data but the middleware cannot extend its control to other devices on the network. For example, it is impossible to transparently watch TV via the TV card in your colleague's PC, or control remote cameras attached to other PCs or directly to the network.

With the increased deployment of networked and mobile multimedia devices, support for such distributed multimedia operation is becoming increasingly important. We are currently developing a distributed multimedia middleware that takes advantage of existing architectures for multimedia middleware and transparently extends them to the network. Of course this requires the redesign of some fundamental services such as synchronization, device control and data transport.

Such a distributed multimedia system must allow a user to create, configure, and manage a complex flowgraph without having to deal with low level details such as data formats and how certain devices must be connected to be compatible with others. New devices and associated new data formats may become available to a system at any time and should be seamlessly supported by the multimedia middleware and thus all of its applications.

For our purposes the term "device" includes hardware devices as well as new software components, including new compression algorithms, network protocols, and file formats. We define "format" as the metadata that describes a multimedia data stream. This includes such properties as sampling rate, resolution, color space, protocol encapsulation and many others. Associated with each of these parameters is a "quality" specified with a weighting function, where a high value expresses a preference for a certain parameter value. A more detailed definition is given later in this paper (see Section 4.1).

New formats from components at the edges of a multimedia flowgraph, such as data sources (e.g. cameras) and sinks (e.g. displays), can often be handled by providing suitable conversion algorithms to formats already supported by the middleware. However, format decisions at the edges can have global effect on a flowgraph as they can propagate along a media flow. A common example is a preferred audio sampling rate of an output device, which should be used throughout the flowgraph in order to avoid sampling rate conversion and its associated problems.

New components that will be used as internal nodes in a flowgraph are more challenging as they can have more impact on the optimal data processing. For instance, optimally using a newly added hardware device that allows efficient DV-to-MPEG transcoding might require re-routing of data across the network to the transcoder instead of using local software transcoding.

Existing systems either require the user to choose and specify the details of the complete flowgraph or rely on a simple template mechanism for selecting missing flowgraph components. Such simple techniques work for the traditional environment with a restricted configuration space where new devices are added infrequently. However, they are inadequate for the dynamic environment of distributed multimedia operation.

In this paper we propose a fully automatic approach to selecting and configuring necessary components for an incomplete flowgraph specified by an user or an application. Given the set of all available multimedia components and their input and output formats, the system uses a modified version of Dijkstra's algorithm for solving the Single-Source-Shortest-Path (SSSP) problem to find the possible connections between two components of the user graph. Additionally this connection should provide the best quality. In order to support complex user graphs the local SSSP algorithm operation is augmented with a global propagation component that forwards local decisions along the chosen paths. Finally, possible solutions are evaluated depending on their computational costs and a complete and valid multimedia flowgraph is created.

We start the paper with a brief review of current systems and previous work in the next section. In Section 3 and 4 we define our environment for specifying multimedia flowgraphs from individual components and their associated data formats. The format negotiation algorithm is then presented in Section 5 with an example given in Section 6.

2 Background and Previous Work

Microsoft's DirectShow [1] is probably the most widely used multimedia middleware. It uses the common approach of providing a large set of small components (called Filters) to be connected in the form of a flowgraph that operates on the multimedia data streams. DirectShow classifies multimedia formats by major type, minor type, format type and optional parameters. The major type includes audio, video and stream formats; the minor type contains extended information about the major type, like the specific YUV format. The local operating system contains a registry of all filters, which allows enumeration of all filters with certain format requirements. In the later versions of DirectShow a simple template mechanism is used for augmenting incomplete flow graphs. As mentioned above this mechanism is insufficient for dynamic and distributed environments.

SGI's Digital Media Library [3] provides a more advanced definition of multimedia formats that is organized in a shallow hierarchy where individual parameters are stored in a list. It provides functions for common operations on formats, such as equality. However, SGI's middleware that is the basis for the new cross platform "open multimedia library (OpenML)" [4] does not provide any automatic mechanism for connecting flowgraphs.

Apple's Quicktime [2] provides an automatic data transform mechanism, which converts input data automatically into the preferred format of a media codec but does not provide a general flowgraph mechanism. Sun's Java Media Framework [5] offers a set of methods to compare formats. A breath-first search algorithm is employed to set up flow graphs but no criterion like costs or quality is used to find a global optimum solution. In summary, all multimedia frameworks are restricted to querying format properties of media processing components and the application is responsible for establishing optimal component connections.

Home networking middleware like HAVi [6], Jini [7] or UPnP [8] offers sophisticated device discovery mechanisms, but only HP JetSend technology directly introduces a concept for format negotiation between components [9]: devices store a preferred encoding format out of their list of supported formats. In a negotiation step, the receiving device is responsible for choosing the encoding. Again, this local model is inadequate for more general media processing.

Little research has been done on application-level format negotiation as described above. However, many algorithms have been developed for automated QoS negotiation in distributed multimedia systems, using for example an agent-based approach [10] or an optimization approach [11]. Rothermel et al. [12] proposed a QoS and format negotiation protocol, which supports arbitrary multimedia flowgraphs. Yet, this approach is limited to determine the QoS parameters of an already fully connected flowgraph. Our approach focuses on augmenting incomplete flowgraphs by automatically adding necessary components, while at the same time trying to achieve the best possible quality and configuring the flowgraph accordingly. Computational costs are only considered to decide between two or more solutions with equal quality.

3 Basic System Design

We follow a common approach for specifying multimedia flowgraphs: devices (e.g. a camera) and software components (e.g. a converter) are represented as *nodes*, which potentially have several multimedia data inputs and outputs; in our case called *jacks*. By connecting input and output jacks, complex flowgraphs can be built. Associated with each jack are one or more supported *formats*. A format provides the metadata that describes the multimedia data to be streamed across a jack. The format negotiation procedure must select exactly one format for each jack and configure all of its parameters. More details on formats are given below in Section 4.1.

Our system distinguishes between six different types of nodes: A *source* produces data and has one output jack. A *sink* consumes data, which it receives from its input jack. A *filter* has one input and one output jack. It only modifies the data of the stream and does not change its format or format specific parameters. A *converter* also has one input and one output jack but can change the format of the data (e.g. from raw video to compressed video) or may change format specific parameters (e.g. the video resolution). A *multiplexer* has several input jacks and one output jack; a *demultiplexer* has one input jack and several output jacks.

There are two different types of dependencies which have to be modeled: First, a converter, multiplexer or demultiplexer might only support certain combinations of input and output formats. We use a concept called *IO-partner*: Each input format is associated with one or more output formats and vice versa. Furthermore, during format negotiation, format parameters will be changed to reflect the actual negotiation process, for instance, a video filter which can process any kind of x- and y-resolution has to reflect the actual chosen video resolution of its input format in its output format.

4 Format Definition

4.1 Format Classification and Specification

A sophisticated format classification and specification mechanism is necessary to support automated format negotiation. The goal of the *format classification* is to divide all possible multimedia formats into possible main categories; in our approach, formats are classified by *type* and *subtype*. The *format specification* then states more precisely the actual parameters within each category. Each parameter is described by *key* and *value*. For example, to completely specify a format like *video/raw*, additional information is needed, like framerate, resolution and color space. The values of parameters are stored as a *set of values*, or as a *set of ranges* (non-intersecting). If no constraints are given on a certain parameter, a *wildcard*-attribute can be used. For example, a display node might support RGB color space (set with one entry), framerates of 1 to 30 fps (set with one range), and arbitrary video resolutions (wildcard).

When trying to connect an output jack to an input jack, one has to check for compatible formats. A *intersection format* of two formats exists if their major and minor types are equal, all parameter keys in one format exist in the other format and vice versa, and all intersections of the ranges of values of corresponding parameter keys are a non-empty set. The existence of an intersection format is called a *match.*

4.2 Extending the Format Definition

In order to perform a quality driven format negotiation, the definition of a format has to be extended. Each entry in a set of possible parameter values is assigned a weight reflecting its respective quality, e.g. a framerate of 30 fps receives a higher quality value than a framerate of 15. This weight is in the range of 0 to 1. For values which are specified as a range, the weights of the lower and upper limits have to be specified. Wildcards, which are not resolved by creating intersection formats, are assigned maximum weight. The weight of a format is computed as the average of its parameters' weights. An additional weighting factor for each parameter can be used to stress the importance of a particular parameter. The weight of an intersection format is determined accordingly.

As mentioned above, a quality driven format negotiation is performed which only takes "costs" into account if two or more solutions with the same quality exist. Since the total costs of an operation performed inside a node depends not only on the type of operation but also on the used input and output formats, we need three different measurements: the input and output costs associated with a format and its specific parameter values and the costs of the operation itself. Since all these costs strongly depend on the chosen values of parameters (e.g. the video resolution), the costs have to be updated during negotiation. While cost measurement is an interesting topic, it is not addressed in the context of this paper.

5 Format Negotiation

After introducing the basic elements of the underlying model, we now define the format negotiation problem: *Given a high-level description of a desired multimedia flowgraph (which is independent of physically possible connections and formats), try to find a solution which provides the highest quality and meets defined requirements. If two or more possible solutions are found, find a cost optimal solution.*

We will give an overview of our approach for solving the format negotiation problem. Then, we will describe this approach in detail and point out the interesting aspects, such as computational complexity.

5.1 Overview

The format negotiation is performed in three steps: First, the *user graph* has to be specified. Basically, this graph only stores the structure of the desired multimedia flowgraph. It contains the wanted sources, multiplexers, demultiplexers, filters, and sinks, and connections between these; converters can but do not have to be added. The format negotiation will create a valid connected multimedia flowgraph. Although the user graph is independent of formats, additional information can be associated with connecting edges. For example, a certain framerate or resolution of a video stream can be specified. If no additional information is given, the format negotiation method described below will try to find the solution with the best quality. There are several ways to obtain the user graph. A user of the system could model a desired configuration; the application could provide a user graph; or, finally, for simple examples with only sources and sinks, the graph could be generated automatically.

The *format negotiation graph* is a representation, which is derived from the user graph and which is used in the second step, the format negotiation. With this extended representation, several sub-negotiations, or requests, are performed to find an optimal solution in respect to the desired parameter, e.g. quality, and format dependencies as described in Section 3. This step uses a modified algorithm for solving the shortest-path problem. Afterwards, solutions from different requests have to be merged. In this step values of format parameters are set globally. Solutions which provide the same quality, are ranked according to their costs. The following section describes the format negotiation in detail.

Finally, the *result flowgraph* can be created. This flowgraph reflects the user graph in the way that the structure of both is the same, but additional necessary converters are included into the result flowgraph and the individual nodes and connections are properly configured in terms of formats.

5.2 Format Negotiation Procedure

As the edges in the user graph can be specified independently of possible connections (in the sense of matching output and input formats), this graph can not be used for format negotiation. An extended representation, the format negotiation graph, is needed. It contains all nodes of the user graph, but all former edges are removed because they do not necessarily represent possible connections. Instead, all connections which represent a match are added as new edges (see Section 4.1). These edges are denoted with the appropriate intersection formats. It is possible that no new edges might be added during this step, so nodes could remain unconnected. This is the case in the example of Figure 1(a): both devices support the same resolutions, e.g. 640x480 and 800x600, but the camera produces video data in YUV format, whereas the display is only able to present RGB video frames. The only way to connect these two devices is to insert a matching converter between them.

Therefore, in the next step, all existing "matching" converters are inserted into the graph[1]. Then, all possible edges are created and denoted with intersection formats. This includes edges from already existing nodes to converters and

[1] This implies having a node registry mechanism, where all existing converters are stored with their possible input formats.

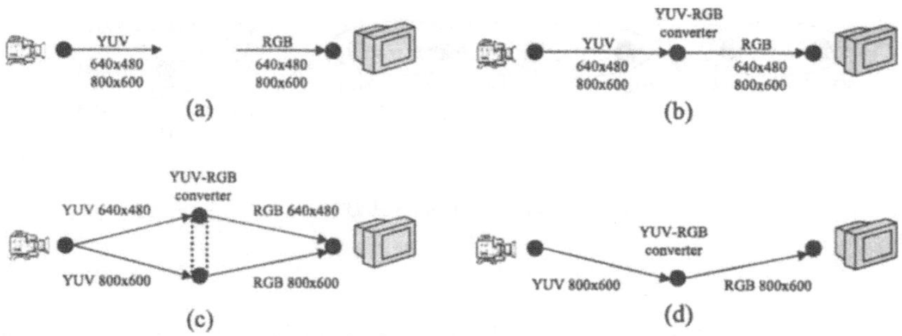

Fig. 1. Basic format negotiation procedure.

vice versa, but also edges from converters to converters. Figure 1(b) shows the result of this step for our example. For simplicity, only one converter is added, as this is capable of performing the required conversion and processing video frames of arbitrary resolution.

Since converters might support several input and output formats, it is necessary to take possible dependencies into account. For example, only specific combinations of input and output formats are allowed (see *IO-partner* in Section 3). Thus, converters are split in the format negotiation graph: for each supported combination of input and output formats, its respective node is split. Since the used format definition allows sets of values as described in Section 4.1, splitting is not only performed per IO-partner, but also per entry in the set of supported parameter values. Figure 1(c) shows the result of the splitting operation.

Due to the fact, that all edges can be labelled with a weight which represents the quality of the corresponding format (as defined in Section 4.2), the format negotiation problem can now be treated as a graph problem. We are interested in finding the path which maximizes the lowest weight on it. This edge is called the "bottleneck" because it determines the overall quality of the solution. Since all weights are positive, one can apply a modified version of Dijkstra's algorithm for solving the Single-Source-Shortest-Path-Problem (SSSP) [13]. Only the initialization function and the relaxation function, which "guides" the search, have to be modified [14]: First, the starting node is labelled with infinite weight, all other nodes with 0. During execution of the algorithm, these values are updated with the current value of the "bottleneck" of the paths leading to this node. The running time of Dijkstra-algorithm is $\mathcal{O}(n \log n + m)$ with n denoting the number of nodes and m the number of edges in the graph. Figure 1(d) shows the result of this step; the higher resolution was chosen because it provides a better quality which is reflected in a higher weight. While a single execution of the algorithm solves the format negotiation problem for simple graphs like the one in Figure 1, in graphs with many multiplexers and demultiplexers a m:n-relationship between sources and sinks is given. That is why we use a divide-and-conquer approach, by dividing the graph into subgraphs. Figure 2 shows the different

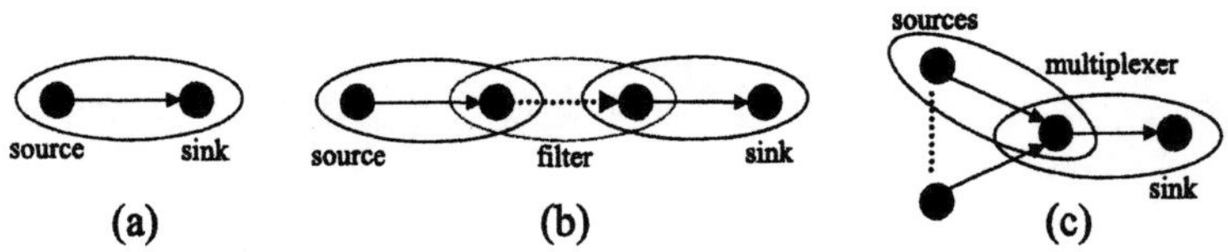

Fig. 2. Different subgraphs.

types of subgraphs. Subgraphs with only one source and sink can be handled with one execution of the algorithm (a). In subgraphs with filters, each filter is first treated as being a sink, and then during the next request as being a source (b). Each input of a multiplexer is treated as a source; the multiplexer itself as a sink (c). Subsequently, the multiplexer is treated as a source. Demultiplexers are treated in a similar way.

Since a solution for one subgraph may lead to an unresolvable conflict or a solution with lower quality later on, all possible solutions for all subgraphs have to be computed. Fortunately, this number is very small in practice, since it is only influenced by the number of converters for a specific format. The results of all requests are then combined to obtain a valid solution. Again, the number of possible combinations is very small because typically only a few solutions for subgraphs can be found which fit together. As parameters are set at this stage, possible dependencies as described in Section 3 have to be taken into account. A general solution which can be used for arbitrary graphs would be the protocol described in [12]. In the special case when there is one edge through which all multimedia data flows, another approach can be used. This includes graphs with one source or one sink only, but also more advanced graph layouts with many sources, sinks, multiplexers and demultiplexer, as long as there exists a "narrowest" location in the graph. Starting from this location, all parameters can be set by simply propagating them upstream to all sources and downstream to all sinks and the total costs can be evaluated.

6 Example

A more advanced example is shown in Figure 3. The user graph in (a) specifies part of a video conference application. The idea is to insert the locally taken picture into the picture of the counterpart. The picture-in-picture multiplexer blends two video streams, one with a small resolution, the other with a high resolution; in this application, the video data generated by a camera (the local picture) and the video data, which is received compressed over a network connection (the picture of the counterpart). The multiplexer can handle raw video data in RGB or YUV format. A filter node, blending a certain logo like the current clock, and a display node as sink complete the user graph. Both nodes can only process RGB video data. Note, that the user graph does not have to include any converters or format specific details.

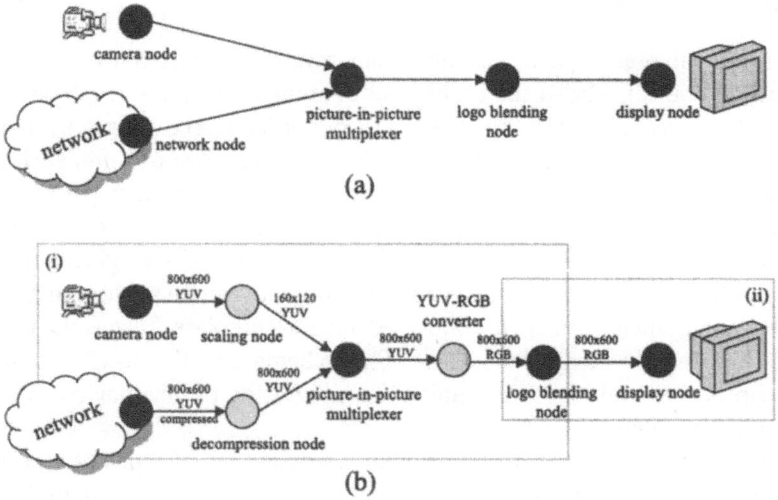

Fig. 3. User graph and result flowgraph of a video conference application.

Figure 3(b) shows the final result of the format negotiation: A converter for decompression has been inserted to fulfill the format constraints of the multiplexer, which can only handle uncompressed video data. The other input-stream of the multiplexer is scaled by an additional converter, since the second input of the multiplexer can only handle small resolution pictures. The color space converter from YUV to RGB is also inserted for connecting the specified logo node. All these steps are performed in one subgraph, denoted in Figure 3(b) by (i). Afterwards, the subgraph (ii) is resolved. As the given formats match, there is no need to insert a converter.

It is noticeable that the YUV to RGB converter is inserted behind the multiplexer. Another solution would have been to convert the video data of both streams individually before they are merged. Since this possibility provides the same quality but needs two relatively expensive conversions instead of only one, this solution was not generated.

7 Implementation

The format negotiation has been implemented in C++ within the Network-Integrated Multimedia framework [15] for Linux. The modified Dijkstra's algorithm uses a STL priority queue to achieve best results. Even with the current non-optimized implementation, the running time of the initialization, format negotiation and construction of a multimedia flowgraph with a total of 20 formats, 15 nodes and 24 edges in the negotiation graph takes only 40ms. A more advanced example with 50 nodes and 100 edges takes 60ms on a standard PC (P-III, 800 MHz) under Linux.

8 Results and Discussion

Given the flexible and quickly changing environment of distributed multimedia applications, we considered the problem of defining a valid flowgraph while minimizing the necessary input by a user. In our scheme the user only needs to specify an incomplete "user graph" containing the key components such as the media sources and specific processing components. The format negotiation then automatically selects additional components that are necessary for a consistent flowgraph which provides the highest "quality" in terms of a weighting function. Additionally, the total costs are considered if more than one solution exists. The resulting components are then connected into a complete flowgraph that can directly be used for media processing. This scheme avoids inflexible template-based approaches and allows to immediate integration of new devices with new format requirements.

We consider this format negotiation an essential part of a distributed multimedia middleware. We plan on extending the basic technique presented here to include cost driven format and QoS negotiation as well as resource allocation (in particular for network bandwidth). Furthermore, further work is required on the fast reconfiguration of flowgraphs given dynamic changes in stream requirements and the environment.

References

1. Microsoft: DirectShow Architecture. http://msdn.microsoft.com/ (2000)
2. Apple: Quicktime 5 API Reference. http://developer.apple.com/quicktime/ (2001)
3. Creek, P., Moccia, D.: Digital Media Programming Guide. Silicon Graphics (1996)
4. Khronos Group: OpenML White Paper V2.0. http://www.khronos.org/ (2001)
5. Sun: Java Media Framework 2.0 API Guide. http://java.sun.com/products/javamedia/jmf/ (1999)
6. HAVi: Specification of the home audio/video interoperability (havi) architecture, version 1.1. http://www.havi.org/techinfo/ (2000)
7. Sun: Jini Specifications v1.1. http://www.sun.com/jini/ (2000)
8. Microsoft: Universal Plug and Play Architecture. http://www.upnp.org/ (2000)
9. Hewlett-Packard: JetSend Technology. http://www.jetsend.hp.com/ (2000)
10. Guedes, L., Oliveira, P., Faina, L., Cardozo, E.: QoS Agency: An Agent-based Architecture for Supporting Quality of Service in Distributed Multimedia Systems. In: IEEE Conference on Protocols for Multimedia Systems - Multimedia Networking. (1997)
11. Hafid, A., Bochmann, G., Kerherve, B.: A Quality of Service Negotiation Procedure for Distributed Multimedia Presentational Applications. In: Fifth international IFIP Symposium of High Performance of Distributed Processing. (1996)
12. Rothermel, K., Dermler, G., Fiederer, W.: QoS Negotiation and Resource Reservation for Distributed Multimedia Applications. In: Proceedings of the 1997 International Conference on Multimedia Computing and Systems (ICMCS '97). (1997)
13. Cormen, T., Leiserson, C., Rivest, R.: Introductions to Algorithms. MIT Press (1997)
14. Wayne, K.: Theory of Algorithms. Technical report, Princeton University (2001)
15. Computer Graphics Lab, Saarland University: Network-integrated Multimedia Framework. http://graphics.cs.uni-sb.de/NMM/ (2001)

A Server-based Interactive Remote Walkthrough

Daniel Cohen-Or[1,2], Yuval Noimark[3], and Tali Zvi[1]

[1] Enbaya Ltd.
[2] Computer Science Department, Tel-Aviv University
[3] IBM Research Lab in Haifa

Abstract. This paper presents a server-based remote walkthrough system. The client is assumed to be a thin client, like a handset or a mobile device, with no strong processor but with some embedded video chip. The server holds the large environment, generates the frames, encodes and transmits them to the client. The encoded frames are transmitted as a video stream to the client, which then decodes the stream and displays it. We show how the computer generated frames can be efficiently encoded using layering techniques to yield a lighter stream, which enables its transmission over narrow bandwidth channels and minimizes the communication latency. To enable the interactivity of the system, the rendering engine generates the frames in real-time according to the client input, and feeds the frames to an accelerated video encoder based on the available optical flow.

1 Introduction

With the increasing availability of the Web and the advances in graphics hardware, the network bandwidth becomes a critical bottleneck. Remote walkthrough in complex computer-generated environments is an emerging challenge in computer graphics, since the entire model cannot be downloaded from the server to the client. Even dynamically downloading relevant portions of the model on demand with respect to the client position is not possible as it may consist of a prohibitive number of polygons or textures. There are different techniques that simplify the representation of the objects to accelerate the walkthrough [6, 14, 18, 17, 3]. Others have focused on Web-based remote walkthrough [13, 7, 20]. Hybrid-rendering methods, where the client and the server both commonly participate in the rendering of the frames are a possible solution that various researchers have taken [11, 15, 23, 5]. Streaming technologies can alleviate the problem by reducing the bandwidth requirement, but require extensive computational power from the client.

For most applications, the server should effectively serve as many clients as possible simultaneously. Thus, it is desirable to shift most of the computation to the client, and to ease the server load. However, there are scenarios where the client is thin and most or all of the computation load should be on the server. This is especially relevant to commercial handsets (e.g. cellphone or PDA) that contain a weak processor for economic reasons. Typically, a handset is built with an old processor that costs much less and whose computation power cannot support graphical 3D applications. In such a case the server should generate the frames and transmit them to the thin client, which then needs only to display them. However, naively transmitting the frames is too expensive since the current available network bandwidth is extremely narrow.

The proposed solution, presented in this paper, is to use a server-based approach. The server renders the sequence and encodes the frames into a video stream. The stream is received by the client, which displays the stream using an MPEG-4 video chip. Fast online encoding is essential for real-time experience of the remote walkthrough, and therefore special techniques are needed to reduce the encoding complexity.

The rest of this paper is organized as follows: In Section 2 we give a brief overview of the system. In Section 3 we describe the MPEG-4 encoding scheme. Section 4 describes our per-layer encoding technique. The real-time encoding is presented in Section 5. We finalize this paper with some results (Section 6), conclusions and future work (Section 7).

2 System Overview

Our system is server-based, as illustrated in Figure 1. The 3D model of the scene is held on the server. Once interaction starts, the Interactive Rendering Engine renders the frames. It provides scene information to the Macro-block Analysis module for generating layering information and motion hints. The layering information is used to vary the quantization level locally over the frame (see Section 4), and motion hints are used for fast encoding (see Section 5).

An interaction back-channel is used for real-time walkthrough in the model. A Control Data back-channel is used for bandwidth adaptation and for packet loss information. The Control Data enables the Frame Encoder to retransmit a lost packet or to adapt the compression ratio and the quality to the available network bandwidth. The frames generated by the rendering engine are fed into the Frame Encoder as plain RGB frames. We choose to encode the frames with the MPEG-4 video standard since today there are already devices that provide MPEG-4 video decoding. Recently more and more companies have announced that cellphones capable of decoding MPEG-4 video will soon be available. We can also expect that in the near future, PDAs and other mobile devices will have such capabilities in hardware.

3 MPEG-4 Encoding Scheme

MPEG-4 is the new ISO/IEC multimedia standard developed by MPEG (Moving Picture Experts Group); its format designation is ISO/IEC 14496 [2]. The standard defines media objects as the primitives in the scene. These objects can be of synthetic or natural origin and can be visual or aural ones. It also defines how to multiplex and synchronize these objects to enable their transportation over the network. One of the media objects defined is MPEG-4 video [1]. As we

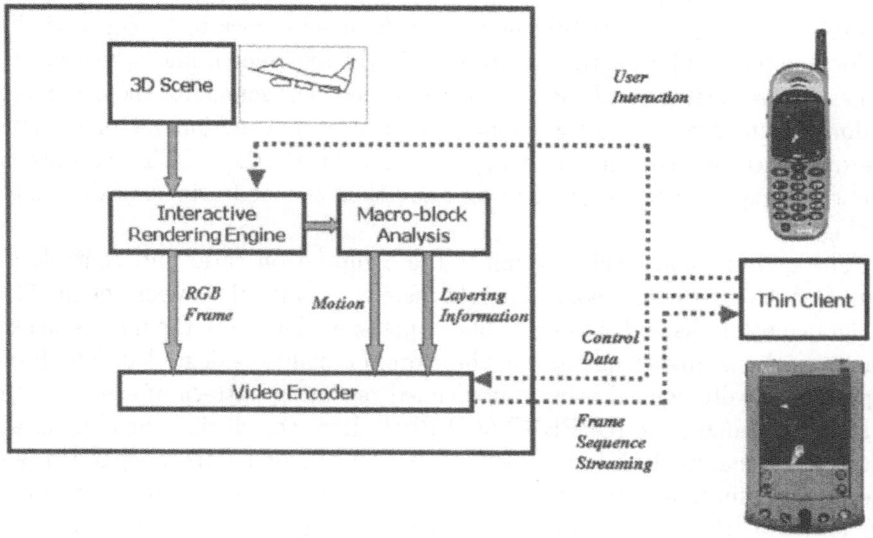

Fig. 1. The systemoverview

mentioned in the Introduction, we have implemented our Frame Encoder with the MPEG-4 video standard as more and more of today's devices are enabled to display MPEG-4 video content using on-chip decoders [16, 19, 4]. These devices can display real-time video according to the user's preferences and the device's location. However, the technique introduced here is not limited to this standard and could be applied to other block-based video compression schemes.

3.1 Frame Coding Scheme

An MPEG-4 video stream consists of three types of frames: intra frames I, predictive frames P, and bi-directional predictive frames B. The I frames are encoded independently of the other frames in the sequence, while the P and B frames are encoded using motion estimation and interpolation techniques. The P and B frames are substantially smaller than the I frames. The motion estimation of the P frames is based on preceding P or I frames. The motion estimation of B frames is based on preceding P or I frames and/or on successive P or I frames. The P or I frames used for motion estimation are referred to as reference frames.

More specifically, a frame is encoded at the macro-block (MB) level. Each frame is partitioned into macro-blocks of 16x16 pixels that are encoded independently of the other macro- blocks. An Intra macro-block (I-MB) is one whose data is fully encoded. An Inter macro-block (P-MB) is one whose data is encoded using motion estimation. The I-MB is encoded by applying DCT (Discrete Cosine Transform) to its data, quantizing the resulting coefficients, and encoding them using variable length coding. The P-MB is first motion-estimated by searching the reference frame for the best match for the macro-block to be encoded. The co-located macro-block is the macro-block in the reference frame, which has the same relative location as the P-MB to be encoded. The search for the best match is done in an area around the co-macro-block. Once a motion vector is found, the difference between the matching area and the P-MB is DCT-transformed. The resulting coefficients are quantized and then encoded using variable length coding.

The quantization level determines the compression ratio and controls the degree of the lossy compression. Clearly there is a trade-off between the qualities of the macro-blocks and the degree of compression. The more the macro-block is compressed (i.e. higher quantizer), the more its quality is degraded. The frame types are usually defined using a predefined repeating pattern of a sequence of I, P and B frames, like IBBPBBP or IPPBIP. However, during encoding of a P frame, each macro-block can be defined as an I-MB or P-MB independently of the global definition of the entire frame. Identifying different types of encoding per macro-block imposes an overhead of predicting the estimated error. When the estimation error is too large, prediction is not used and an I-MB is used instead.

Encoding a P (or B) macro-block imposes a search for the best candidate macro-block in the reference frame. A benefit of MPEG-4 is that is does not restrict the search area. However, searching for a candidate is a complex and time-consuming task. In Section 8 we describe a technique we use to reduce the computation complexity of the search to enable a real-time encoding.

3.2 Macro-block Quantization

An important parameter in the encoding process is the quantization value. The DCT coefficients are quantized and encoded into a variable size length of 3-26 bits. A successful choice of the quantizer is critical for an efficient encoding. Usually the quantization value is defined globally aiming at generating some given frame rate. The value is chosen according to the trade-off between better quality and higher bitrate; the higher the quantizer the better compression to be achieved and the more degrading quality. The quantization factor varies from 1 to 31 in steps of 1. A step change in the quantizer can improve the compression ratio while the degradation in quality is almost unnoticeable. MPEG-4 defines two types of quantization. In the first method, the same quantization value is used for all DCT coefficients of the macro-block. In the second, a matrix of quantization values for the macro-block is used where each coefficient can be quantized with a different value according to the matrix (see [1], Section 7.4.4.1). Further in this paper we refer to the quantization method in which one quantizer is used for all coefficients. Choosing a quantizer and a quantization method is an active area of research. Quantizing the correct coefficients with the correct value gives the best compression ratios while maintaining quality as far as possible. Another usage of the quantizer is for bit-rate control purposes. A bit-rate mechanism usually modifies the quantizer on a per-frame base. Current approaches make use of the human visual system (HVS) to modify the quantizer on a per macro-block base (see [1], Annex L.).

Figure 2 is an example of the effect of different quantization values. In (a), one can see the quality of a sequence encoded with a quantizer value of 2. In (b), the quantization value is 18 and the quality degrades significantly.

(a) (b)

Fig. 2. The effect of applying different quantization values. The quantization value in (a) is 2, and 18 in (b).

4 Per-layer Quantization

Efficient frame encoding can be achieved by choosing the correct quantization value per macro-block according to its visual importance. This necessarily requires some image understanding of the scene represented in the sequence.

If depth information is given or some other knowledge about the model in the image, a frame can be segmented into layers, and each layer can then be assigned a different visual importance value. However, automatic segmentation of an image, or a sequence of images, into layers is not simple and still an active area of research (e.g., [21, 8]) Moreover, real-time segmentation of video sequences is very complex and is not feasible yet.

When the frame sequence encodes views of a computer-generated model, the layering problem is trivial. For example, one can easily segment the image into background and foreground macro-blocks as shown in Figure 3. The figure shows an image segmented and classified into two layers (see Figure 3(b)). The macro-blocks containing the foreground objects are colored in white; the less visually important macro-blocks are in black. Our server-based system is based on the ability to properly select different quantization values on a per macro-block level to yield better compression ratios, while degrading only the background macro-blocks.

The quantization value for background and foreground can differ in several levels. For example, one can assign a quantization value of 10 to the background and a quantization value of 2 to the foreground. However, such an approach can cause artifacts, as the transition from foreground to background might be noticeable. Our approach uses a gradual change of the quantization value, so that the transition from foreground to background is not abrupt and noticeable (see Figure 3(c)).

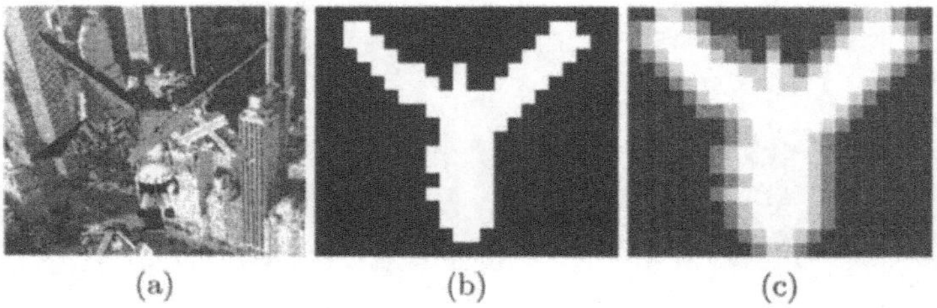

Fig. 3. A frame from the Studio sequence in (a), and its foreground/background layering in (b). In (c) a smoothing of the layering

Using a different quantization value for each layer, our method yields better compression ratios. The quality is degraded only in areas that are defined as background. These areas are not in the viewer focus and therefore less visually important. There are other methods which assign different quantization values on a per macro-block base [10]. However, these methods do not take into consideration regions of interest. Our approach is based on the knowledge of the model and on the visual importance of its different parts. Thereby, regions that are less visually important are compressed with a higher ratio, while preserving the appropriate quality for regions of higher importance to the viewer.

5 Real-time Encoding

5.1 Selecting the Encoding Pattern

The computer-generated model can be further exploited to compress the frame sequence by selecting an I frame when it is known to be needed. In a conventional encoder, a pre-defined pattern is used to determine the type of frame to encode. Patterns, such as IPPPP or IPBBBPBBI, are used to determine which frame should be independently encoded and which should be encoded using motion estimation. Playing a video sequence from a new location in time is termed seek. I frames (except for the first frame) are used in the encoding process to enable seek capability at the end viewer and to reduce the propagated error of P frames over error-prone networks.

Most of the frames types, as defined in the encoding pattern, are motion estimated ones. In cases of scene cuts, where the whole scene changes in a given frame, no motion vectors can be found. A scene cut, encoded as a P frame, imposes a redundant search for each of its macro-blocks. The search does not find a suitable motion vector since the motion estimation error is too high and the macro-block ends up being encoded as an I-MB.

Using the scene's model, one can use I frames only when necessary. The frame encoding pattern is not pre-defined but determined in real-time as a function of the walkthrough. The system uses its ability to detect scene-cuts and informs the Frame Encoder to avoid the search for motion, and to encode the current frame as an I frame. The Frame Encoder's complexity is considerably reduced for these frames and the processing power can be diverted to other time-consuming tasks. Another case, in which the system informs the Frame encoder to encode a frame as an I frame, is when the network is error-prone. As back-channel exists, the client can transmit to the server the statistics of lost frames. As the number of lost frames increases, the server may increase the number of I frames to reduce the propagated error of P frames.

5.2 Accelerating Motion Estimation

Searching for a motion vector is the most time-consuming task in the encoding, and several search algorithms have been proposed to accelerate its computation [12, 9]. There is a tradeoff between the complexity of the search and its resulting motion vectors. Typically, there is a direct relation between the complexity of the search algorithm and quality of the match. An exhaustive search yields the best possible match, but of course, it is overly expensive, since algorithms with relatively low complexity can provide acceptable results for real-time applications.

Wallach et al. introduced in [22] a technique to find the motion vectors based on the available optical flow information using common graphics hardware. The Macro-block Analysis module also exploits the known model and accelerates the search algorithm by providing approximate motion vectors to the Encoder module. In our implementation we use the Logarithmic motion estimation algorithm [12]. This is a hierarchical search that checks the corners, sides, and centers of a 2Nx2N pixel square, for the best match and continues recursively on the best result as the new center. This means that in each iteration there are nine possible motion vectors (4 corners, 4 sides, 1 center). Based on the available scene model and the available camera parameters, the macro-block analysis module can compute an approximate optical flow for a given macro-block. This is used as the initial location of a Logarithmic search by the Encoder. This saves the first level search and gains a speed-up of nine in encoding and yields a real-time encoding throughput. The speed-up gained in the Logarithmic search time does not come without cost, since the computation of the optical flow is also time-consuming. However, in our system this overhead is hidden since the Macro-block Analysis and the Frame Encoder work simultaneously in a pipeline fashion. Thus, the acceleration of the encoding improves the overall performance of the system and enables its usage as in real-time scenarios.

6 Results

We have implemented our technique within the framework of MPEG-4. The encoder is implemented in C, the decoder is pure Java and can be used on any Java-enabled platform, while the rendering engine is based on a proprietary implementation. Table 1 compares the stream size of the frame sequences encoded with a constant quantization value and those encoded with our method. The size of each frame in the sequence is CIF (Common Intermediate Format; 352x288). The figures show that our method provides better compression ratios while only degrading the quality of the background regions. The background regions have less importance to the viewer and therefore the degradation in quality is acceptable. We use the same quantization value for the foreground as in the constant quantization and a higher quantization value for the background. In the table, the left column shows the quantization range used (high-low). The lower value is used for foreground quantization and the higher value is used for background quantization. The "2-levels" column shows our resulting stream sizes which are lower than the sizes of the streams in the "low" columns. The "high" column shows the sizes of streams encoded with the same value we used for the background. Although its size is lower, its quality is worse than in our 2-levels approach. This is especially noticeable in the areas of the foreground object itself. We have repeated the same analysis for a QCIF (Quarter CIF; 176x144) size type. The results are similar, however the compression gained is somewhat less than in CIF size. This is because the macro-block size is fixed and therefore the ratio between the foreground and the background macro-blocks is a bit higher for QCIF.

Figure 4 compares images encoded by our technique and naive quantization, in which the same quantization value is used for all macro-blocks. The two sequences have been encoded with different ranges. The left column is from the "Pilot" sequence, encoded in the range of 10-4. The right column is from the "Studio" sequence, encoded in the range of 12-6. In the upper row, the lowest value is used as the constant quantization value. While in the lowest row, the higher value is used. The middle row shows frames of our two-layer technique. Note that the quality of the foreground object is as high as that in the upper row. The movies and a player, are available for download at: http://www.cs.tau.ac.il/~dcor/mpeg4/

7 Conclusions and Future Work

We have introduced a server-based system that alleviates the processing power required by a thin client to render an interactive remote walkthough. The technique exploits the fact that a thin client has the ability to decode video sequences independently of its computational power. Since we are streaming computer-generated video, we benefit from the available model of the scene to better compress the sequence and reduce the required bandwidth and communication latency. Current bandwidth issues might delay the immediate adoption of this

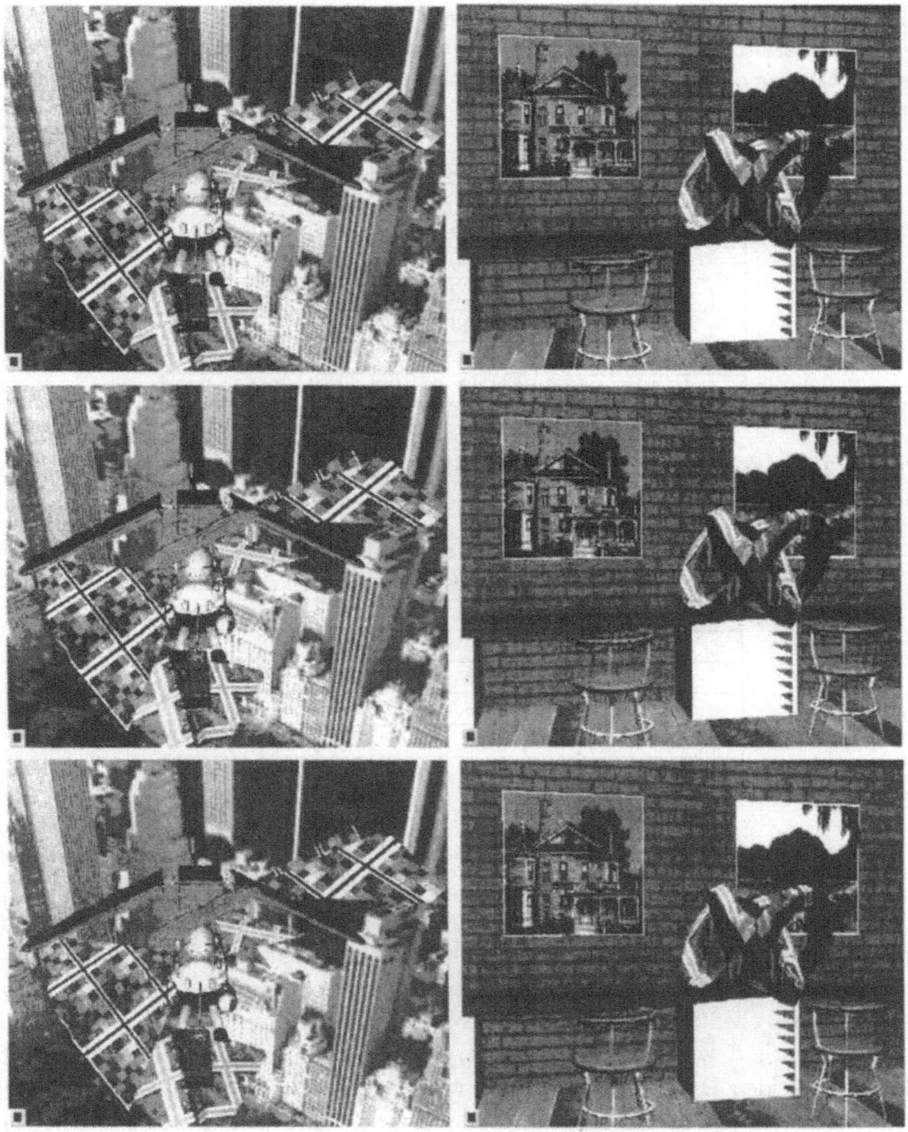

Fig. 4. A comparison of images encoded by our technique and naive quantization. In the upper row, the lowest value is used as the constant quantization value. While in the lowest row, the higher value is used. The middle row shows frames of our two-layer technique.

Table 1. The stream sizes (KBytes) of CIF (352x288 frame) in different quantization levels. Each line represents a different range of quantization values. The column "low" shows the size of a stream quantized with the lowest value in the range; the "high" shows the size of the stream with the highest value, and the "2-level" column shows the size using our per-layer technique .

Quantization	Studio Sequence			Pilot Sequence		
	high	2-levels	low	high	2-levels	low
8-2	1,813	3,038	7,307	1,657	3,404	6,947
10-4	1,388	1,980	3,851	1,249	2,121	3,596
12-6	1,105	1,459	2,516	979	1,514	2,326
14-8	908	1,143	1,813	788	1,151	1,657
16-10	767	932	1,388	652	912	1,249
18-12	660	783	1,105	548	744	979

Table 2. The stream sizes (KBytes) of QCIF (176x144 frame) in different quantization levels as in Table 1.

Quantization	Studio Sequence			Pilot Sequence		
	high	2-levels	low	high	2-levels	low
8-2	512	1,160	2,257	430	1,190	1,788
10-4	378	699	1,158	319	698	938
12-6	291	485	735	244	476	609
14-8	230	359	512	191	347	430
16-10	188	278	378	152	264	319
18-12	157	223	485	124	207	244

technique. We expect this technique to be adopted as emerging networks gain more bandwidth. However, it does not require broadband networks. This technique can be applied in interactive network games where the server needs to serve several clients playing in a common virtual environment.

The method we have presented in this paper focuses on the basic set of MPEG-4 Video [1]. MPEG-4 defines various types of other "media objects" rather than video objects. However, today's devices are still limited to MPEG-4 video decoding and do not provide the ability to display a whole MPEG-4 scene. Moreover, the devices cannot compose several video objects overlaid. Such a capability would enable us to enhance this technique and further improve its performance.

8 Acknowledgment

The authors wish to thank the following people for their various contributions: Efi Fogel and Amit Shaked from Enbaya Ltd., Zohar Sivan and Konstantin Kupeev from IBM Research Lab in Haifa.

References

[1] Information Technology - Coding of Audio-Visual Objects - Part2: Visual. ISO/IEC 14496-2, Dec. 1999.

[2] Overview of the MPEG-4 Standard (ISO/IEC JTC1/SC29/WG11 N3747). http://www.cselt.it/mpeg/standards/mpeg-4/mpeg-4.html, Oct. 2000.

[3] D. G. Aliaga and A. A. Lastra. Architectural walkthroughs using portal textures. In R. Yagel and H. Hagen, editors, *IEEE Visualization '97*, pages 355–362, Nov. 1997.

[4] M. Budagavi, W. Rabiner, J. Webb, and R. Talluri. Wireless mpeg-4 video on texas instruments dsp chips. In *Acoustics, Speech, and Signal Processing, 1999. Proceedings., 1999 IEEE International Conference on*, volume 4, pages 2223–2226, 1999.

[5] D. Cohen-Or, Y. Mann, and S. Fleishman. Deep compression for streaming texture intensive animations. In *Computer Graphics* Proceedings, Annual Conference Series, pages 261–268, Aug. 1999.

[6] T. A. Funkhouser and C. H. Séquin. Adaptive display algorithm for interactive frame rates during visualization of complex virtual environments. In *Computer Graphics* Proceedings, Annual Conference Series, pages 247–254, Aug. 1993.

[7] G. Hesina and D. Schmalstieg. A network architecture for remote rendering. In A. Boukerche and P. Reynolds, editors, *Proceedings of Second International Workshop on Distributed Interactive Simulation and Real-Time Applications*, pages 88–91, July 1998.

[8] H. Huang, W. Lin, Y. Hung, and C. Fuh. New video object segmentation technique based on flow-thread features for mpeg-4 and multimedia systems. In *Image and Video Communications and Processing 2000*, pages 204–212, 2000.

[9] A. kHI RN, O. Au, and M. Liou. Fast motion estimation using circular zonal search, 1999.

[10] H.-J. Lee, T. Chiang, and Y.-Q. Zhang. Scalable rate control for very low bit rate (vlbr) video. In *Proceedings of the 1997 International Conference on Image Processing (ICIP '97)*, volume 3, 1997.

[11] M. Levoy. Polygon-assisted jpeg and mpeg compression of synthetic images. *Proceedings of SIGGRAPH 95*, pages 21–28, August 1995. ISBN 0-201-84776-0. Held in Los Angeles, California.

[12] R. Li, B. Zeng, and M. Liou. A new three-step search algorithm for fast motion estimation. *IEEE Trans. Circuits Syst. Video Technol.*, 4:438–442, 1994.

[13] M. R. Macedonia, D. P. Brutzmann, M. J. Zyda, D. R. Pratt, P. T. Barham, J. Falby, and J. Locke. NPSNET: A multi-player 3D virtual environment over the internet. In P. Hanrahan and J. Winget, editors, *1995 Symposium on Interactive 3D Graphics*, pages 93–94. ACM SIGGRAPH, Apr. 1995.

[14] P. W. C. Maciel and P. Shirley. Visual navigation of large environments using textured clusters. In *1995 Symposium on Interactive 3D Graphics*, pages 95–102, Apr. 1995.

[15] Y. Mann and D. Cohen-Or. Selective pixel transmission for navigating in remote virtual environments. *Computer Graphics Forum*, 16(3):201–206, August 1997.

[16] T. Nishikawa, M. Takahashi, M. Hamada, T. Takayanagi, H. Arakida, N. Machida, H. Yamamoto, T. Fujiyoshi, Y. Maisumoto, O. Yamagishi, T. Samata, A. Asano, T. Terazawa, K. Ohmori, J. Shirakura, Y. Watanabe, H. Nakamura, and S. Minami. A 60 mhz 240 mw mpeg-4 video-phone lsi with 16 mb embedded dram. In *Solid-State Circuits Conference, 2000. Digest of Technical Papers. ISSCC. 2000 IEEE International , 2000*, pages 230 –231, 2000.

[17] G. Schaufler and W. Stürzlinger. A three dimensional image cache for virtual reality. *Computer Graphics Forum*, 15(3):227–236, August 1996.

[18] J. Shade, D. Lischinski, D. H. Salesin, T. DeRose, and J. Snyder. Hierarchical image caching for accelerated walkthroughs of complex environments. In *Computer Graphics* Proceedings, Annual Conference Series, pages 75–82, 1996.

[19] H. Stolberg, M. Berekovic, P. Pirsch, H. Runge, H. Moller, and J. Kneip. The m-pire mpeg-4 codec dsp and its macroblock engine. In *Circuits and Systems, 2000. Proceedings. ISCAS 2000 Geneva. The 2000 IEEE International Symposium on*, volume 2, pages 192–195, 2000.

[20] E. Teler and D. Lischinski. Streaming of complex 3d scenes for remote walkthroughs. *to appear in Computer Graphics Forum (Proceedings of Eurographics 2001)*, 2001.

[21] K. Vaithianathan and S. Panchanathan. Analysis of object segmentation methods for vop generation in mpeg-4. In *Image and Video Communications and Processing 2000*, pages 191–203, 2000.

[22] D. S. Wallach, S. Kunapalli, and M. F. Cohen. Accelerated mpeg compression of dynamic polygonal scenes. *Proceedings of SIGGRAPH 94*, pages 193–197, July 1994. ISBN 0-89791-667-0. Held in Orlando, Florida.

[23] I. Yoon and U. Neumann. Web-based remote rendering with ibrac (image-based rendering acceleration and compression). *Computer Graphics Forum*, 19(3):321–330, August 2000.

Sobol Partial Distortion Algorithm for Fast Full Search in Block Motion Estimation

Davide Quaglia and Bartolomeo Montrucchio

Dipartimento di Automatica e Informatica, Politecnico di Torino,
corso Duca degli Abruzzi 24,
I-10129 Torino (Italy)
{davide.quaglia,montru}@polito.it
http://multimedia.polito.it/quaglia, http://www.polito.it/~montru

Abstract. Block motion estimation is a cpu intensive task for video encoding. Many fast algorithms have been developed to solve this problem, trying to improve both block searching and block matching. Some of them reduce the image quality compared to the full search method in order to improve performance. The algorithm presented in this paper, called Sobol Partial Distortion (SPD) algorithm, is a full search (lossless), fast matching, block motion estimation algorithm, applying partial distortion elimination. It uses a new matching strategy to quickly compute distortion and reduce block matching computation. Image-dependent computation is not required, since the matching strategy does not depend on the frame sequence. The proposed algorithm performs well in terms of computational speedup in comparison with other existing full search algorithms.

1 Introduction

Motion compensation is used in video encoding to improve the efficiency of the prediction from past or future frames. Motion estimation [1][2] is the process of evaluating movements between adjacent frames. The so-called block matching algorithms are the most important of these estimation methods, especially in coding schemes based on the discrete cosine transform. Pel-recursive, frequency domain, and gradient motion estimation methods are less frequently used.

For each test block in the current frame, the block matching methods try to find the most similar candidate block in the previous frame. The displacement between these two blocks is the motion vector for the given test block. Unlike in pel-recursive methods, the motion vector refers to all pixels of the block.

The most accurate block matching method is the Full Search (FS), that compares every possible candidate block in the search window with the test block; in this way, it produces accurate results, but it is slow.

The block matching technique is used in well-known video encoding standards, such as MPEG-1, MPEG-2, MPEG-4, H.261 and H.263. In these standards, full search motion estimation requires up to 70% of the encoding time, and hardware and software encoders suffer from these modest speed performances.

For this reason, several alternative and faster techniques have been developed, which can be classified into two categories. The first is based on lossy motion estimation algorithms, with some degradation of the predicted image compared with FS; recent examples are [3–9]. The second is based on several lossless algorithms [10–15]. Particularly important among them are the Successive Elimination Algorithm (SEA) [10], an improved version of it called Extended SEA (ESEA) [16], and the Partial matching Distortion Elimination (PDE) [13], which also uses an adaptive matching scan and the selection of representative pixels [15].

Viewing the problem from another angle, two approaches can be chosen to reduce computation in block matching algorithms. The first reduces the number of candidate blocks in the search window (e.g. [3]), while the second reduces the number of pixels involved in each candidate-test block comparison (e.g. [6]). Both these methods in general are lossy; however lossless methods use the same concepts. SEA reduces safely the search space through the elimination of impossible candidates, and ESEA introduces tighter bounds for the sum of absolute differences (SAD) and exploits the already calculated lower bounds during the calculation of the matching criterion (ESEA also extends SEA for the application of the MSE). PDE allows stopping the candidate-test block comparison if the partial sum of matching distortion (SAD) is larger than the matching error for the most similar candidate block found so far. Picking candidates in a particular order within the search window often leads to finding the global minimum of distortion faster, so that many comparisons can be prematurely stopped. Therefore PDE has been improved both by changing the searching method with the SpiralPDE [13, 14], in which the searching order follows a center-biased spiral, and by changing the matching method [15]. In particular in [15] a strategy for finding representative pixels (and doing an adaptive matching scan) has been shown to further reduce the comparison time in block matching (with respect to SpiralPDE).
It is important to note that SEA and PDE can be combined together [7].

In [15] the order in which pixels are considered during block matching is a function of the frame content (through gradient). In this paper we will show that further improvements can be achieved using Sobol's sequence to order pixel checks within a block without needing to perform computations based on the image. This sequence is independent of the image and it can be precomputed to avoid any overhead.

Therefore, the algorithm presented in this paper is a new full-search (lossless), fast-matching, block motion estimation algorithm, using partial distortion elimination, called the Sobol Partial Distortion (SPD) algorithm.

Experimental results show that this way of comparing pixels during block matching improves computational performances up to 20% with respect to SpiralPDE.

Since the algorithm does not require any pre-processing step, its migration towards a hardware implementation could be easier, and will be the subject of future work.

This paper is organized as follows. Section 2 describes the basic idea used in the algorithm, while Section 3 introduces Sobol's sequence. Section 4 explains the SPD algorithm in detail, and the results are presented in Section 5. Finally, conclusions and future work are reported in Section 6.

2 The Basic Idea

The block matching operation is based on the assumption that all pixels in the block move by the same amount. Therefore a good motion estimation can be often obtained by using only a subset of representative pixels in the block. A possibly good way to identify representative pixels without additional computation is to use a pseudo-random uniform distribution. In particular, Sobol's distribution can be fruitfully employed since a block comparison can be stopped at any moment (applying the partial distortion elimination approach) without losing the property of uniformity. On the other hand, regular grids are more uniform than Sobol's sequence though they can not be stopped at any point without losing their properties.

In this paper we will show that Sobol's sequence in effect provides interesting results without any a priori knowledge of the image.

3 Sobol's Sequence

Sobol's pseudo-random sequence was first introduced for Monte Carlo integration by I. M. Sobol [17] in 1967. The sequence generates numbers between zero and one in an S-dimensional space; successive points uniformly fill a region of the space [18].

The sequence, scaled into a 16×16 block, is used to define the order in which pixels are checked within the block: this order is specified in Fig. 1.

The computation of the sequence is fast, although in this work the sequence is precomputed to avoid overheads. The main feature of Sobol's sequence is a more regular uniformity of points compared to a uniformly distributed random sequence. Only a regular grid has better uniformity, but a regular grid can not be prematurely stopped without altering its properties.

4 SPD Algorithm

The SPD algorithm is based on partial distortion elimination. According to this approach, the SAD evaluation for a block stops if the partial sum becomes larger than the matching error for the most similar candidate block found so far. The number of operations of this approach depends both on the visiting order of the pixels within a block to compute SAD (matching strategy) and on the comparison order of candidate blocks to the test block (search strategy). In fact, the more different are the pixels, the earlier the SAD computation will

133	129	125	251	167	41	213	83	102	228	24	154	206	76	176	50
237	107	143	17	69	195	55	185	136	10	246	116	32	162	94	220
179	53	201	71	27	157	97	223	210	80	172	46	122	248	4	134
89	215	35	165	241	111	139	13	60	190	66	192	148	22	234	104
203	77	177	47	99	229	25	151	170	40	212	86	2	128	124	254
33	159	91	221	137	7	243	117	68	198	58	184	236	110	146	16
119	249	5	131	207	81	173	43	30	156	96	226	182	52	200	74
149	19	231	105	61	187	63	193	240	114	142	12	88	218	38	164
101	227	23	153	205	75	175	49	0	130	126	252	168	42	214	84
135	9	245	115	31	161	93	219	238	108	144	18	70	196	56	186
209	79	171	45	121	247	3	255	180	54	202	72	28	158	98	224
59	189	65	191	147	21	233	103	90	216	36	166	242	112	140	14
169	39	211	85	1	127	123	253	204	78	178	48	100	230	26	152
67	197	57	183	235	109	145	15	34	160	92	222	138	8	244	118
29	155	95	225	181	51	199	73	120	250	6	132	208	82	174	44
239	113	141	11	87	217	37	163	150	20	232	106	62	188	64	194

Fig. 1. Sobol's sequence for a 16 × 16 grid

be stopped. Moreover, if the best candidate block is found early, then many comparisons will be skipped.

PDE matching strategy consists in the computation of the partial distortion row by row (where a row is made up of 16 pixels); the implementation of the search strategy is also row by row, from top to bottom. SpiralPDE (PDE improvement) search strategy follows a center-biased spiral, in order to exploit the center-biased distribution of motion vectors.

SPD algorithm involves:

- spiral search strategy in the search window,
- Sobol's sequence order (see Fig. 1) for the matching strategy (partial distortion computation),
- comparisons made for each group of 8 pixels (equivalent to a half row of SpiralPDE).

In PDE, the test on the partial distortion comparison is performed for each row of 16 pixels. Among possible choices (1,2,...,16 pixels), we have chosen 8-pixel-groups for Sobol's sequence in the SPD algorithm since this approach leads to the highest speedup over SpiralPDE as explained in Section 5 and shown in Fig. 3.

It is worth noting that our algorithm (like others derived from PDE) can be successfully combined with SEA or its improved versions [11] [16] to achieve maximum speedup.

5 Experimental Results and Remarks

We tested the performances of the SPD algorithm with respect to SpiralPDE. A large set of sequences has been encoded using a modified MPEG-2 encoder derived from ISO/IEC [13]. From the implementation point of view, in order to be fair, we have used the same programming techniques both for SpiralPDE and SPD; for this reason a comparison of the two algorithms is also feasible in terms of the total encoding time.

We have used a total of 17 sequences in various formats: QCIF (176×144), CIF (352×288) and CCIR-601 (720×486). They are well-known sequences, covering a large spectrum of applications from cinema to videoconference; some of them have large motion and others, commonly called "head-and-shoulders", are almost inactive. Sequences used are: "bream0", "bream1", "carphone", "claire", "container", "foreman", "garden", "glasgow", "grandmother", "miss america", "mobile", "mother&daughter", "news", "salesman", "silent", "suzie" and "trevor". The number of frames for each sequence varies from 80 up to 800. The search range is ± 15 pixels, while the block size is 16×16. We have used several Intel-based processors to test and evaluate our algorithm; in all cases results show the same behavior.

Results are reported in Figs. 2, 3 and Table 1.

Figure 2 shows averages and standard deviations for all sequences of the percentage reduction in numbers of rows checked before discarding the block. For SPD a row-equivalent value is obtained by dividing the number of checked pixels by 16. The gain is a maximum when the granularity of partial distortion is one pixel.

In Fig. 3 a similar plot is shown for the percentage of cpu time reduction for SPD with respect to SpiralPDE. Results are in percentage total cpu time for the encoding of all frames and are plotting for partial distortion comparison every 1,2,4,8,16 pixels. In average the advantage is a maximum for 8 pixels, although it depends slightly on the chosen video sequence. This maximum is due to the trade-off between the overhead produced by the number of comparisons (increasing toward left on the Figure) and by the number of pixels considered before the subsequent comparison (increasing toward right on the Figure).

Table 1 reports the average value of checked rows for SEA, PDE, SpiralPDE, the "Proposed 2" (P2) algorithm from [15] and SPD. In this case SPD does comparisons every 8 pixels and, therefore, a row-equivalent value is reported. Data for all algorithms are for these five sequences: "carphone", "claire", "foreman", "grandmother" and "trevor", common between [15] and our tests. Data for SEA, PDE, SpiralPDE and P2 are taken from [15]. SPD shows an average computational gain of up to 20% with respect to SpiralPDE algorithm.

It is worth remarking that results in Fig. 2 and Table 1 are different from those in Fig. 3: this is because the number of checked rows affects the motion estimation time which is only a part of the total encoding time considered in Fig. 3. Moreover Fig. 2 does not take into account the different comparison overhead with respect to SpiralPDE that does comparisons every 16 pixels.

We can conclude that the SPD algorithm performs well with respect to other algorithms; the method rejects impossible candidates faster than other PDE based algorithms, without any additional frame-based computation.

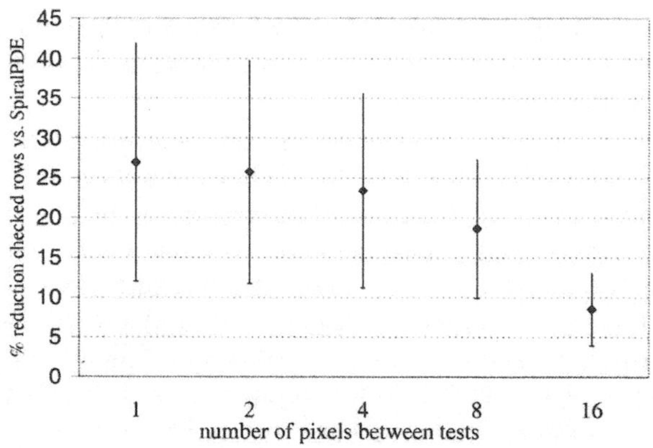

Fig. 2. Average value and standard deviation of the percentage of reduction of checked rows for SPD with respect to SpiralPDE with partial distortion comparison every 1,2,4,8,16 pixels, for all tested sequences

Table 1. Average checked rows for various algorithms with respect to SpiralPDE. P2 is the "Proposed 2" in [15]. Data for all algorithms are for these five sequences: "carphone", "claire", "foreman", "grandmother", "trevor", also used by [15]. (*) SPD does comparisons every 8 pixels (equivalent to a half row) as discussed in Section 5.

SEA	PDE	SpiralPDE	P2	SPD
3.38	7.62	3.62	3.06	2.93*

6 Conclusions and Future Work

In this paper we have presented a new full-search (lossless), fast-matching, block motion estimation algorithm, which uses the partial distortion elimination approach; this algorithm is denoted as Sobol Partial Distortion (SPD).

It uses a new matching strategy, based on Sobol's sequence instead of row by row top to bottom scanning order, to quickly compute minimum distortion, and reduce block matching computation. No image-dependent computations are required.

The proposed algorithm performs well in comparison with other existing full search algorithms. In particular our experimental evaluations have reported an

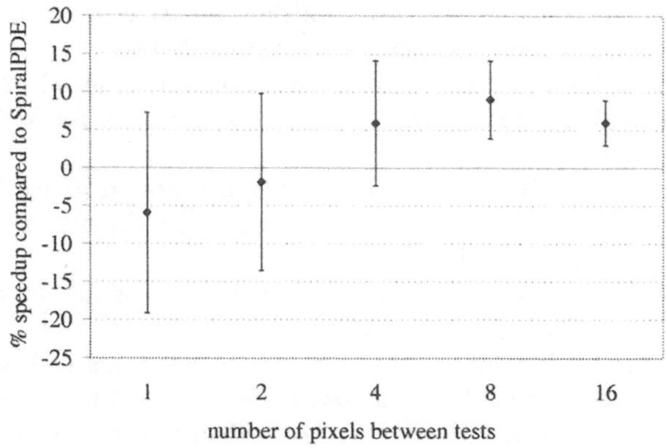

Fig. 3. Average value and standard deviation of the percentage of reduction in total encoding cpu time for SPD with respect to SpiralPDE with partial distortion comparison every 1,2,4,8,16 pixels, for all tested sequences

average computational gain of up to 20% with respect to SpiralPDE algorithm, as reported in Table 1. The proposed algorithm is independent of methods based on SEA and can be used with them to improve global speedup.

The results which we have obtained are a stimulus for further exploration of the proposed methodology in the light of improved performances and of fast special purpose architecture. Future work aims to further improve the matching strategy. The uniformity of Sobol's sequence could also be used in a lossy method based on pixel decimation in the matching phase.

References

1. Dufaux, F., Moscheni, F.: Motion estimation techniques for digital TV: A review and a new contribution. Proceedings of the IEEE, **83** 6 (1995) 858–876
2. Stiller, C., Konrad, J.: Estimating motion in image sequences. IEEE Signal Processing Magazine **16** 4 (1999) 70–91
3. Po, L.M., Ma, W.C.: A novel four-step search algorithm for fast block motion estimation. IEEE Trans. On Circuits and Syst. for Video Technol. **6** 3 (1996) 313–317
4. Lu, J., Liou, M.L.: A simple and efficient search algorithm for block-matching motion estimation. IEEE Trans. On Circuits and Syst. for Video Technol. **7** 2 (1997) 429–433
5. Cheng, F.H., Sun, S.N.: New fast and efficient two-step search algorithm for block motion estimation. IEEE Trans. On Circuits and Syst. for Video Technol. **9** 7 (1999) 977–983
6. Wang, Y., Wang, Y., Kuroda, H.: A globally adaptive pixel-decimation algorithm for block-motion estimation. IEEE Trans. On Circuits and Syst. for Video Technol. **10** 6 (2000) 1006–1011

7. Wang, H.S., Mersereau, R.M.: Fast algorithms for the estimation of motion vectors. IEEE Trans. On Image Processing **8** 3 (1999) 435–438
8. Cheung, C.K., Po, L.M.: Normalized partial distortion search algorithm for block motion estimation. IEEE Trans. On Circuits and Syst. for Video Technol. **10** 3 (2000) 417–422
9. Lengwehasatit, K., Ortega, A.: Probabilistic partial-distance fast matching algorithms for motion estimation. IEEE Trans. On Circuits and Syst. for Video Technol. **11** 2 (2001) 139–152
10. Li, W., Salari, E.: Successive elimination algorithm for motion estimation. IEEE Trans. On Image Processing **4** 1 (1995) 105–107
11. Oh, T.M., Kim, Y.R., Hong, W.G., Ko, S.J.: A fast full search motion estimation algorithm using the sum of partial norms. Proc. ICCE 13–15 June (2000) 236–237
12. Coban, M.Z., Mersereau, R.M.: A fast exhaustive search algorithm for rate-constrained motion estimation. IEEE Trans. On Image Processing **7** 5 (1998) 769–773
13. Eckart, S., Fogg, C.: ISO/IEC MPEG-2 software video codec. Proc. SPIE Vol. 2419 (1995) 100–118
14. Telenor R&D, ITU-T recommendation H.263 software implementation, Digital Video Coding Group (1995)
15. Kim, J.N., Choi, T.S.: A fast full-search motion-estimation algorithm using representative pixels and adaptive matching scan. IEEE Trans. On Circuits and Syst. for Video Technol. **10** 7 (2000) 1040–1048
16. Brünig, M., Niehsen, W.: Fast full-search block matching. IEEE Trans. On Circuits and Syst. for Video Technol. **11** 2 (2001) 241–247
17. Sobol, I.M.: On the distribution of points in a cube and the approximate evaluation of integrals. USSR Computational Mathematics And Mathematical Physics **7** 4 (1967) 86–112
18. Press, W.H., Teukolsky, S.A., Vetterling, W.T., Flannery, B.P.: Numerical Recipes In C: The Art Of Scientific Computing. 2nd edn. Cambridge University Press (1993)

DynaVideo - A Dynamic Video Distribution Service

Luiz Eduardo Leite, Renata Alves, Guido Lemos, and Thais Batista

Informatics Department - DIMAp
Federal University of Rio Grande do Norte - UFRN
{leduardo, renata, guido, thais}@natalnet.br
http://www.natalnet.br

Abstract. Most solutions proposed to implement audio and video distribution services have been designed for specific infrastructures or have been tailored to specific application requirements, such as stream and clients types which will be supported by the service. Other important aspect in this context is that the performance of distributed services is becoming increasingly variable due to changing load patterns and user mobility. This paper presents the Dynamic Video Distribution Service - DynaVideo. The service may be designed to distribute video in a way that is independent of the video format and to interact with different types of clients. The main feature of DynaVideo is the ability to configure the service dynamically to a specific demand.

1 Introduction

The cost reduction of high-speed networks, the development of powerful and cheaper microprocessors and the consolidation of audio and video standards to applications such as Digital TV, Video on Demand, High Definition Television and Interactive TV are factors that motivate the development of video distribution services over digital networks, such as the Internet. This paper presents the Dynamic Video Distribution Service - DynaVideo. The service is designed to distribute video in a way that is independent of the video format and to interact with different types of client. The service may be used to distribute video over any digital network, however, it is focused on the Internet. The main feature of DynaVideo is the ability to configure the service dynamically to a specific demand. Applications that deal with video distribution, such as broadcast digital television, normally have to deal with abrupt variations on its demand. The number, type and location of clients of the service can vary rapidily. This could occur every time the broadcast of an interesting programme starts. Nowadays, many systems can distribute video over digital networks like the Internet. Real System of the Real Networks [5] encodes the video streams in many formats, but its focus is on the support of its proprietary format RM. This system may transmit video with IP Multicast, TCP, UDP or HTTP. The Microsoft Windows Media Service [7] proprietary format is ASF. The following video formats BMP, WAV,

WMA, WMV, ASF, AVI, and MPEG-1 [3] are also supported and can be transmitted with UDP, TCP, HTTP/TCP or IP Multicast. The IBM VideoCharger [6] transports MPEG-1, MPEG-2 [4], AVI, WAV, LBR and QuickTime video streams, using RTP [9], TCP, HTTP or IP Multicast. Once configured, distribution services based on these platforms remain unchanged and cannot automatically adjust configurations to varied demands. This paper is structured as follows: Section 2 presents the DynaVideo Architecture; Section 3 discusses the implementation details of the DynaVideo components; Section 4 presents some experiments results. Finally, Section 5 contains the conclusions.

2 Dynavideo Architecture

The DynaVideo service can be dynamically configured. This is its main feature. This flexibility allows the service to automatically adjust itself to demand variations. The service continually tries to find an optimized configuration to respond to a given demand. In DynaVideo the demand is defined by the number, type and location of the service clients. The target applications of the service are Digital Television broadcast and Video on Demand. In such applications, the demand can change from a few users to millions of them in a short time. Fig. 1 shows the DynaVideo architecture using the UML component diagram [2].

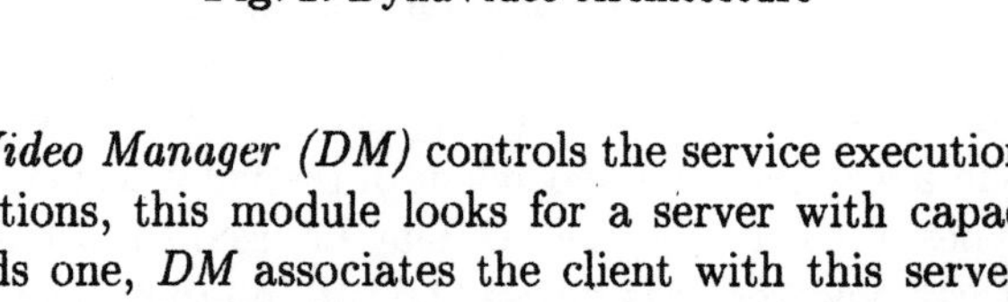

Fig. 1. DynaVideo Architecture

The *DynaVideo Manager (DM)* controls the service execution. When clients request connections, this module looks for a server with capacity to support them. If it finds one, *DM* associates the client with this server. Otherwise, a *Secondary Server* is initialized to support the client. Notice that initially the service policy is to try to serve the client as fast as possible, and not to find an optimized configuration to the video distribution.

The *Primary Servers (PS)* have direct access to video sources, which can be real time encoders or video file servers. *PS* captures a video stream from the source and transmits it to the service clients.

The *Secondary Servers (SS)* are different from *PS* because they do not have direct access to video sources. They receive the video stream from a *PS* and forward it to the service clients, acting as a reflector. The main feature of the DynaVideo *SS* is its ability to move through the network. This way, when it is necessary to optimize the service configuration, *DM* can determine that a certain *SS* moves to a given node of the network.

The arrival of a client determines a change in the service configuration. This event activates the *Traffic Monitor (TM)* [1] to find the routes from the active servers to the client. This way, the role of *TM* is to create and update a data structure, the *route graph*, which records routes from the active servers to the service clients.

When the *route graph* is updated, *DM* activates the *Configuration Optimizer (CO)* module to compute an optimal configuration of the service. *CO* is executed in the background, searching for a better configuration of the video distribution service, considering the current demand represented by the route graph. Once a configuration better than the existing one is found, *CO* requests *DM* to:

- move clients from a server to another one;
- add or delete *Secondary Servers*;
- move *Secondary Servers* from one locality to another.

The goal is to tune the service configuration to optimize the use of transmission, processing and storage resources. Fig. 2 illustrates an example of a reconfiguration, showing the evolution from a configuration with unnecessary streams traversing links and routers over the network to another where this does not occur. One *SS* is added and three clients are transferred from *PS* to *SS*. The other modification was the creation of a multicast group with three clients. This optimization takes into account that R2 does not support multicast, so the only way to eliminate unnecessary transmissions in the route that traverses R2 is to use a *SS*.

Finally, the *Fault Manager (FM)* goal is to identify failures in the service components and to arrange replacements through a service reconfiguration. For example, if a server fails, *FM* detects this event and asks *DM* to move its clients to other servers.

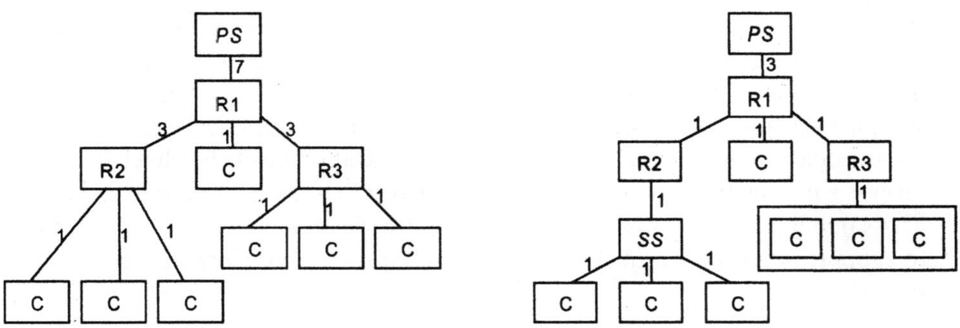

Fig. 2. DynaVideo Reconfiguration Example

In the following sections, we discuss the specification and implementation of *DM*, *PS*, and *SS* Modules. The *TM* module was described in [1]. *CO* and *FM* are under development.

3 Implementation Issues

3.1 DynaVideo Manager

The *DynaVideo Manager (DM)* provides mechanisms to:

- Register *Primary Servers*;
- Add and delete clients;
- Add, delete, and move *Secondary Servers*;
- Select a primary or secondary server to attend a client request.

DM is divided into three parts: *Server Interface*, *Client Interface* and *Manager Controller*. The *Server Interface* function is to control the communication between *DM* and the modules *SS* and *PS*. The *Client Interface* receives a connection request and forwards it to the proper server (primary or secondary). The *Manager Controller* enables service management by controlling which server is active and which server supports each client. This class updates the data structures *ServerTable*, *ClientTypeTable* and *ServiceConfiguration* through the execution of the routines *ServerRegistration()*, *AddClient()*, *AddServer()*, *PrimaryServerRegister()*, *DeleteClient()* and *MoveServer()*. The choice of the server to support a new client is made by the *SelectServer()* routine, which searches at the *ServiceConfiguration* tree (similar to the tree shown in Fig. 2) for a server with capacity to support the new client.

One of the target application of the DynaVideo service is to distribute Television video. Considering this application as an example, when a user wants to play a video using a third part player (DynaVideo client), he must do the following actions: the user must access a Web page and select a TV channel link. At the client browser, an applet will be executed to send a *StreamRequest()* to *DynaVideo Manager*, providing the proper information about the video player that will be used. *DM*, executing the *SelectServer()* method, searches for an appropriate server to support the client. If there is one, it is selected and *AddClient()* is executed to associate this server with the client. Then, the video stream begins to be transmitted to the client. The transmission ends when the client sends a *StopStream()* to *DM*. In response, *DM* removes the client from the service with the execution of the *RemoveClient()* method, as shown in Fig. 3. The same figure illustrates a situation in which there is not an available server to support a new client. In this case, *DM* initializes a *Secondary Server* to serve the new client.

3.2 Primary Server

The *Primary Server (PS)* can be configured to meet service needs (video format, transmission rate and protocol). *PS* supports different kinds of clients (for instance, Microsoft-Media Player, Real Player and MTV). The interface between *PS* and the data sources is based in two classes: *SourceManager* and *SourceInterface*. These class specifications depend on the stream generator entity. If there

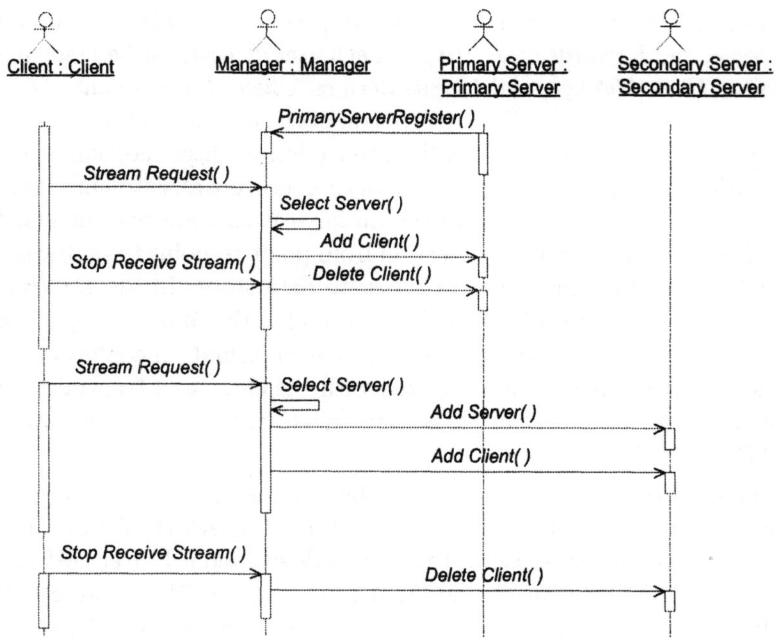

Fig. 3. Add Client Case Sequence Diagram

is more than one data source, an instance of each of these classes is used for each source. The *SourceInterface* class receives video data segments and stores them in an instance of the *DataBuffer* class, invoking the *PutDataOnBuffer()* method of the *MainManager* class. The *SourceManager* class acquires parameters of the data source. For example, if it is a TCP transmitter, the jitter is measured and reported to the *MainManager* class through the *SetParameter()* routine. The *MainManager* class controls the exchange of information between the other classes of *PS*. It controls data insertion and recovery in a *DataBuffer* object, using the methods *PutDataOnBuffer()* and *GetDataFromBuffer()*. This class also stores and retrieves the *PS* parameters configured by the service administrator or defined by some other object, through the *SetParameter()* and *GetParameter()* routines. The *MainManager* class interprets and executes commands through the *Execute()* routine and adds and removes clients using *AddClient()* and *DeleteClient()* routines.

The *DataBuffer* class contains, in addition to a buffer used to store the data stream, mechanisms that provide mutual exclusion between buffer accessing objects. This class has also a *timestamp* that indicates the time of data insertion into the buffer. This feature allows the classes which access objects to decide whether they will use those data or not. The interface between the service administrator and the *MainManager* class, which enables the system administration, is implemented by the *UserInterface* class. The *ManagerInterface* class acts as an interface between *PS* and *DM*. It interprets commands from the *DM*, executes some, and forwards others to *SS*. Each user of *PS* must be associated with the classes *ClientManager* and *ClientInterface*. *ClientManager* controls each new client's connection without the intervention of the administrator, negotiating its initial parameters. It also notifies the connection or disconnection of clients to the *MainManager* class. The *ClientManager* class controls stream transmission to the clients and can renegotiate the initial transmission parameters. For example, it can change a client connection from point-to-point to multicast in real time. *ClientInterface* class controls access to data stored in the *DataBuffer* object, invoking the *GetDataFromBuffer()* method of the *MainManager* class. The *ClientInterface* class also adjusts the data stream format, in conformity with requirements of the client type associated with the class, and transmits the data. For instance, this class adapts MPEG streams to allow their transmission using the RTP protocol.

Primary Server was implemented to allow transmission of MPEG streams to the following clients: MTV (MPEG-1 using TCP, UDP, HTTP and IP Multicast); VideoLan (MPEG-2 using UDP); Windows Media Player (MPEG-1 and MPEG-2 using HTTP); RealAudio (MPEG-1 using HTTP) and JMF (MPEG-1 using RTP). In the experiments done at NatalNet Laboratory at UFRN, MPEG streams were obtained in real time from an Apollo capture card. The card is installed in a PC Pentium II 400 with 64 MB of RAM and a Microsoft Windows NT 4.0 operating system. A *Named Pipe* with an 8 MB buffer was created. The Apollo software was configured to write the video stream into the pipe. A program named *Streamer* was implemented using two *threads*. One thread waits for connection requests and accepts them if there is no other client (*PS*) connected. The other one continues to read the MPEG stream from the pipe and transmits it to *PS* using a TCP data connection. When the buffer of the *Named Pipe* becomes full, the *streamer* empties the buffer and notifies *PS* using a TCP signaling connection.

PS was implemented using C++ and was installed in a Linux platform. As already mentioned, *SourceInterface* class was implemented to receive the video stream. *SourceManager* class receives control data from the *Streamer*. *SourceInterface* object stores the data segments of the video stream in a *DataBuffer* object, using the *PutDataOnBuffer()* method of the *MainManager* class. *ClientManager* and *ClientInterface* classes were specified and implemented in a different way for each protocol supported by *PS*;

To transmit MPEG-1 streams using the TCP protocol, the *ClientManager* class implementation has a main method that remains blocked until it receives a connection request. When a connection request arrives, it is accepted, its descriptor is placed in a *wait list* and a request is sent to the *MainManager* class to insert a new client through the *AddClient()* method. After this, the method remains blocked, waiting for new requests;

The *ClientInterface* class has a main method that reads data from the buffer and sends them to all clients whose descriptors are in a *send list*. If it is not possible to send data to a given client, its descriptor is removed from the list and a request is sent to an object of the *MainManager* class to remove this client. If there is some client in the *wait list*, the method searches for an MPEG sequence initial code. When this code is found, the stream is sent to all the clients whose descriptors are in the *wait list* and these descriptions are moved from the *wait list* to the *transmission list*. Then the method returns to reading the buffer, restarting the whole process;

To transmit MPEG-1 streams using the HTTP protocol, the *ClientManager* class was implemented in a similar way to those used for TCP transmission. The only difference is that before inserting a client in the *wait list*, a handshake using HTTP protocol is performed. During this handshake, the server uses the header fields "Pragma: no-cache" and "Cache-Control: no-cache" to tell the client that the content must not be cached. The format of the stream is set up through the header field "Content-Type: video/mpeg". The length in bytes of the video file is set up in the field "Content-Length: 45000000". This field is necessary and must be configured with a high value because some players start video and audio execution only when the file is completely loaded. *ClientInterface* class was implemented in a similar way to those used with TCP protocol;

To transmit MPEG-1 using UDP protocol, *ClientManager* class was implemented to allow insertion and removal of clients. When a client is inserted, a socket is created to it and its identifier is inserted in a *transmission list*. The *ClientInterface* class has a method that reads data from the buffer and sends it to all the clients whose identifiers are in the *transmission list*. For transmissions of MPEG-1 using IP Multicast, the *ClientManager* and *ClientInterface* classes are similar to those used for a UDP transmission. The only difference is that the *ClientManager* class receives a class D IP address, instead of an IP unicast address;

To transmit MPEG-1 video streams using the RTP transport protocol, the *ClientManager* class was implemented in a similar way to those used for UDP transmission. The *ClientInterface* class has a method that reads data from the buffer and scans it in order to identify the data structures of MPEG standard as well as some MPEG Frames header fields whose values are placed in specific RTP permanent header fields. In this way, MPEG-1 video is packed in conformity to the rules posed in [10]. To transmit MPEG-2 streams, part of the code of *VideoLan Server* [8] was used to produce the transmission packets. The code was adapted to read a stream from the buffer and to send it to a *ClientInterface* object. One *ClientInterface* class was implemented to receive *VideoLan Server* streams, instead of reading it from the buffer.

3.3 Secondary Server

One of the main features of DynaVideo is its ability to adjust the service configuration dynamically. The idea is to identify network links with unnecessary connections to try to eliminate them. When it is not possible to use multicast, a good solution is to instantiate *Secondary Servers (SS)* agents. *SS* has two classes. The *controller class* interprets commands received from *DM* requiring: to start or to finish sending streams (Start/Stop Server); to add or to remove a client

(Add/Delete Client); and to move or to clone *SS* (Move/Clone Server). The commands are sent by *DM* in ***Protocol Data Units.*** Each command has a code and optional information such as the client IP and port number. The *Streamer* class receives the video stream from *PS* and sends it to the clients in the *ClientTable.* *SS* is started through an *Agent Dispatcher*, which is responsible for the creation, destruction, cloning, moving and forwarding commands to *SS*. *SS* presents the following methods:

- *AddClient*: controller adds an IP address and an associated port in *ClientTable.* To send streams, *SS* scans this table.
- *DeleteClient*: controller removes the IP address and the port from the *ClientTable.*
- *StartServer*: controller requests *SS* to wait for UDP packets from the *PS.* When *SS* receives a packet, it scans the client vector in order to forward this packet.
- *MoveServer*: controller requests *SS* to stop sending streams. It moves *SS* (with all its clients) to the location determined by *DM.*
- *CloneServer*: a copy of an agent is created in another context.
- *StopServer*: controller requests *SS* to stop sending streams. It ends the execution of an agent.
- *DecodeCommand*: controller receives, interprets and executes the commands sent by *DM.*

To validate the *SS* design, we have implemented it using two different environments: IBM Aglets [14] and Agent Lua [11].

Aglet One implementation of *SS* was made using the Aglet library [14], developed by IBM. This library is composed of a set of classes written in Java. These classes have methods that allow the agent to move or to clone from one execution context to another (***dispatch/clone***) and to be extended with other functions. Tàhiti [14] is one application that implements the Aglet execution context concept and was used in this work.

The *SS* Aglet agent has two classes: the *Controller* and the *Streamer*. The *Controller* uses the methods inherited from the Aglet class to move (***dispatch***) or to clone (*clone*) the agent to another context. When an Aglet needs to go to another place, the method ***OnDispatch*** is executed to prepare the Aglet to travel. This method calls ***Stop Stream*** from the *Streamer* class. When the agent arrives at its target, it executes the method *OnArrival* that askes the *Streamer* to *Start Stream.* The *Streamer* starts to receive the video stream from the *PS* and sends it to the same list of clients that it had at the original place. To start a new *SS*, an *Agent Dispatcher* must be running. When it receives a command from *DM* to start an agent in another place, it clones itself to that place. The new *SS* will, then, use the *controller* to communicate with *DM* and receive commands such as *Add Client* or *Delete Client.* The class *Streamer* receives PDUs from *PS* and sends them to the clients in the list that are initially empty.

Agent Lua The DynaVideo *Secondary Server* was also implemented using the Agent Lua library (aLua) [11]. The aLua distributed programming mechanism is an event-driven extension of the interpreted language Lua [12]. It offers support to send messages to remote processes containing codes to be executed at destination. In aLua, each agent is an independent process that communicates with another agent through asynchronous messages. This mechanism has two important features. It is a non-blocking one, once it uses an event-driven approach and considers each event as an atomic block that must be executed as a whole. Since aLua runs in an interpreted environment, it is easy to modify *SS* whenever necessary without disturbing other DynaVideo modules. This feature introduces flexibility to the *SS* implementation.

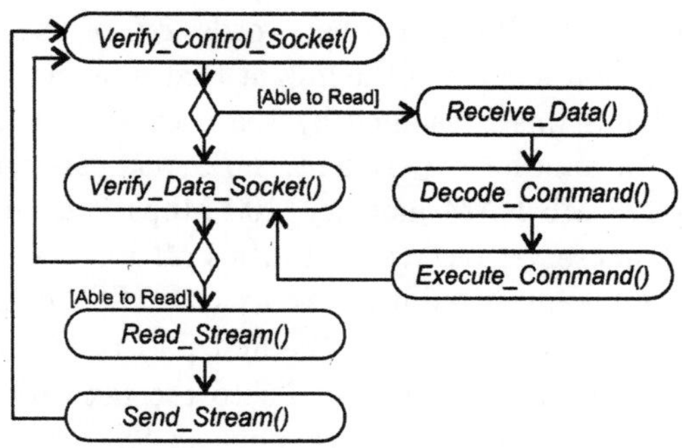

Fig. 4. *SS* Activity Diagram in an aLua Enviroment

The *SS* initialization in the aLua environment happens in this way. Firstly, it is necessary to implement a component that acts as an *agent dispatcher*. Then, *DM* asks the *agent dispatcher* to prepare execution contexts, by sending to it the command *Conf (address)*. In response to this command, the *agent dispatcher* issues a *spawn* command to the respective address. After this, an aLua environment becomes ready in the new location. In order to trigger the execution of a *SS*, *DM* sends an activate command to the *agent dispatcher*. In response, it sends the Lua code of the secondary server to the newly created aLua environment. When the code is received, it begins to be executed.

The activity diagram shown in Fig. 4 describes the *SS* implementation using aLua. An infinite loop verifies if there are, in a control socket, commands available for reading. In this case, the commands are decoded and executed. It also verifies if there are, in a data socket, data available for reading. In this case, it sends them to all the clients listed in the client table.

To move an *SS* from a location to another, *DM* asks the *agent dispatcher* to initialize a secondary server code in the new location. When the sent code is running, it adds all the clients of the old location in the new one. Then, the manager orders the primary server to stop sending video to the old location, and to begin sending it to the new one. And finalizes the agent being moved, by issuing a *Com_Exit()* command.

4 Results

In order to test the performance of the DynaVideo service we did some experiments on the following scenarios. The *Primary Server (PS)* was configured in a PC Pentium MMX 300 with 128 Mb RAM memory, a 100 Mbps Ethernet card and Linux operating system. A 4 Mbps real time MPEG-2 stream was generated and transmitted from the *streamer* to *PS*. This stream was generated by an Apollo card installed in a PC Pentium II 400 with 64 MB RAM memory and with Microsoft Windows NT 4.0 operating system. The utilization of the link that connects *PS* to an IBM 8265 Switch, when *PS* was transmitting UDP datagrams to a multicast address, was 9.5% (9.5Mbps). Since a video stream was being generated at a constant rate of 4 Mbps, the reception and transmission of this stream consume 8 Mbps, in other words, 8% of the band. Considering that no other application was using the link at that moment, we have concluded that 1.5 % of the band was consumed by the overhead of transport, link and network protocols. In another experiment, a *PS* was configured in a PC Pentium III 600 with 128 Mb RAM memory, 100 Mbps Ethernet card and Linux operating system. This server received a 4 Mbps MPEG-1 video stream directly from the *streamer* and transmitted it to twenty (20) MTV clients using the UDP protocol. This scenario is illustrated by the first part of Fig. 5. In this case, the utilization of the link that interconnects *PS* to the network reaches 100%. To prove the feasibility of the *SS* concept, we move an *SS* to a machine at the LCC network. In this scenario (second part of Fig. 5), we can serve 29 clients: *PS* transmitting to 19 clients and to *SS*, and *SS* transmitting to 10 clients. With this experiment, we confirm the scalability of the DynaVideo approach.

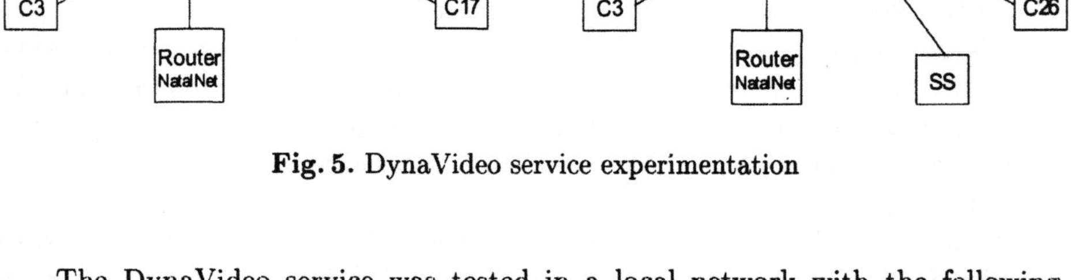

Fig. 5. DynaVideo service experimentation

The DynaVideo service was tested in a local network with the following clients: MTV (MPEG-1 using TCP, UDP, HTTP and IP Multicast), VideoLan (MPEG-2 using UDP), Windows Media Player (MPEG-1 and MPEG-2 using HTTP), RealAudio (MPEG-1 using HTTP), and JMF (MPEG-1 using RTP). In all clients, the video was played at a good quality. Fig. 6 shows an MPEG-1

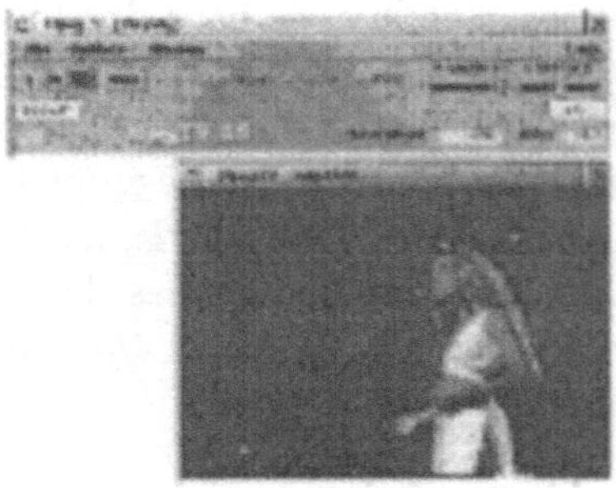

Fig. 6. MPEG-1 Video exhibited by MTV client

Fig. 7. MPEG-2 Video exhibited by VLC client

video being exhibited by an *MTV* client. Fig. 7 shows an MPEG-2 video being exhibited by a *VideoLan* client.

5 Conclusions

This paper has presented the architecture and implementation of the Dynamic Video Distribution Service (DynaVideo) designed for generic data communication environments, supporting different video formats and different client types. In this paper, we have described the following DynaVideo components: *Dynavideo Manager* that controls the service execution; *Primary Server* that has direct access to video sources and whose function is to capture a video stream from the source and to transmit it to the service clients; and *Secondary Server* that acts like a reflector, receiving the video stream from a *Primary Server* and forwarding it to the service clients.

The main feature of the *Secondary Server* is that it can move through the network. This allows the dynamic reconfiguration of the service. The importance of dynamic reconfiguration of video distribution systems is also discussed in [13]. This report proposes an infrastructure to distribute video and uses agents to update and to fix bugs in the code of the replicas. Other works [15][16] have adopted the replication idea, but do not provide support to service reconfiguration during real time video transmissions. DynaVideo allows the transmission of MPEG streams to the MTV clients (MPEG-1 using TCP, UDP, HTTP and IP Multicast), VideoLan clients (MPEG-2 using UDP), Windows Media Player clients (MPEG-1 and MPEG-2 using HTTP), RealAudio clients (MPEG-1 using HTTP) and JMF clients (MPEG-1 using RTP). In the experiments done, the video received by these clients was at good quality. In the implementation, we have adopted a configuration-based approach to the *DynaVideo Manager*. This module integrates the other modules of DynaVideo and acts as a mediator, sending and forwarding commands to other modules. The configuration-based approach facilitates the change of one module without disturbing the others. This issue promotes the reuse and allows integration of new services in DynaVideo whenever necessary. To support *Secondary Server* mobility, we have developed two implementations. One of the implementation uses the Aglet library, an IBM product. The other one uses aLua, an event-driven mechanism that offers support to move processes. The implementations validated the feasibility of the approach, which is a good alternative to services dealing with unstable demands, like TV distribution. The implementation of the *Traffic Monitor* module was done in another work and it is described in [1]. Currently, the *Configuration Optimizer* and the *Fail Manager* modules are under development.

References

1. Madruga, M., Batista, T., Lemos, G.: SMTA: Um Sistema para Monitoramento de Tráfego em Aplicaçẽs Multimídia. CLEI'2000 (2000)
2. Booch, G., Jacobson, I., Rumbaugh, J.: The Unified Modeling Language for Object-Oriented Development. Documentation Set Version 0.91 Addendum UML Update (1996).
3. Coding of Moving Pictures and Associated Audio for Digital Storage Media up to About 1,5 Mbits/s. ISO/IEC International Standard 11172 (1993).
4. Generic Coding of Moving Pictures and Associated Audio Information. ISO/IEC International Standard 13818 (1994).
5. Realserver Administration Guide RealSystem G2. http://www.real.com/serveradminguideg2.pdf (2001).
6. VideoCharger Server Key Features. VideoCharger, IBM DB2 Digital Library, http://www-4.ibm.com/software/data/videocharger/vcserverkey.html (2000).
7. Windows Media Technologies. http://www.microsoft.com/windowsmedia/ (2001).
8. VideoLan. Ecole Centrale Paris, http://www.videolan.org (2001).
9. Schulzrinne, H., Casner, S., Frederick, R., V. Jacobson: RTP: A Transport Protocol for Real-Time Applications. RFC 1889 (1996).
10. Hoffman, D., et al.: RTP Payload Format for MPEG1/MPEG2 Video. RFC 1849 (1998).
11. Ururahy, C; Rodriguez, N.: Alua: An event-driven communication mechanism for parallel and distributed programming. PDCS'99, Fort Lauderdale, FL (1999).
12. Ierusalimschy, R, Figueiredo, L, Celes, W.: Lua - an extensible extension language. Software: Practice and Experience, 26(6):635-652 (1996).
13. Kon, F., Campbell, R. et al.: Dynamic Reconfiguration of Scalable Internet Systems with Mobile Agents. Technical Report, Department of Computer Science at the University of Illinois Urbana-Champaign (1999).
14. Lange, D., Oshima, M.: Programming and Deploying Java Mobile Agents with Aglets. Addison Wesley (2000).
15. Parveen Kumar, L. H. Ngoh, A. L. Ananda.: A Programmable Audio/Video Streaming Framework for Broadband Infrastructures. Network Storage Symposium - NetStore '99. Seattle, WA (1999).
16. Brian Noble, Ben Fleis, Minkyong Kim, Jim Zajkowski.: Fluid Replication. Network Storage Symposium - NetStore '99, Seattle, WA (1999).

Content Based Retrieval of VRML Objects – An Iterative and Interactive Approach

Michael Elad[1], Ayellet Tal[2], and Sigal Ar[2]

[1] HP Laboratories
Haifa, Israel
elad@ee.technion.ac.il

[2] Department of Electrical Engineering
Technion – Israel Institute of Technology
Haifa, Israel
{ayellet, ar}@ee.technion.ac.il

Abstract. We examine the problem of searching a database of three-dimensional objects (given in VRML) for objects similar to a given object. We introduce an algorithm which is both iterative and interactive. Rather than base the search solely on geometric feature similarity, we propose letting the user influence future search results by marking some of the results of the current search as 'relevant' or 'irrelevant', thus indicating personal preferences. A novel approach, based on SVM, is used for the adaptation of the distance measure consistently with these markings, which brings the 'relevant' objects closer and pushes the 'irrelevant' objects farther. We show that in practice very few iterations are needed for the system to converge well on what the user "had in mind".

1 Introduction

The problem of automatically comparing objects and detecting which ones are alike is a difficult problem. After all, "similarity is in the eye of the beholder". Objects' similarity is a subjective matter, dependent on the human viewer, since objects have semantics and are not only geometric entities. Does a parasaurolophus (Figure 1) look more like a kangaroo or more like an allosaurus?

A Parasaurolophus A Kangaroo An Allosaurus

Fig. 1. Which one is more alike?

Finding similarity between geometric objects has been a lively topic of research in computational geometry [5, 22, 29]. Objects are considered similar if their geometric features are close, given a metric measuring the distance [6]. A lot of work has been done matching sets of points in two dimensions under various transformation sets [8, 9, 28]. The *Hausdorff distance* has been frequently used to measure the distance between point sets [18, 19].

Polygonal shapes have also been considered. Algorithms for computing the minimum Hausdorff distance between polygons were proposed by [2, 3, 12, 20]. Hausdorff distance has some limitations as it is not robust for outliers. Comparing polygons as turning functions is proposed in [7]. In [4] the *Frechet distance* is used to compare polygons. In [17], a *reflection metric* is defined and computed for two unions of line segments.

Less work has been invested in the three-dimensional case [11, 13, 20, 26]. In particular, extending methods of comparing polygonal curves in two dimensions to higher dimensions is non-trivial, both in theory and in practice [23]. However, as VRML objects are becoming more popular on the World-Wide Web, this problem is expected to have many applications, one prominent example being in e-commerce.

Much of the research on similarity has been done in the context of images [24, 1]. On one hand, finding similarities between three-dimensional models seems like it should be easier than finding similarities between their projections to images. After all, the whole object can be "seen", thus occlusions, self-occlusions, lighting effects and reflections, are avoided. On the other hand, three-dimensional models can be harder to handle since they do not have a simple parameterization, and registration and feature correspondence are more difficult to find.

In this paper, we focus on finding similarities between three-dimensional geometric objects. Rather than dealing solely with the choice of features and the definition of a distance measure on these features, we want to give the user the added ability of influencing the search as it is being conducted by means of relevance feedback [14, 21, 25]. We suggest an iterative method where each user can specify how relevant the results are according to this user's preferences.

The scheme we propose is as follows. Given an object, the system searches a database for similar ones. Once a set of results is obtained, the user is presented with the best (most-similar) objects and is given a chance to mark a subset of them as 'relevant' or as 'irrelevant'. Using this feedback from the user, the distance function is updated and another iteration of the search may be conducted. A new set of results, of the updated search, is presented to the user to mark and re-iterate the process, if need be. Thus, with the same database and the same object, each user may get different objects as the closest to the chosen one.

Figure 2 illustrates the intent of the algorithm, as well as some results obtained by the system implementing it. In Figure 2(a), an initial set of the top thirty similar objects is presented, when a search for figures similar to "man4" is conducted on a database of more than a 1000 VRML objects. After the user marked a subset of the results as relevant or irrelevant, and a couple of iterations were run, the final set of results is produced and shown in Figure 2(b). The latter set of results can be contrasted with the initial set. Not only more human figures were found among the top thirty, but also their ranking among the top thirty has been improved. Moreover, figures which differ geometrically, such as 13 ("allien2") where the legs are open, and 16 ("man8") where one leg is folded and an arm is pointing forward, were selected and reflect sematic similarity.

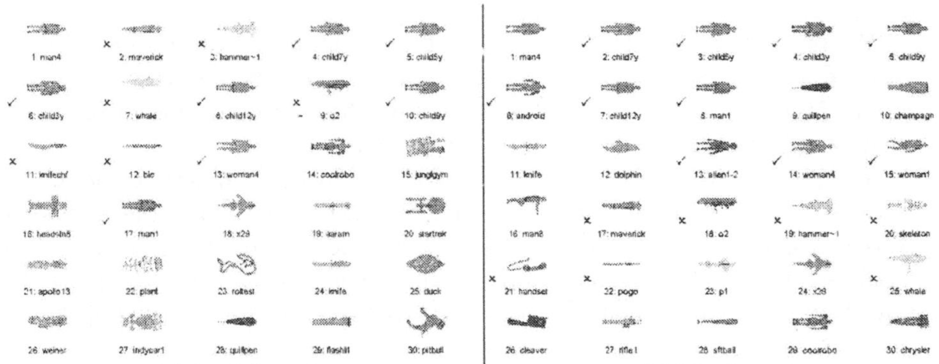

(a) Initial results (b) Final results

Fig. 2. Searching the database for objects similar to 1:man4

Three main issues are tackled in this paper. The first issue is the choice of features. The goal is to have a representation which is compact, suffices to uniquely identify each object, and reflects similarities (and dissimilarities) between objects. Such features can be considered as a *signature* associated with each three-dimensional object, just as a few keywords are associated with each document and are used when searching large databases or the web. The second main issue is the choice of a distance measure which should not only reflect object similarities/dissimilarities well, but should also be amenable to adaptations, to enable refinement of searches. The third issue is finding an adaptation rule on the distance measure.

We will show that the moments of the three-dimensional objects' surfaces, up to some order, are a relevant choice for features as only a handful of them are needed to represent the essence of the data. We will also show that the weighted Euclidean distance leads to an efficient and effective adaptation scheme, based on the user's feedback. Finally, based on the user's input, we find the optimal weights for the weighted Euclidean metric in a way which reflects the user's desire and warps the space such that the 'relevant' results are brought closer and the 'irrelevant' results are pushed farther. Using ideas based on Support Vector Machine learning algorithms (SVM) [30], we formulate an optimization problem in which the weights are the unknowns and their optimal values correspond to the maximal margin between the distances. The obtained optimization problem is convex (QP), thus ensuring a unique solution.

We view the contributions of this paper to be threefold. First, We propose a novel algorithm for retrieving three-dimensional VRML objects, an area which is relatively unexplored. Second, we propose to use moments as features representing three-dimensional objects, and in particular we show how to use moments within a relevance feedback scheme. While moments can have problems in pictures due to occlusions and self-occlusions, they can very well characterize three-dimensional models which are given wholly. Last but not least, we show how to use relevance feedback in the context of SVM.

We tested the algorithm with a database containing over a 1000 objects, given in VRML. Simulations of the search mechanism exhibit very promising results. With very few iterations (usually, 1–4), the search process converges on what sample users had in mind for these searches.

The rest of this paper is organized as follows. Section 2 describes the object features we use. Section 3 describes the similarity measure and the actual iterative search process. In Section 4 we show some runs of the algorithm on a database of three-dimensional VRML objects, and explain the workings of the algorithm by way of demonstration. Finally, Section 5 concludes the paper.

2 Object Features

We assume an object is given in VRML, i.e. it is a three-dimensional object represented by a set of vertices and a set of polygonal faces embedded in three dimensions. The features we choose to represent the objects are the moments, computed for object surfaces, assuming all objects are hollow. For object D, we denote the surface by ∂D. D's (p,q,r)-th moment is the given by

$$m_{pqr} = \int_{\partial D} x^p y^q z^r \, dx dy dz \ . \tag{1}$$

The set of moments $\{m_{pqr}\}$ have a property of fundamental importance: they uniquely determine, and are uniquely determined by, the object. Thus, the triple sequence of moments constitutes a full and complete object description, and a partial object description can be obtained by using some subset of them [16].

Sampling to Approximate the Moments

At the crux of our algorithm lies the computation of a subset of the (p,q,r) moments of each object, which are used as the feature set. Thus, we perform a pre-processing stage where the features are calculated for each database object.

A practical way to evaluate the integral defining moments is to compute it analytically for each facet of the object, and then sum over all the facets. We use an alternative approach, yielding an approximation of the moments. The algorithm draws a sequence of points, (x,y,z), distributed uniformly over the object's surface. The number of points drawn from each of the object's facets is proportional to its relative surface area. If we denote the list of points for a given object by $\{x_i, y_i, z_i\}_{i=1}^{N}$, the (p, q, r)-th moment is then approximated by

$$\hat{m}_{pqr} = \frac{1}{N} \sum_{i=1}^{N} x_i^p y_i^q z_i^r \tag{2}$$

NORMALIZING THE OBJECTS

We want the similarity measure to be invariant to spatial position, scale and rotation of the different objects. We therefore need to normalize the feature vectors of all objects.

The first moments m_{100}, m_{010} and m_{001} represent the object's center of mass. Thus, the normalization starts by estimating the first moments for each object represented as a set of surface sample points, and subtracting them from each of these points:

$$\forall i = 1, 2, \ldots, N \;\; [x_i, y_i, z_i]^T \leftarrow [x_i - \hat{m}_{100}, y_i - \hat{m}_{010}, z_i - \hat{m}_{001}]^T \; . \tag{3}$$

This amounts to positioning all objects so that their center of mass is at coordinates $(0, 0, 0)$, thus removing any dependence on translation, or spatial position. This also sets each of $\hat{m}_{100}$, $\hat{m}_{010}$ and $\hat{m}_{001}$ to 0 for all objects, and thus renders them useless for further computations.

The second moments – m_{200}, m_{020}, m_{002}, m_{110}, m_{101} and m_{011} – represent the object's rotation and scale in the following manner. When the second moments, calculated for the object re-centered at $(0, 0, 0)$, are ordered into a matrix:

$$M = \begin{bmatrix} m_{200} & m_{110} & m_{101} \\ m_{110} & m_{020} & m_{011} \\ m_{101} & m_{011} & m_{002} \end{bmatrix} \tag{4}$$

and Singular Value Decomposition is performed, the result may be written as:

$$U \Delta U^T = SVD(M) \; , \tag{5}$$

where the unitary matrix U represents the rotation and the diagonal matrix Δ represents the scale in each axis, ordered in decreasing size.

The normalization continues with a second stage approximating the second moments for each object, by computing them from the updated surface point data sets, using equation 2, into $\hat{M}$. After performing the SVD decomposition of the second moment matrix $\hat{M}$, we multiply each point by U to rotate the object back to a canonic position. We also divide each point by $\Delta(1, 1)$ to rescale the object so that its largest scale is 1. To summarize, each point is replaced by

$$[x_i, y_i, z_i]^T \leftarrow \frac{1}{\Delta(1, 1)} \cdot U \cdot [x_i, y_i, z_i]^T \; . \tag{6}$$

Finally, the algorithm should also determine each object's orientation, relative to each axis. To do this, we count the number of points on each side of the center of the body. In order to normalize such that all the objects have the same orientation, we flip each object so that it is "heavier" on the positive side. In counting the number of points and flipping according to it, we are actually forcing the median center to be on a predetermined side relatively to the center of mass.

After applying all the normalization stages to each object, the moments are computed once more, up to the pre-specified order. As we indicated, the normalization fixed $\hat{m}_{100}$, $\hat{m}_{010}$, $\hat{m}_{001}$ and $\hat{m}_{200}$ to 0, 0, 0 and 1, respectively, for each and every object. These are therefore no longer useful as object features.

3 Iterative Refinement

Having two finite sets of moments in vectors X and Y, constituting partial descriptions of database objects D_X and D_Y respectively, we can measure the distance between the objects using (the square of) the Euclidean distance

$$d(D_X, D_Y) = ||X - Y||^2 \tag{7}$$

Using the Euclidean distance alone, the automatic search of the database will indeed produce objects that are geometrically close to the given one. However, these may not be what the human user had in mind when initiating the search. Therefore, we employ further "parameterization" of this distance by adding weights and a bias value:

$$d(D_X, D_Y) = [X - Y]^T W [X - Y] + b\ . \tag{8}$$

where W may be any matrix, yet in the following we assume it is a diagonal matrix.

Given a set of search results, a human user may consider some of them relevant and some of them irrelevant, in spite of them all being geometrically close. The adaptation of the distance function can be done by recalculating distances, based on the user preferences. The additional requirement is that the new distance between the given object and the relevant results be small and, obviously, the new distance between the given object and the irrelevant results needs to be large.

In essence, this is a classification, or a learning problem. A way to formulate the requirements is by defining weights on the components of the distance function and writing a set of constraints. Denote the vector moments of the object for which the system is to search by O, the vectors of moments of the 'relevant' results by $\{G_k\}_{k=1}^{n_G}$ and the vectors of moments of the 'irrelevant' results by $\{B_l\}_{l=1}^{n_B}$. The constraints posed on the weight function are then

$$k = 1, 2, \ldots, n_G,\ d(D_O, D_{G_k}) = [O - G_k]^T W [O - G_k] + b \leq 1 \tag{9}$$

$$l = 1, 2, \ldots, n_B,\ d(D_O, D_{B_l}) = [O - B_l]^T W [O - B_l] + b \geq 2\ .$$

This creates a margin between the 'relevant' and 'irrelevant' results. The above inequalities are linear with respect to the entries of W.

Denoting the main diagonal of W by ω, we may rewrite the constraints as

$$k = 1, 2, \ldots, n_G, \quad d(D_O, D_{G_k}) = [O - G_k]^2 \cdot \omega + b \leq 1 \tag{10}$$

$$l = 1, 2, \ldots, n_B, \quad d(D_O, D_{B_l}) = [O - B_l]^2 \cdot \omega + b \geq 2 \, ,$$

where the notation V^2, for a vector V, means multiplying each vector entry by itself.

An additional constraint is that the entries of W are all non-negative. Note though, that we do not require b to be non-negative, and may therefore end up with a non-metric similarity measure.

It can be shown (see for example [27, 10, 15, 30]), that the maximal margin of separation between the two sets of results is achieved by the ω with the smallest (square of the) norm – $min_\omega(||\omega||^2)$. Choosing the ω with the smallest norm also renders the solution to the constraint system robust to the number of examples from each of the two subsets – 'relevant' and 'irrelevant', and also the size of the rest of the database. This is good when the above constraints are insufficient, when $n_G + n_B << \mathcal{M}$, $\mathcal{M}$ being the arity of the feature vectors. That is, there are more unknowns than inequalities, and therefore multiple possible solutions $\{\omega, b\}$ all satisfying the constraints.

Thus, at each refinement iteration we essentially need to solve the following for ω:
Minimize $||\omega||^2$
Subject to:

$$k = 1, 2, \ldots, n_G, \quad d(D_O, D_{G_k}) = [O - G_k]^2 \cdot \omega + b \leq 1$$

$$l = 1, 2, \ldots, n_B, \quad d(D_O, D_{B_l}) = [O - B_l]^2 \cdot \omega + b \geq 2 \tag{11}$$

$$\omega \geq 0$$

This Quadratic Optimization problem may be solved either directly or through the dual problem [30, 15, 10], which proves easier when the number of constraints is much lower than the number of unknowns, i.e., $n_G + n_B << \mathcal{M}$. The use of the bias in the formulation is crucial since it frees us from considering the boundary values and therefore choosing these values to be 1 and 2 does not lose generality.

ITERATING THE SEARCH

The system may use the new, refined distance function to perform a new search, offering the user a set of results to better suit personal preferences. The user may, on this new set of results, mark preferences as was done for the previous search results. The new 'relevant' and 'irrelevant' results sets may now be used to further refine the distance function.

There is no limit by the system on the number of refinement iterations allowed. However, our experiments showed that very few iterations were needed for any example, before a human user is satisfied with the proposed search results.

4 Experimentation and Results

We tested the algorithm with a database containing over a 1000 objects, given in VRML. First, the database was pre-processed. All objects were sampled, with $10,000$ points representing each object, and then normalized as described in Section 2. Further pre-processing included computing a feature vector of the moments up to a pre-specified order (usually, 4–7 is sufficient), for each object. At that point every VRML object has a small signature (the vector of features) associated with it. Note that in the World-Wide Web setup every signature need be calculated only once, upon creation, and then used as a key for all subsequent searches, without ever having to access the VRML object itself.

At each test search, we chose an object from the database, and asked the system to produce the thirty closest objects. These results are organized by their increasing distance from the desired object. Given these, we marked some as 'relevant', and others as 'irrelevant', according to what seems reasonable to a human viewer. We then re-iterated the search to take these preferences into account, as described above in Section 3.

In Figure 3 we show the Allosaurus, an object to be searched. In Figures 4–7 we show the search results, and their evolution from one iteration to the next, based on the user's markings. First, Figure 4 shows the results of the first search iteration, with unweighted Euclidean distance. These results include four dinosaurs (in addition to the one being searched), and one of them was ranked as 28th. We marked these four dinosaurs as 'relevant' and four other objects as 'irrelevant'. Figure 5 shows the best thirty results of the new search, after the distance function had been weighted according to our preferences. This added three more dinosaurs and they all ranked high. The last two iterations brought in all the dinosaurs of the database (ten, including the original allosaurus) and all of them are ranked at the top. As can be seen from this example, the search results improve with each iteration both in terms of the match of the results to the desired one and also in terms of the order in which the results are given (reflecting their closeness to the desired object). Note, again, that the dinosaurs may differ geometrically. Yet, they are considered close because the user considered them semantically so.

5 Conclusions

We propose a new algorithm for determining the content-based similarity of three-dimensional objects, given in a standard representation, such as VRML. Three main issues are considered. The first is the selection of features that can represent the object in a compact manner, and can thus be considered as a signature for the object, similar to the way keywords representing documents. The second issue is the selection of a distance measure that is adaptable and can enable learning in a way that takes semantics into account. The third issue is he selection of an adaptation rule on the distance measure.

Using the normalized moments as features, a weighted-Euclidean function as the distance measure, and the SVM algorithm to 'train' the distance measure, we

Fig. 3. Allosaurus

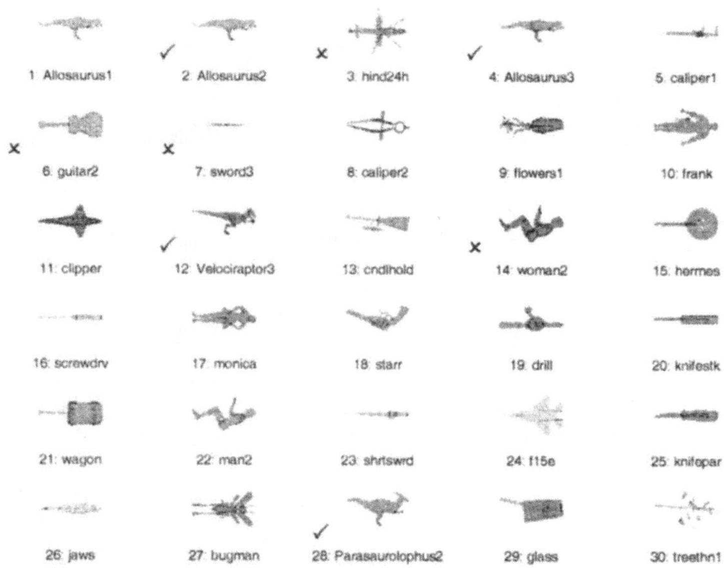

Fig. 4. Allosaurus – Results of the initial search

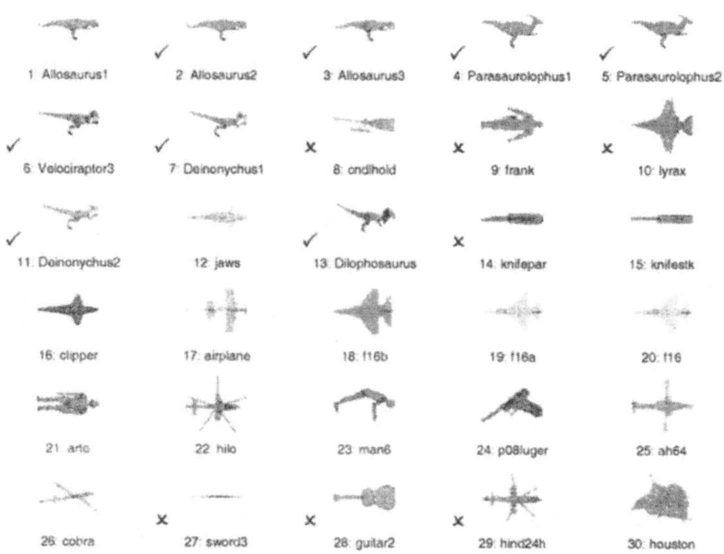

Fig. 5. Allosaurus – Results of 2*nd* search iteration.

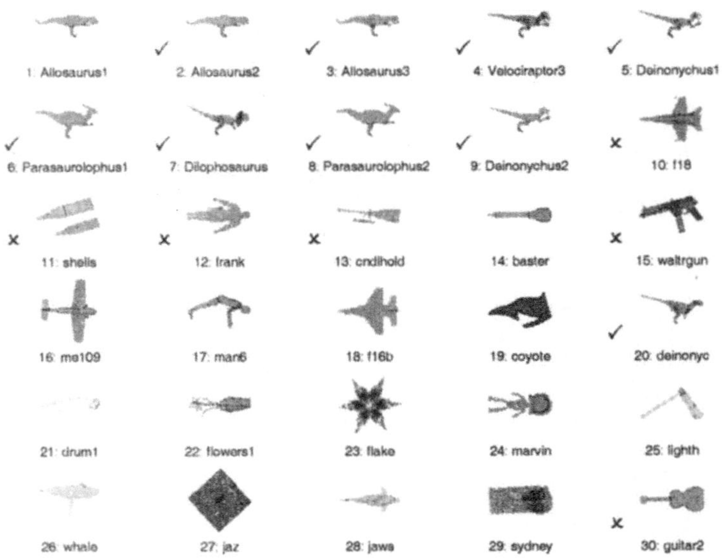

Fig. 6. Allosaurus – Results of 3*rd* search iteration

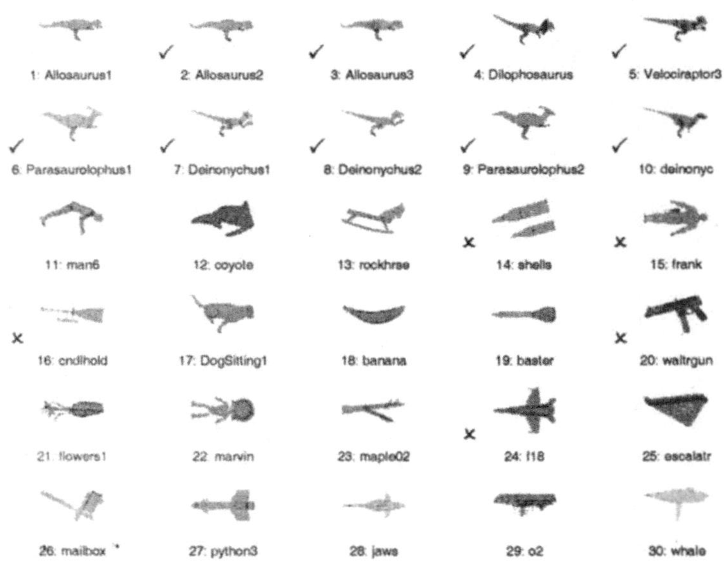

Fig. 7. Allosaurus – Results of the 4*th* (final) search iteration

introduce a novel learning mechanism, that enables adaptation of the distance measure, based on a user's preferences.

Experiments on a database of more than a 1000 objects exhibit very good results. Not only did more "semantically similar" objects rank close to the query object, from among those found to be "geometrically similar", but also objects which differ geometrically rank high. An order of moments of only 4–7 is sufficient to represent the objects well. Less than five iterations need be run before the system converges to what the user had in mind.

The main aspects of this work can be extended. Other features, such as topological traits, colors and textures can be considered as well. We apply the basic search paradigm in one simple version, namely let the search system present the user with results and allow the user to mark any results the user wishes as either 'relevant' or 'irrelevant'. However, one may think of other variants warranting experimentation: Let the user mark only the results viewed as 'relevant' and consider all other search results proposed by the system as 'irrelevant'; Impose further restriction, requiring not only that all 'relevant' results are close to the searched object, but also that they be close to each other; Impose yet further restrictions, requiring, in addition, that each 'relevant' result be far from each 'irrelevant' result.

References

1. IEEE Computer (1995). special issue on content based image retrieval, 28, 9.
2. Agarwal P.K. , Sharir M. and Toledo S. *Applications of parametric searching in geometric optimization*, Proc. 3rd ACM-SIAM Sympos. Discrete Algorithms, 1992, 72–82.
3. Alt H., Behrends B. and Blömer J. *Approximate matching of polygonal shapes*, Proc. 7th Annu. ACM Sympos. Comput. Geom, 1991, 186–193
4. Alt H. and Godau M. *Measuring the resemblance of polygonal curves*, 8th ACM Symposium on Computational Geometry (1992), 102-109.
5. Alt H. and L.J. Guibas. Resemblance of Geometric Objects. In J.-R. Sack and J. Urrutia, editors *Handbook of Computational Geometry*. North-Holland., Amsterdam, 2000.
6. Alt H., Melhorn K., Wagener H. and Welzl E. *Congruence, Similarity and symmetries of geometric objects*, Discrete Computational Geometry, Vol 3 (1988), 237-256.
7. Arkin E.M., Chew L.P., Huttenlocher D.P., Kedem K. and Mitchell J.S.B. *An efficiently computable metric for comparing polygonal shapes*, IEEE Trans. Pattern Anal. Mach. Intell., 13(3), 1991, 209–216.
8. Arkin E.M., Kedem K., Mitchell J.S.B., Sprinzak J. and Werman M. *Matching points into pairwise-disjoint noise regions: combinatorial bounds and algorithms* ORSA J. Comput., 4(4), 1992, 375–386.
9. Atallah M.J. *A matching problem in the plane*, J. Comput. Systems Sci. 31 (1985), 63-70.
10. Bertsekas D.B. *Non-Linear Programming*, Athena Scientific, Belmont Massachusetts, 1995.
11. Chew L.P., Dor D., Efrat A. and Kedem K. *Geometric pattern matching in d-dimensional space*, Third European Symposium on Algorithms, ESA '95 (1995), 264-279.

12. Chew L.P., Goodrich M.T., Huttenlocher D.P., Kedem K., Kleinberg J.M. and Kravets D. *Geometric pattern matching under Euclidean motion* Comput. Geom. Theory Appl., 7, 1997, 113–124.
13. Chew L.P. and Kedem K. *Improvements on approximate pattern matching problems*, Third Scandinavian Workshop on Algorithm Theory, (1992), 318-325.
14. Cox I.J., Miller M.L., Minka T.P., Papathomas T.V. and Yianilos, P.N. The Bayesian Image Retrieval System, PicHunter: Theory, Implementation, and Psychophysical Experiments. IEEE Transactions on Image Processing, Vol 9, No 1, January 2000.
15. Cortes C. and Vapnik V. *Support Vector Networks*, Machine Learning, Vol. 20 No. 3, September 1995, 273–297.
M.
16. Duda R.M. and Hart P.E. *Pattern Classification and Scene Analysis*, Wiley, 1973.
17. Hagedoorn M. Overmars M. and Veltkamp R.C. *A Robust Affine Invariant Similarity Measure Based on Visibility* 16th European Workshop Comput. Geom. 2000, 112–116.
18. Huttenlocher D.P. and Kedem K. *Computing the minimum Hausdorff distance for point sets under translation*, ISAAC, (1996).
19. Huttenlocher D.P., Kedem K. and Kleinberg J. *On dynamic Voronoi diagrams the minimum Hausdorff distance for point sets under Euclidean motion in the plane*, 8th ACM Symposium on Computational Geometry (1992), 110-119.
20. Huttenlocher D.P., Kedem K. and Sharir M. *The upper envelope of Voronoi surfaces and its applications*, Discrete Computational Geometry, 9, (1993), 267-291.
21. Minka T. P. and Picard R. W. Interactive learning using a "society of models. Pattern Recognition, 30(4), 1997
22. O'Rourke J. and Toussaint G.T. Pattern Recognition. In J. O'Rourke and J. E. Goodman, editors, *Discrete and Computational Geometry*, pages 797–813. CRC Press., New York, 1997.
23. Paquet E. and Rioux M. *A Content Based Serach Engine for VRML Databases*, Proceedings of IEEE Conference on Computer Vision and Pattern Recognition, 1998.
24. Rui Y. and Huang T. S. and Chang S-F. Image Retrieval: Current Techniques, Promising Directions, and Open Issues. Journal of Visual Communication and Image Representation, 10, (1), 1999, pp. 39-62.
25. Rui Y. Huang T. S. and Mehrotta S. Content based image retrieval with relevance feedback in MARS. Proceedings of IEEE ICIP '97.
26. Schwarz J.T. and Sharir M. *Identification of partially obscured objects in two and three dimensions by matching of noisy characteristic curves*, Int. J. Robotics Research, 6(2) (1987), 29–44.
27. Scholkopf B. Support Vector Machines IEEE Intelligent Systems, Vol.13, No. 4, (July-August, 1998), 18–28
28. Sprinzak J. and Werman M. *Exact Point Matching*, Proc. Israeli Symposium on AI, Vision and Pattern Recognition, Elsevier Science Publishers. 1990.
29. Toussaint G.T. Computational Geometry and Computer Vision. In B. Melter, A. Rosenfeld and P. Bhattacharya, editors, *Vision Geometry*, pages 213–224. Amer. Math. Soc., Providence, 1991.
30. Vapnik V. *The Nature of Statistical Learning Theory*, Springer-Verlag, Ney-York, 1995.

Authentication of Volume Data Using Wavelet-Based Foveation

M. S. Kankanhalli[1], E.-C. Chang[1], X. Guan[2], Z. Huang[1], and Y. Wu[1]

[1] Department of Computer Science
{mohan, changec, huangzy, wuyinghu}@comp.nus.edu.sg
http://www.comp.nus.edu.sg/
[2] Department of Computational Science
National University of Singapore
guanxin@cz3.nus.edu.sg
http://www.cz3.nus.edu.sg/

Abstract. 3D volume data has been increasingly used in many applications. The digital nature of the data allows easy creation, copying and distribution. However, it also allows ease of manipulation which can enable wilful or inadvertent misrepresentation of the content. For an application like medical imaging, this can have serious diagnostic and legal implications. Thus there is a strong need to establish the integrity of a particular volume data-set. We argue that the traditional data authentication mechanisms like digital signatures or cryptographic methods are not very useful in this context due to their extreme fragility. What is required is a method that can detect the integrity for allowable content-preserving manipulations. We have developed a novel authentication procedure which is robust against benign content manipulation. The volume data can be robustly authenticated under normal operations such as scaling, resampling and additive Gaussian noise. On the other hand, it offers protection against any malefic or unintentional data manipulation which significantly changes the content of the volume data-set. Such manipulations include cropping, changing of voxel values etc. Our method uses segmentation, wavelet-based foveation, and encryption to achieve this. We have implemented the method and tested its robustness for several manipulations.

Keywords: Volume Data, Authentication, Foveation, Wavelets

1 Introduction

3D volume data has been increasingly used in many applications [11]. Medical imaging is one area which generates an enormous amount of volume data. Recently, there has been increasing awareness about the problem of copyright protection of digital images, video and audio [10]. Researchers have started raising concerns about the copyright protection and piracy of 3D data as well. In fact, there is a growing interest in developing digital watermarking techniques for 3D mesh as well as volume data [15, 9]. However, all these techniques address the copyright problem, not the integrity problem. In this paper, we address the problem of authenticating 3D volume data i.e. verification of the *genuineness* of the data-set. For example, given a medical volume data set which shows a medical condition like a tumor, we do not want the patient to fraudulently alter the data-set so that the tumor is removed and thus mis-represent the medical condition to an insurance company. Similarly, we would not like a medical institution to alter the data-set in order to introduce artifacts which represents some abnormality and make a patient go through unnecessary expensive medical procedures. In such situations, preserving and checking the veracity of a data-set assumes tremendous importance. Even for volume data sets which represent art objects or manufactured objects, the accuracy and integrity of the data-set needs to be preserved. Basically, a secure authentication system can prove that no tampering has occurred during situations where the credibility of the volume data may be questioned. In the two hypothetical scenarios present, there is a need to detect that some illegal manipulation has taken place. On the other hand if some allowable modification (like re-sampling of the data-set) is done, it should detect this manipulation but it should indicate that the data-set is still usable.

We propose that this problem can be addressed by use of a *content-based* digital signature which is robust yet effective. The idea is that at the time of data creation (which is through either some physical scanning device like a CT Scanner or through some software), a content-based digital signature associated with the data-set is simultaneously created. For all further authenticity checks, this data-set can be verified against this digital signature. If there is a mis-match, then the data is considered unreliable and it should not be used.

Two solution possibilities naturally arise when considering this problem. One could argue that either traditional general message authentication techniques can be used or perhaps semi-fragile watermarking techniques could be used. We will now argue why neither of this possibility is applicable for 3D volume data.

Traditional message authentication techniques like hashing-based digital signatures or cryptographic authentication [20] cannot be used because of their extreme fragility. These techniques do not tolerate flipping of even one bit of information of a message. For example, we could use the traditional message digest based digital signature for a volume data-set. Even if one least significant bit of a voxel is changed, the authentication procedure will flag this data-set as unreliable. However, for volume data, certain operations such as scaling, resampling etc. are valid operations in which cases the manipulations are benign. They are not intended to change the significant content of the data-set and thus they do not impact the integrity of the data. One example is the content-based digital signature proposed in [16] which used the histogram of divided data blocks as the content to be hashed. If the voxel values are uniformly deduced by one unit, or more generally, a Gaussian noise with a non-zero mean is added, this signature may fail to authenticate the data. Therefore, we need a novel digital signature method which allows content-preserving manipulations. In other words, the digital signature must authenticate the data set for such cases. However, if somebody really tampers with the content, e.g. crops out the tumor region, then the digital signature should indicate that data-set has been tampered with and thus is unreliable. Thus traditional digital signatures are not useful but *robust authentication* (robustness to allowable manipulations) is required.

The second possibility is the use of semi-fragile watermarks for the purpose of authentication [13]. Many techniques have been developed for 2D digital image data which could perhaps be adapted for 3D volume data. Unfortunately, this is not possible for two reasons. Firstly, the image watermarks usually exploit the characteristics of the human visual system (HVS) in order to hide the secondary watermark information. In case of volume data, the HVS cannot be exploited because we can only visualize the 3D volume data through surface and volume rendering. Secondly, there is an even more serious problem. All watermarking techniques involve the modification of the voxel values for the purpose of embedding the watermark. However, for the case of volume data (and especially related to medical imaging), distortion of the voxel values is not allowed. Even if small perturbations in the voxel values were allowed, there is no watermarking method which can provably bound the distortion of the voxel values. While the Parseval's theorem [6] can guarantee the bounding of the overall watermark signal energy, simultaneously limiting the maximum distortion level in the spatial domain and frequency domain appears to be very difficult. Therefore, watermarking techniques are also not useful for authenticating 3D volume data.

In this paper, we present a new technique for authenticating 3D volume data using a *robust content-based digital signature.* This signature is derived from the significant features of volume data so that if any of these features are altered significantly, the signature will not match the data-set. The term *content-based* refers to the fact the important features of the data (whose integrity we are interested in certifying) should be somehow incorporated into the digital signature. The rationale being that if some important content feature is deleted/modified/added, then the digital signature should not match the doctored data-set. The term *robust* refers to the fact that any manipulation which does not change the significant features should not affect the veracity of the signature. For such benign operations, the digital signature should indeed authenticate the data-set. Common types of operations on volume data-sets are scaling, thresholding, cropping, cut-and-replace a sub-volume, filtering, addition/removal of noise and affine transformations. As long as these operations do not change the content features, they are considered benign. We use a novel wavelet-based foveation technique to accurately and succinctly capture the significant content features. Moreover, the scheme allows a flexible threshold to be set which can determine the extent of the manipulations which can be considered benign.

2 Overview of the Technique

We will now provide an overall description of the method for generating the robust content-based digital signature and the method for authenticating a volume data-set using this digital signature. For the generation of the digital signature, the following steps are required:

1. *Feature extraction*: The basic idea here is to capture the essential features which need to be preserved for authentication. Since the size of a 3D volume data-set is huge, this also allows us to create a compact key derived from the important features. The process is done in three steps:
   (a) *Volume segmentation*: The voxels of the input 3D volume data are separated into two classes – the significant "foreground" and the relatively less important "background". While we present a method for doing the segmentation in this paper, we recognize that different types of data-sets need their own specialized segmentation technique. Our authentication method is flexible in the sense that it does not really depend on the particular details of the segmentation algorithm used. If required, this part can be customized either for a particular application domain or for an individual volume data-set.
   (b) *Selection of key voxels*: In general, the number of voxels in the foreground is quite large. To reduce the amount of data, a few "key voxels" are chosen for the purpose of data reduction.
   (c) *Wavelet-based foveation*: To make sure that important content throughout the foreground is captured, we apply the foveation technique which is basically a space-variant filtering technique. We believe it is very important to use this since it *summarizes* all the important content throughout the foreground with the key voxels as the foci. Thus all significant features are compactly captured. Additionally since it is a many-to-one mapping, it offers security. Thus, this information can be used as a key.
2. *Encryption*: For additional security, public-key cryptography [20] is utilized to encrypt the key derived in the previous step. Basically, the secret key of the owner of the volume data is used to encrypt the feature key obtained. For the purpose of authentication, the public-key of the owner can be used to decrypt this information and the feature key can be thus recovered. Since this step is well-understood, we will not discuss it further in this paper.

For authenticating a particular volume data-set, the following steps are performed:

1. *Affine transformation parameters recovery*: Since, one of the benign manipulations could be the affine transformation of the volume, the transform parameters are computed first.
2. *Matching*: The content features of the transformed volume are compared with the content features of the original data-set (obtained from the digital signature after decryption using the owner's public key). A match value between the original features and the transformed volume features is computed. If this match value exceeds a certain threshold, then the volume is certified as genuine else it is considered untrustworthy.

3 Creation of the Content-Based Signature

Given a volume data-set, we first extract the feature points (key voxels) after performing segmentation. The number of the feature points must be small in order to guarantee the acceptable small size of the signature. Based on the extracted feature points, a weighted norm is selected. The volume is then lossily compressed using this weighted norm as the measure. The description of the weighted norm and the compressed data are encrypted using public-key cryptography and they constitute the robust content-based digital signature associated with this volume data-set.

3.1 Feature Extraction of Volume Data

In this subsection, we describe the process of extracting from the original volume data a small number of voxel groups that represent the important information (features). It consists of two steps: volume segmentation and key voxel sampling. Volume segmentation is to identify and demarcate into foreground/background the voxel in the original volume data. Note that the foreground voxels can belong to different sub-categories (like bone, skin, soft tissues, etc.). This results in the segments (a connected sub-volume) with each one representing an important feature of the data. It is similar to image segmentation, a common technique used in computer vision. Usually the number of voxels in each segment is too large to be directly used for the signature. Thus, key voxel sampling is used to derive a few key voxels from each segment for the foveation process which effectively summarizes the significant content of the data-set, and will be detailed in the next subsection.

We propose a segmentation method based on the voxel value analysis and bounding box information of the isosurfaces. It can be summarized as follows. We assume that the voxel values are scalar for the ease of description.

1. Partition of the voxel values by data analysis. First, all the voxel values are sorted in the non-descending order. Second, partition the sorted list using the threshold value. The threshold value is specified by the user in our current implementation. However, heuristics can be applied if the domain knowledge is known for the particular class of volume data. For many volume data sets, the density values of significant content components are distinguishable even though the voxels representing them are closely connected to each other. Sometimes, they may perhaps even have similar voxel values in which case domain knowledge could be utilized for distinguishing them. For example, human CT/MRI volumes can be partitioned by using the density values as well as anatomical knowledge.
2. Isosurfacing. From the partition, we derive a set of voxel values that partition different parts. These voxel values are used to derive the same number of sets of the isosurfaces.
3. Segmentation. One segment of voxels can be formed if they are bounded as a closed sub-volume by (1) one isosurface, (2) several isosurfaces, or (3) one or several isosurfaces with the one or several border planes of the volume. It can be efficiently derived using the scan conversion algorithm, an extension of the standard scanline

algorithm used in the rasterization and hidden-surface elimination, to derive and accumulate the intervals bounded by the isosurfaces and border planes iteratively.

4. Feature extraction. It is a process of selection of key voxels. A 3D Gaussian mask is applied on the volume several times as lowpass filtering. Due to the large size of volume data, we simulate the 3D Gaussian filtering as a windowed lowpass filtering dimension by dimension. In the highly blurred resulting volume, the key voxels are chosen to be local maximum voxels which are above a predefined threshold. The key voxels are then used as the input to the foveation procedure.

If the size of volume data is N^3, sorting in the first step takes $O(N^3 logN)$ time. It is $O(N^3 + logh)$ for isosurfacing in step 2 where h is the number of different extreme values (min or max) [5]. It is $O(N^3)$ for the scan conversion in step 3. So the overall time complexity is $O(N^3 logN)$. One example as a result of this procedure is shown in Fig 1.

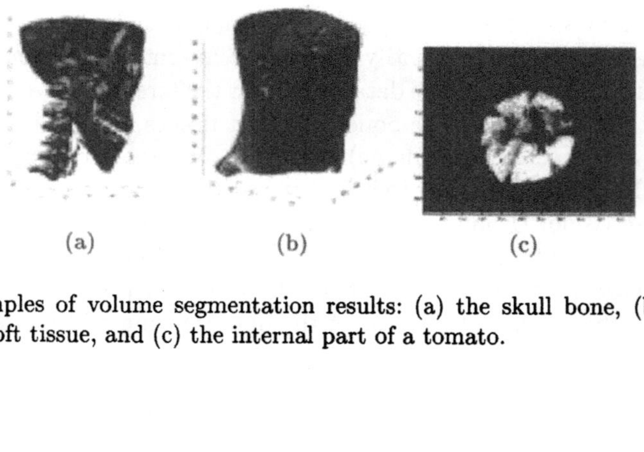

(a) (b) (c)

Fig. 1. Examples of volume segmentation results: (a) the skull bone, (b) the skull muscle and soft tissue, and (c) the internal part of a tomato.

3.2 Content-based Weighted Norm

We now briefly present the idea behind summarizing the volume using a space-variant wavelet based filter. The basic idea is to summarize and compress the important content information. Most 2D/3D imaging systems use a norm (usually the Euclidean 2-norm) to measure their performance. However, the 2-norm treats each pixel/voxel equally. However, in most real-life data, it is possible to determine some regions that are more interesting for the application at hand. For example, through feature detection, we can find significant voxels in a given data-set. In such cases, a weighted norm is more appropriate. The weighted norm $\|\cdot\|_w$ for the volume $V(x, y, z)$ with a weighting function w is given by:

$$\|V\|_w^2 = \sum_{x,y,z} w(x, y, z) V(x, y, z)^2,$$

where $w(\cdot, \cdot, \cdot)$ is the weighting function. In our authentication system, a content-based weighted norm is used for measurement of the distortion caused by allowable and illegal operations. The weight of each voxel is determined through a combination of segmentation and feature detection schemes. In the digital signature creation process, the original volume data is lossily compressed under the weighted norm. The highly compressed data S, together with the description of weighting function W, forms the signature (S, W). This signature can then be further encrypted. Because the description of the weighting function is part of the signature, to satisfy compactness, w cannot contain the full information of the original data set. We now describe in detail the whole procedure.

3.3 Wavelet-based Foveation Technique

Our visual system has a space-variant nature where the resolution is high in a point (fovea) but falling off towards the peripheral[17]. This distribution of resolution provides a fast and simple way of reducing information in the visual field, without sacrificing the size of the visual field and the resolution around the fovea. As the biological visual system is highly effective, this space-variant nature has inspired the design of many computer vision systems which resembles the biological foveated vision [3, 1, 18], video conferencing [2, 7], and visualization systems [12].

The foveated volume is obtained from a uniform resolution volume through a space-variant smoothing process where the width of the smoothing function is small near the fovea but gradually increases towards the peripheral. The process of going from a uniform volume to a foveated volume is known as *foveation.* The *foveation* of a function $V : \mathbf{R}^d \to \mathbf{R}$ is determined by a *smoothing function* $g : \mathbf{R}^d \to \mathbf{R}$, and a *weight function* $w : \mathbf{R}^d \to \mathbf{R}_{\geq 0}$.

$$(TV)(\mathbf{x}) := \int_{\mathbf{R}^d} V(\mathbf{t}) w(\mathbf{x}) g\left(w(\mathbf{x}) \|\mathbf{t} - \mathbf{x}\|_2\right) d\mathbf{t}. \tag{1}$$

The weighting function w depends upon three parameters and takes the form

$$w(\mathbf{x}) = \left(\alpha \|\mathbf{x} - \gamma\|^d + \beta\right)^{-1} \tag{2}$$

We call α the *rate* as it determines how fast resolution falling off, call γ the fovea as it determines the point of highest resolution, and call β the *foveal resolution* as it determines the resolution at the fovea. Both α and β are non-negative and the smoothing function g is normalized so that $\int_{-\infty}^{\infty} g(\mathbf{x})\, d\mathbf{x} = 1$. In general, we could replace the weighting function by any non-negative function. This generalization is useful when we are interested in volumes with multiple foveae. Given two weighting functions w_1,w_2, the blended w_3 is

$$w_3(\mathbf{x}) = \max\{w_1(\mathbf{x}), w_2(\mathbf{x})\}. \tag{3}$$

Foveated volumes can also be treated as the approximation of an volume using a fixed number of bit, using a weighted norm as the underlying measure. This weighted norm can be derived from (1) and has the form,

$$\|V\|_w = \int_{\mathbf{R}^d} \frac{V(\mathbf{x})}{w(\mathbf{x})} d\mathbf{x}, \tag{4}$$

where the weighting function w is the function in (2).

Wavelet bases have important applications in mathematics and signal processing due to their ability to build sparse representation for large classes of functions and signal [14]. It is a natural choice for foveated volume due to their locality in space and frequency. Interesting, the choice of the weighting function (2) gives a self-similarity across scales [4], which is illustrated in Fig 2. This property leads to a simple but fast extraction algorithm [4].

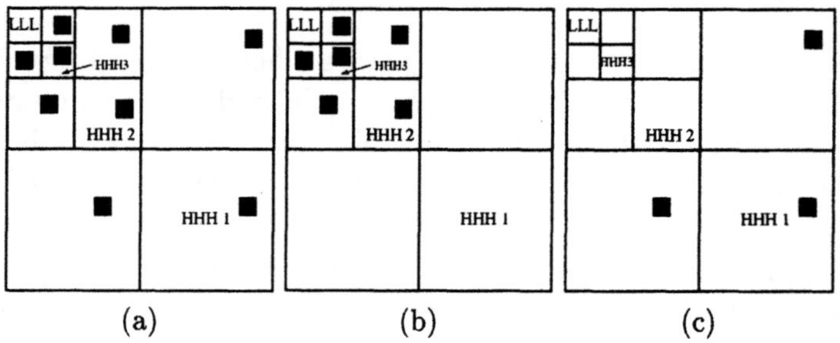

Fig. 2. Allowable Lowpass Filtering: (a) Original wavelet coefficients (C_w); (b) After allowable lowpass filtering (C'_w); (c) Remaining coefficients ($C_w{}^*$). $C_w - C'_w = C_w{}^*$.

3.4 Extracting the Coefficients

Recall that the first part of the signature (S, W) is the highly compressed volume. To obtain S, one could first compute the foveation (1) with respect to the multi-foveae weighting function, and then compress the foveated volume using a known lossy or lossless compression technique for uniform volumes. Because computing (1) directly is computational intensive, we use the approximation (5).

$$(T^{\text{fov}} I) \approx \text{IDWT}(M \cdot \text{DWT}(I)). \tag{5}$$

In our implementation, S is extracted from the volume by quantizing the wavelet coefficients M DWT(I), followed by a lossless compression using **gzip**. For an intuitive illustration, we use a 2D image to show its compression result (Fig 3). The (S, W) can then be encrypted and be stored as the digital signature for that image.

Note that **gzip** is a general lossless compression tool, which does not exploit properties of volumes, especially the coherence of wavelet coefficients across space and scale. Thus it is not the best technique for our application. A possible improvement can be done by incorporating the well-known zero-tree algorithm [19] into our scheme.

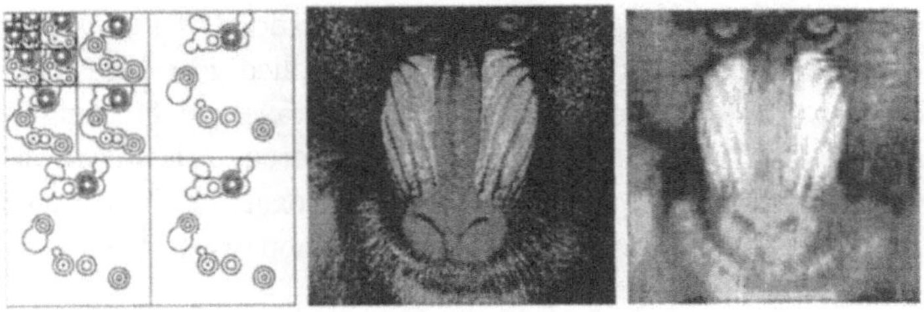

(a) (b) (c)

Fig. 3. (a) The mask M for the weighting function. (b) The original image (262Kbytes). (c) The compressed image (4Kbytes) using the mask M.

4 Implementation and Experiment Results

The first phase of the authentication process is detection of the allowable affine translation applied to the volume data-set. For consistency, the norm used in the detection is the weighted norm whose weighting function is part of the signature. That is, the detection finds the affine transformation $T_{\min}$ such that $h_0 = \|T_{\min}(S) - V\|_w$ is minimum. Through our preliminary experiment, we find that such $T_{\min}$ can be accurately determined for translation and rotation. In the rest of this section, we assume that no affine transformation has been applied to the data-set.

In the second phase of authentication, the similarity value $h_0 = \|S - V\|_w$ is compared with a predetermined threshold $A_0 H$, where A_0 is a normalizing factor depending only on the size and mean of the volume data-set. If h is smaller, then the volume is declared to be authenticated. Otherwise, it is rejected and hence considered unreliable. The choice of the H depends on the level of allowable attacks. It can be determined analytically by assuming a certain distribution on the voxel, or through experiment conducted a-prior to the signature creation. In our experiments, we choose $H = 0.08$, which is analytically determined by assuming that the allowable low-pass will filter out only the first level wavelet coefficients as illustrated in Figure 2.

We did experiments on two volume data sets with 256 gray levels, SKULL ($64 \times 64 \times 64$) and TOMATO ($128 \times 128 \times 64$). In the selection of key voxels, we used a windowed lowpass filtering for five times with the window size 9 and the threshold 1.5. The resulting numbers of key voxels are 25 for SKULL and 124 for TOMATO. The sizes of the signatures are 8K and 19K bytes respectively.

Five experiments were done with these two volume data sets. The first three experiments examine the signature robustness under global manipulation like low-pass filtering, sharpening, and lossy compression, whereas the last two experiments consider local manipulation like cropping and localized modification. In the first experiment, the volume data-sets are subjected to low pass filtering. The low filtering is achieved by a rectangle window. From Figure 4(a), the signature remains authentic even under a 7x7x7 rectangular filtering. In the second experiment, Figure 4(b), Gaussian white noise is added. To test the robustness of our signature under lossy compression, we applied zero-thresholding to the volume data-set. That is, given a threshold T, all wavelet coefficient C satisfying $|C| < T$ are replaced by zeros. The results for different T is shown in Figure 5.

Figure 6 (a) shows the robustness after the voxels in the center region are replaced by zeros, and Figure 6(b) shows the robustness after the volume is cropped.

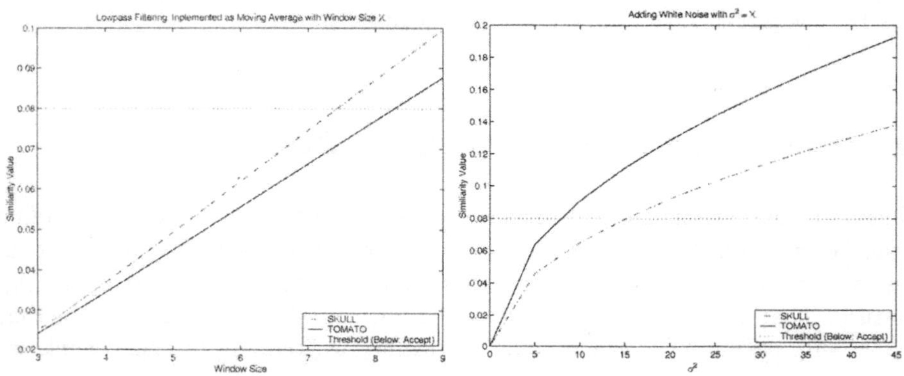

(a) (b)

Fig. 4. Results for Lowpass Filtering (a) and Addition of White Noise (b)

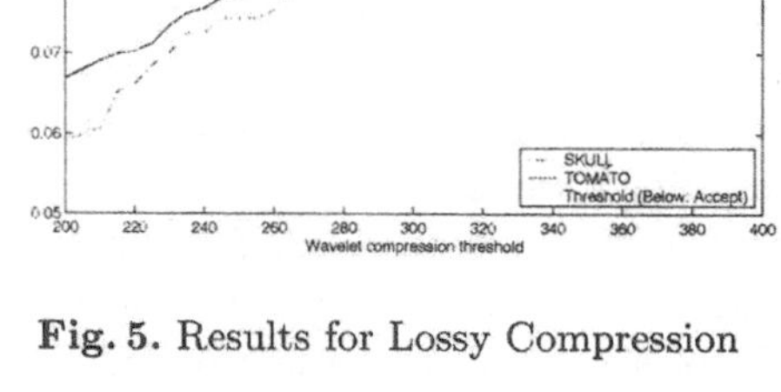

Fig. 5. Results for Lossy Compression

Modification of information of a volume data can take three forms. One is to modify a particular part of the voxel values to other values, e.g., set all voxel values to zero (Fig 6 (a)). The second is to crop the volume to a subset of the original one (Fig 6 (b)). Removal is acceptable as long as important information remains. Since our method of important feature extraction does not aim at a particular region of the volume, it is enough to give false-signature alarm when too much information has been removed. This can be seen in Fig 6. In real-world applications, users can define the regions-of-interest for feature extraction, for example, tumors or abnormal bones. The third modification is the addition of previously non-existent content feature. This is handled in a manner similar to the one for the removal case. Thus, with the proposed robust digital signature scheme, the signature will match only when all (and no more) regions-of-interest can be detected.

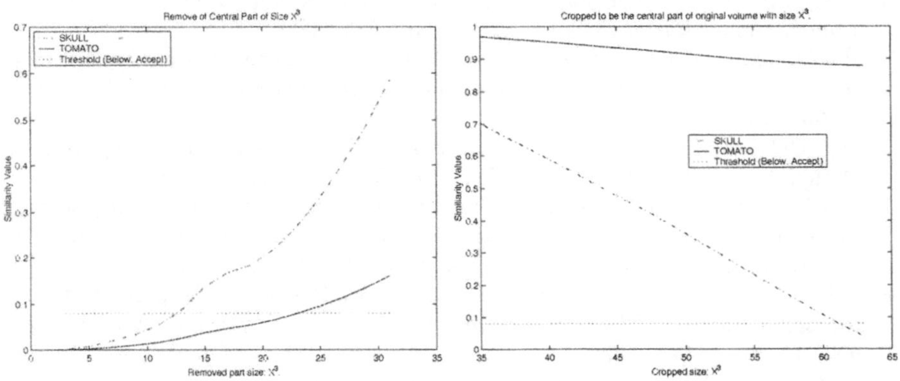

(a) (b)

Fig. 6. Results for Removal (a) and Cropping (b)

5 Conclusion

We have described a novel robust content-based authentication technique for volume data. The technique uses segmentation followed by key voxel selection which are used as fovea for a wavelet-based foveation procedure to derive the content-based key for the volume data-set. This key is then encrypted using public-key cryptography and used as a robust digital signature. For authenticating a questionable volume data-set, the affine transformation parameters are first determined and feature extraction is done for the transformed volume. The feature for the transformed volume is then matched against the feature values in the original digital signature to determine whether the volume data is reliable or not. The method has been implemented and tested against various manipulations. The experimental results show that this is a very promising approach.

Our future work is to come up with a reliable volume authentication technique which can be incorporated into all types of scanners (like CT Scanners and MRI devices) in order to make them *trustworthy* [8].

The research was partly supported by NUS R-252-000-090-112. We also thank the EGMM 2001 reviewers for the helpful comments.

References

1. J. Aloimonos, I. Weiss and A. Bandyopadhyay. Active Vision. *st International Conference on Computer Vision* London, England, 35-54, 1987.
2. A. Basu and K.J. Wiebe. Videoconferencing using spatially varying sensing with multiple and moving fovea. *IEEE Trans. on Systems, Man and Cybernetics*, 28(2):137–148, 1998.
3. P.J. Burt. Smart sensing within a pyramid vision machine. *Proceedings of the IEEE*, 76(8):1006–1015, 1988.
4. E-.C. Chang, S. Mallat, and C. Yap. Wavelet foveation. *Journal of Applied and Computational Harmonic Analysis*, 9(3):312–335, 2000.
5. P. Cignoni, C. Montani, E. Puppo, and R. Scopigno. Optimal Isosurface Extraction from Irregular Volume Data. *Proceedings of IEEE Symposium on Volume Visualization.* 1996, 31-38.
6. D.J. DeFatta, J.G. Lucas and W.S. Hodgkiss. Digital Signal Processing: A System Design Approach. *John Wiley & Sons.* New York, Second Edition, 1988.
7. A. Eleftheriadis and A. Jacquin. Automatic face location detection and tracking for model-assisted coding of video teleconferencing sequences at low bit rates. *Signal Processing: Image Communication.* Vol. 7, No. 3, 231-248, 1995.
8. G.L. Friedman. The Trustworthy Digital Camera: Restoring Credibility to the Photographic Image. *IEEE Transactions on Consumer Electronics.* Vol. 39, No. 4, 905-910, November 1993.
9. X. Guan, Y. Wu, M.S. Kankanhalli, and Z. Huang. Invisible Watermarking of Volume Data Using Wavelet Transform. *International Conference on Multimedia Modeling - MMM2000.* November 2000, Japan, 153-166.
10. F. Hartung and M. Kutter. Multimedia Watermarking Techniques. *Proceedings of the IEEE.* vol. 87, no. 7, July 1999, 1079-1107.
11. A. Kaufman, D. Cohen and R. Yagel. Volume Graphics. *IEEE Computer.* vol. 26, no. 7, July 1993, 51-64.
12. M. Levoy and R. Whitaker Gaze-Directed Volume Rendering. *Computer Graphics.* Vol. 24, No. 2, 217-223, 1990.
13. E.T. Lin and E.J. Delp. A Review of Fragile Image Watermarks. *Proc. Multimedia and Security Workshop (ACM MM'99).* Orlando, 25-29, October 1999.
14. S. Mallat. A Wavelet Tour of Signal Processing. *Academic Press.* 1998.
15. E. Praun, H. Hoppe, A. Finkelstein. Robust Mesh Watermarking. *Computer Graphics ACM SIGGRAPH '99 Proceedings.* 69-76, September 1999.
16. M. Schneider and S.-F. Chang. A robust content based digital signature for image authentication. *Proceedings of ICIP.* Volume: 3, pages: 227 -230, 1996.
17. E.L. Schwartz. Topographical mapping in primate visual cortex: history, anatomy, and computation. In D.H.Kelly, editor, *Visual Science and Engineering: models and applications*, pages 293–360. Marcell Dekker, Inc, New York, 1994.
18. E.L. Schwartz, D.N. Greve and G. Bonmassar. Space-variant active vision: Definition, Overview and Examples *Neural Networks.* Vol. 8, No. 7-8, 1297-1308, 1995.
19. J.M. Shapiro. Embedded image coding using zerotrees of wavelet coefficients. *IEEE Trans. on Signal Processing.* vol. 41, no. 12, December 1993, 3445-3462.
20. W. Stallings. Cryptography and Network Security: Principles and Practice. *Prentice-Hall Inc.* Second Edition, 1998.

Buoy Indexing of Metric Feature Spaces for Fast Approximate Image Queries

Stephan Volmer

Fraunhofer IGD, Rundeturmstr. 6, 64283 Darmstadt, Germany
stephan.volmer@igd.fhg.de

Abstract. A novel indexing scheme for solving the problem of nearest neighbor queries in generic metric feature spaces for content-based image retrieval is proposed to break the "dimensionality curse." The basis for the proposed method is the partitioning of the feature dataset into clusters that are represented by single buoys. Upon submission of a query request, only a small number of clusters whose buoys are close to the query object are considered for the approximate query result, effectively cutting down the amount of data to be processed enormously. Results concerning the retrieval accuracy from extensive experimentation with a real image archive are given. The influence of control parameters is investigated with respect to the tradeoff between retrieval accuracy and computational cost.

1 Introduction

Interest in digital images has increased enormously over the last few years, fuelled at least in part by the ubiquity of digital media, the availability of large image archives, and the rapid growth of the Internet infrastructure. Users in many professional fields exploit the opportunities offered by the ability to access and manipulate remotely stored images in all kinds of new and exciting ways. Finding an image whose content is truly relevant to the user's need has become the focal point of recent research in information technology.

Problems with traditional methods of image retrieval [5] have led to the rise of techniques for retrieving images on the basis of content descriptors for perceptual features such as color, texture, shape, structure, and spatial relationship – a technology now generally referred to as *content-based image retrieval* (CBIR). CBIR systems employ unsupervised automatic feature extraction algorithms on images by analyzing their pixel distributions. This analysis results in compact feature descriptors, which convey specific aspects of the image's most salient visual properties [8, 10, 13].

Upon presentation of a query, the feature descriptor of the query image is compared with all corresponding descriptors in the database by some well-defined similarity measure. A sequential search through all potential descriptors contained in the database would be very time-consuming and inefficient. Therefore, an indexing scheme becomes necessary in order to limit the number of potential target descriptors from the database and reduce the computational effort needed to sequentially determine their similarity to the query descriptor. This task is generally referred to as *similarity indexing* [14]. The goal of similarity indexing is to reduce the amount of data to be processed by categorizing or grouping similar objects together.

2 Preliminaries

In this paper, we focus on providing a general purpose spatial indexing scheme applicable to any feature derived from images that complies with the postulates of the *metric feature model*. The common framework for the metric feature model is defined in the remainder of this section.

2.1 Metric Feature Model

The metric feature model is based on the assumption that human similarity perception corresponds with a measurement of an appropriate distance between *features* that model the images' characteristic properties.

Let Δ be a *feature extraction algorithm* that transforms images $\boldsymbol{I}$ into compact *feature descriptors* ω:

$$\boldsymbol{I} \overset{\Delta}{\longmapsto} \omega \tag{1}$$

Then (Ω, δ) is called a generic *feature space*, where Ω is a – possibly infinite – set called the *feature domain* whose elements are feature descriptors ω, and δ is a metric on Ω called the *dissimilarity measure*. The metric δ must satisfy the following properties:

Positivity

$$\delta(\omega_i, \omega_j) \geq 0 \tag{2}$$

Self-similarity

$$\delta(\omega_i, \omega_i) = 0 \tag{3}$$

Symmetry

$$\delta(\omega_i, \omega_j) = \delta(\omega_j, \omega_i) \tag{4}$$

Triangle Inequality

$$\delta(\omega_i, \omega_j) + \delta(\omega_j, \omega_l) \geq \delta(\omega_i, \omega_l) \tag{5}$$

It is assumed that the definition of the feature extraction algorithm Δ and its associated dissimilarity measure δ is only based on pre-attentive human similarity. This means they depend only on the perceived stimuli of the visual content of the images, without accounting for any previous knowledge, interpretation or reasoning.

This common framework includes the definition of ubiquitous d-dimensional feature vector spaces ($\Omega \equiv \mathbb{R}^d$), but is not necessarily limited to them.

2.2 Feature Dataset

Let

$$\mathcal{S} = \{\, \omega_1, \omega_2, \ldots, \omega_N \} \tag{6}$$

be a finite subset of a feature domain Ω called the *feature dataset* whose elements are the feature descriptors from a set of N images.

2.3 K-Nearest Neighbor Query

By far the most common query of a CBIR system is a request like "find the first K images most similar to the query example." Such a request can be formulated as a K-*nearest neighbor query* (K-NN query) in metric space: Given an query object $\omega_Q \in \Omega$ and an integer $K \geq 1$, the K-NN query $\mathcal{S}_{NN}(\omega_Q, K)$ selects the K elements from the feature dataset $\mathcal{S}$ which have the smallest distance from ω_Q with the following properties:

$$
\begin{aligned}
&\text{(i)}\ \ \mathcal{S}_{NN}(\omega_Q, K) \subset \mathcal{S} \\
&\text{(ii)}\ \ |\mathcal{S}_{NN}(\omega_Q, K)| = K \\
&\text{(iii)}\ \forall\, \omega \in \mathcal{S}_{NN}(\omega_Q, K)\ \nexists\, \omega' \in \mathcal{S} \setminus \mathcal{S}_{NN}(\omega_Q, K) \\
&\qquad\quad \text{with}\ \ \delta(\omega_Q, \omega') < \delta(\omega_Q, \omega)
\end{aligned}
\tag{7}
$$

3 State-Of-The-Art

The history of recent research on similarity indexing techniques can be traced back to the middle 70's when hierarchical tree structures (e.g. *k-d* tree) for indexing multi-dimensional vector spaces were first introduced. In 1984, Guttman proposed the R-tree indexing structure [7], which was the basis for the development of many other variants. Sellis et al. proposed the R^+-tree [12], and Beckman et al. proposed the best dynamic R-tree variant, the R^*-tree [2] in the following years.

A very extensive review and comparison of various spatial indexing techniques for feature vector spaces can be found in [14]. Motivated by *k-d* tree and R-tree, they proposed the VAM *k-d* tree and the VAMSplit R-tree. Experimentally, they found that the VAMSplit R-tree provided the best performance, however, this was at the loss of the dynamic nature of the R-tree.

Common to all of the cited research is the idea that feature descriptors are stored at the leaf level of a hierarchical index tree structure. Each leaf corresponds to a partition of the feature space and each node to a convex subspace spanning the partitions created by its children. During a similarity query, the search space is reduced by pruning tree branches at nodes that do not meet certain distance requirements. The main problem with this approach is that it requires the calculation of the minimum distance from the query point to the arbitrarily shaped convex subspace represented by the node being examined. The most common approach for simplifying this problem is that partitions are split into sub-partitions along a single axis of the vector space, ultimately creating hyper-rectangular partitions whose sides are aligned parallel to the spanning axes of the underlying feature space.

Most of the hierarchical spatial indexing methods work satisfactorily for lower dimensions, but suffer from the dimensionality curse [11] when applied to feature vectors in medium- or high-dimensional feature spaces ($d > 20$). The dimensionality curse is strictly related to the distribution of the dissimilarity measures between the feature dataset and the query object. If the variance of the dissimilarities for a given query object is low, then conducting an indexed K-NN query becomes a difficult task. A way to obviate this situation is to conduct queries that come up with an approximate solution of the K-NN query problem [1, 3].

In recent research, there have been many attempts to get a grip on the problem of the dimensionality curse – one of them is the reduction of the dimensionality of the underlying feature domain with a principal component analysis (PCA) or its variants. In [9], Ng and Sedighain followed this approach to reduce the dimensionality, and in [6] Faloutsos and Lin proposed a fast approximation of the Karhunen-Loeve Transform (KLT) to perform the dimension reduction. However, even though experimental results from their research showed that some real feature datasets can be considerably reduced in dimension without significant degradation in retrieval quality, the image queries become proportionally less accurate with the loss of dimensions.

The biggest shortcoming of the techniques mentioned is that they are inherently only applicable to feature vector spaces, that is, each feature descriptor can be suitably represented by an adequate vector of fixed dimensionality.

In the following section an indexing scheme is proposed that is applicable to feature domains beyond the traditional vector spaces and enables fast approximate similarity queries through a very simplistic indexing paradigm.

4 Buoy Indexing

The proposed indexing scheme is based on the idea that the feature dataset is decomposed into disjoint non-empty partitions of arbitrary convex shape. However, each partition is NOT represented by a complex description of its extension or its boundaries in the feature domain but rather by a single prototype element that is an element of the feature domain itself. The prototype element serves as a *buoy* for its associated partition. The membership of an element of the feature dataset to a specific partition is solely determined by its metric distances to all buoys placed in feature space – a feature descriptor exclusively belongs to the partition with the closest associated buoy in the feature space. Ideally, each partition should have the same number of feature descriptors as members, and the number of partitions should be an order of magnitude smaller than the number of feature descriptors in the dataset. The buoys for a specific dataset are stored in a simple list or in a more complex hierarchical structure (e.g. M-tree [4]).

In general, the task of partitioning a particular feature dataset $\mathcal{S}$ into k disjoint non-empty subsets $\mathcal{S}_1, \mathcal{S}_2, \ldots, \mathcal{S}_k$ (also called *clusters*)

$$\bigcup_{i=1}^{k} \mathcal{S}_i = \mathcal{S} \tag{8}$$

$$\mathcal{S}_i \neq \emptyset \quad \forall \quad 1 \leq i \leq k \qquad \wedge \qquad \mathcal{S}_i \cap \mathcal{S}_j = \emptyset \quad \forall \quad 1 \leq i, j \leq k, i \neq j \tag{9}$$

is performed by any k-clustering algorithm. The number of clusters k is assumed to be fixed and each descriptor of the feature dataset belongs to exactly one cluster (crisp membership). By far the most common type of k-clustering algorithm is the *optimization algorithm*.

The optimization algorithm defines a cost criterion

$$c : \{\mathcal{S}_1, \mathcal{S}_2, \ldots, \mathcal{S}_k\} \rightarrow \mathbb{R}_0^+ \tag{10}$$

which associates a non-negative cost with each cluster. The goal of the optimization algorithm is then to minimize the global cost

$$c(\mathcal{S}) = \sum_{i=1}^{k} c(\mathcal{S}_i) \tag{11}$$

for a given feature dataset.

If each cluster $\mathcal{S}_i$ is represented by a buoy $\hat{\omega}_i$ that is an element of the feature domain Ω itself, then, the cost criterion of a cluster can be defined as

$$c(\mathcal{S}_i) = \sum_{m=1}^{|\mathcal{S}_i|} \delta(\hat{\omega}_i, \omega_{im}) \tag{12}$$

where ω_{im} is the mth element of $\mathcal{S}_i$, and $|\mathcal{S}_i|$ is the number of elements in $\mathcal{S}_i$.

Naturally, the centroid of the cluster would be chosen to be the buoy $\hat{\omega}_i$ (*k-means clustering algorithm*). However, since many types of dataset do not belong to feature spaces in which the mean is defined (the mean of two elements of the feature domain is required to be an element of the feature domain itself – this is NOT always the case for feature spaces that are not vector spaces), a different buoy for clusters must be chosen for a more general type of feature space (see Sect. 2). Intuitively, the median of each cluster is selected as its representative buoy (*k-medians clustering algorithm*). Note that $\hat{\omega}_i \in \mathcal{S}_i \subset \mathcal{S} \subset \Omega$ and that $\hat{\omega}_i$ is chosen to minimize the cost $c(\mathcal{S}_i)$ of the cluster itself.

4.1 Building the Index

The classic implementation of the optimization problem is an algorithm that tries to minimize (11) iteratively. The algorithm converges if $c(\mathcal{S})$ remains constant for two consecutive iterations. The result is usually a local minimum of the optimization problem. Techniques like simulated annealing can be employed further to improve the result.

The pure k-medians clustering algorithm produces clusters with sizes $0 < |\mathcal{S}_i| \leq N$. In order to support the development of clusters of approximately the same size, additional constraints on the cluster sizes are imposed during each iteration:

$$S_{\min} \leq |\mathcal{S}_i| \leq S_{\max} \tag{13}$$

If any cluster's size exceeds the constraint of (13), the smallest cluster is deleted and accordingly the largest cluster is split randomly into two equally sized clusters. The member descriptors of the deleted cluster are assigned to the clusters with the closest associated buoys. A high level description of the iterative optimization algorithm is shown in Fig. 1.

4.2 Updating the Index

Considering that CBIR systems today are dynamic since new images are continuously added to the image archive, the feature dataset increases with time also. Intuitively, the

```
Initialize clusters by assigning descriptors of dataset
Initialize buoys of clusters
Calculate global cost
repeat
    for all clusters whose size exceed constraints
        Find smallest cluster
        Redistribute descriptors of smallest cluster to other clusters
            according to the descriptors' distance to the clusters' buoys
        Delete smallest cluster
        Split largest cluster randomly
        Update buoys of split clusters
    Reassign descriptors of the dataset to clusters
        according to the descriptors' distance to the clusters' buoys
    Update buoys of clusters
    Calculate global cost
until global cost remains constant
```

Fig. 1. Constrained k-Medians Clustering Algorithm

newly added descriptors are assigned to the cluster with the closest buoy. However, since the buoys are not modified during this process, some clusters might grow extensively, while others might not grow at all. This necessitates an infrequent periodic update to the index in order to compensate for the newly added feature descriptors. The clusters are then simply initialized with the buoys of the old index to avoid starting the iterative algorithm from scratch again.

With the number of descriptors increasing, it might even become necessary to increase the overall number of clusters. In this case, empty clusters are added which are then removed by the size constraint in following iterations.

4.3 Indexed Queries

Upon submission of an indexed query request, the first task is to conduct a k'-NN query on the set of buoys $\hat{\mathcal{S}} = \{\hat{\omega}_1, \ldots, \hat{\omega}_k\}$ of the index in order to find the $k' \ll k$ closest buoys $\hat{\omega}'_i$ to the query object

$$\hat{\mathcal{S}}_{NN}(\omega_Q, k') \subset \hat{\mathcal{S}} \tag{14}$$

Then, the second task is to perform an approximate K-NN query $\mathcal{S}_{ANN}(\omega_Q, K, k')$ on the joint union of all member descriptors of the clusters $\mathcal{S}'_i$ associated with the k' closest buoys $\hat{\omega}'_i \in \hat{\mathcal{S}}_{NN}(\omega_Q, k')$

$$\mathcal{S}_{ANN}(\omega_Q, K, k') \subset \bigcup_{i=1}^{k'} \mathcal{S}'_i \tag{15}$$

where K is the number of results the query is supposed to return (typically $K = \{10, 20, 50, 100\}$). The result is an approximation of the correct result given by a sequential K-NN query based on the whole dataset. The accuracy of $\mathcal{S}_{ANN}(\omega_Q, K, k')$

mainly depends on the selection of parameter k'. This is due to the fact that query objects might be located in areas of the feature space that are less populated by the dataset. As a result, the variance of the distance distribution to the dataset descriptors for this particular query object is low. This yields many potential candidate descriptors with approximately the same distance to the query object. Because the feature space is intentionally limited to a small number of clusters k' prior to the search, some potentially relevant descriptors might not be returned during an indexed query.

Practically, this indexing paradigm yields a number of consecutive sequential NN-searches. However, the overall number of comparisons necessary for an approximate NN-search can be reduced significantly by a smart selection of the parameters k and k' with respect to the total number of descriptors N present in the dataset. The interaction between computational cost and retrieval accuracy is investigated in the next section.

5 Results

The overall retrieval accuracy of an approximate K-NN query $\mathcal{S}_{ANN}(\omega_Q, K, k')$ with the proposed indexing scheme depends on the following features:

- the statistical distribution of a given feature dataset $\mathcal{S}$ in the feature domain Ω
- the specific characteristics of the metric δ
- the number of clusters k and the initialization conditions of the constrained k-medians clustering algorithm
- the query object ω_Q and the parameters k' and K of an indexed K-NN query

The first and second features are directly associated with the selection of a particular feature extraction algorithm and its associated dissimilarity measure. The third is related to the visual content of the images that are inserted into the dataset, and therefore, has a random aspect. As a result, their influence cannot be made quantitatively tangible. However, if the feature space and the dataset are selected carefully for an experimental analysis, a general statement about the method's performance can be made.

5.1 Experimental Setup

Database The image database consisted of a total of $N = 25000$ color JPEG images in screen preview quality (approximate size 300 × 200). The images were taken from CD image catalogues with a variety of topics, e.g. people, sports, art, travel, animals, nature, industry, and business. Thus, the visual content of the database was quite heterogeneous and can be considered domain independent.

Feature Space The feature domain was generated by extracting the color histogram with a total of 116 distinct color bins obtained by fuzzy quantization of the cylindrical HSL colorspace. The L_1-metric was used for comparing the color histograms in terms of similarity.

Clustering The feature dataset was clustered into $k = 500$ clusters. The expected average cluster size is $\overline{|S_i|} = \frac{N}{k} = 50$. The influence of the number of clusters on the retrieval accuracy is not investigated in this paper.

Queries A total sample of 500 query images that were not part of the image database itself were submitted as requests to the query engine in order to collect the experimental results.

5.2 Retrieval Accuracy

A total of 3 different indices were evaluated in order to depict the influence of the size constraint on the k-medians clustering algorithm. Table 1 shows the corresponding parameters used for the generation of the single indices along with the final global cost. The resulting destribution of cluster sizes is depicted in graph (I) of Fig. 2. Clearly, the unconstrained index (IIa) tends to produce many small and few large clusters. This undesired effect is eliminated by introducing minimum and maximum size constraints on indices (IIb) and (IIc).

Table 1. Evaluated Indices

Index	k	$S_{\min}$	$S_{\max}$	$c(\mathcal{S})$
(IIa)	500	—	—	6580.0022
(IIb)	500	10	100	5976.8084
(IIc)	500	25	75	5879.8690

The retrieval accuracy $P(\omega_Q, K, k')$ for the experimental setup was determined by comparing the correct result $\mathcal{S}_{NN}(\omega_Q, K)$ of the non-indexed K-NN query with the approximate result $\mathcal{S}_{ANN}(\omega_Q, K, k')$ of the indexed K-NN query according to

$$P(\omega_Q, K, k') = \frac{|\mathcal{S}_{ANN}(\omega_Q, K, k') \cap \mathcal{S}_{NN}(\omega_Q, K)|}{K} \tag{16}$$

The graphs (IIa) through (IIc) in Fig. 2 show the retrieval accuracy's dependency on the number of clusters k' that were included in the approximate NN-query. It can be seen that the retrieval accuracy quickly approaches 100% as k' increases. The lower dashed line corresponds to the lower boundary with 90% confidence in the experimental results, that is, 90% of all results are expected to be better than this boundary. The same applies to the lower boundaries with 50% and 75% confidence respectively. In the majority of cases a retrieval accurary of more than 95% can be achieved for $k' = 30$. Furthermore, the retrieval accuracy for the constrained indices (IIb–c) is considerably better in comparison to the unconstrained index (IIa) for larger values of k'. This is due to the fact that the distribution of clusters in feature space is more balanced in terms of size.

5.3 Computational Cost

The computational cost of an NN-query with the proposed indexing scheme is

$$C(N, k, k') \approx k' \cdot (\overline{|S_i|} + 1) \approx k' \cdot (\frac{N}{k} + 1) \tag{17}$$

$C(N, k, k')$ specifies the number of necessary computations of the metric distance between the query object and the indexed descriptors. In comparison, a linear search requires exactly N computations. A smart choice of the parameters k and k' can lead to a

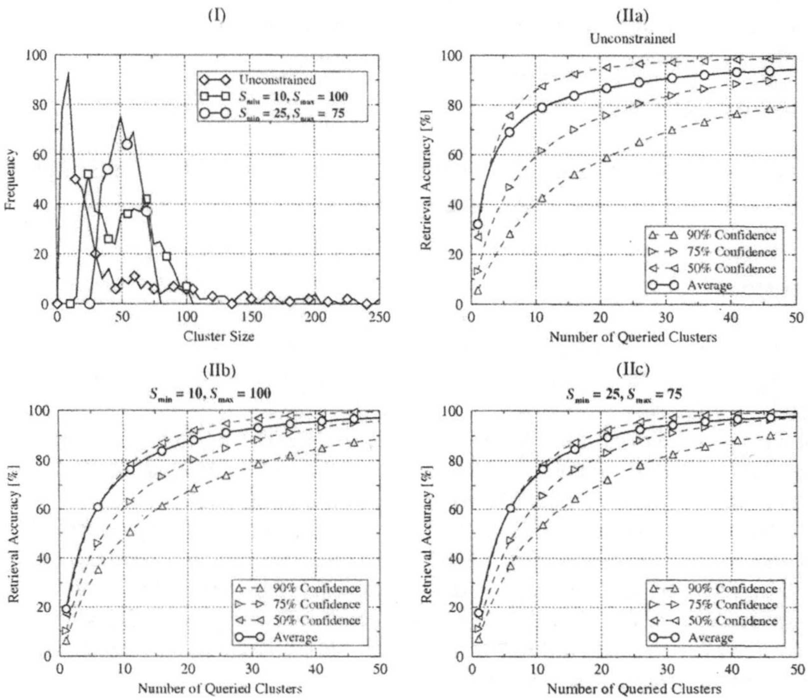

Fig. 2. Distribution of Cluster Sizes for Different Indices (I) and Retrieval Accuracy of Indexed K-NN-Queries (IIa–c) for $K = 100$

significantly lower computational cost while still resulting in a high retrieval accuracy. In the examined cases, the retrieval accuracy was almost 95% for most queries while requiring only 10% of the computational effort of a sequential search.

In fact, with a suitable choice of the parameter k', any query request can be guaranteed to complete in a given time frame after submission (depending on the system's hardware). Of course, this is at the potential loss of some retrieval quality for small time frames.

6 Future Research

The influence of the parameters, namely the number of cluster buoys k, the minimum and maximum cluster constraints $S_{\min}$ and $S_{\max}$, and the number of queried clusters k' during an approximate NN-query, has to be examined more thoroughly in order to fully understand their relationship on retrieval accuracy and computational cost.

The generation of the index through the constrained k-medians clustering algorithm needs considerable processing time that increases with the number of clusters k and the number of feature descriptors N of the dataset. Although the generation is generally computed off-line, there is a point where the load in terms of processing power and memory resources has to be distributed on multiple computers.

Acknowledgements

This work was supported by the European Commission with the ESPRIT Project #28773 COBWEB "Content-based Image Retrieval on the Web."

References

1. Arya, S., Mount, D.M., Netanyahu, N.S., Silverman, R., Wu, A.Y.: An Optimal Algorithm for Approximate Nearest Neighbor Searching in Fixed Dimensions. *Journal of the ACM*, 45(6):891–923, November 1998.
2. Beckmann, N., Kriegel, H.P., Schneider, R., Seeger, B.: The R^*-tree: An Efficient and Robust Access Method for Points and Rectangles. In *Proc. of the ACM SIGMOD Int'l Conf. on Management of Data*, pp. 322–332, Atlantic City, USA, May 1990.
3. Ciaccia, P. and Patella, M.: Using the Distance Distribution for Approximate Similarity Queries in High-dimesional Metric Space. In *Proc. of the 10th Int'l Workshop on Database & Expert Systems Applications*, pp. 200–205, Florence, Italy, September 1999.
4. Ciaccia, P. and Patella, M. and Zezula P.: M-tree: an Efficient Access Method for Similarity Search in Metric Spaces. In *Proc. of the 23rd Int'l Conf. on Very Large Databases*, pp. 426–435, Athens, Greece, September 1997.
5. Enser, P.G.B.: Pictorial Information Retrieval. *Journal of Documentation*, 51(2):126–170, June 1995.
6. Faloutsos, C., Lin, K.I.: FastMap: A Fast Algorithm for Indexing, Data-Mining and Visualization of Traditional and Multimedia Datasets. In *Proc. of the ACM SIGMOD Conf.*, pp. 163–174, San Jose, USA, May 1995.
7. Guttman, A.: R-tree: A Dynamic Indexing Structure for Spatial Searching. In *Proc. of the ACM SIGMOD Int'l Conf. on Management of Data*, pp. 47–57, Boston, USA, June 1984.
8. Kovalev, V., Volmer, S.: Color Co-occurence Descriptors for Querying-by-Example. In *Proc. of the 5th Int'l Conf. on Multimedia Modeling*, pp. 32–38, Lausanne, Switzerland, October 1998.
9. Ng, R., Sedighian, A.: Evaluating Multi-dimensional Indexing Structures for Images Transformed by Principal Component Analysis. In *Storage and Retrieval for Image and Video Databases IV*, vol. 2670, pp. 50–61. SPIE, La Jolla, USA, January 1996.
10. Pass, G., Zabih, R.: Comparing Images Using Joint Histograms. *ACM Journal of Multimedia Systems*, 7(3):234–240, May 1999.
11. Pestov, V.: On the Geometry of Similarity Search: Dimensionality Curse and Concentration of Measure. *Information Processing Letters*, 73(1–2):47–51, January 2000.
12. Sellis, T., Roussopoulos, N., Faloutsos, C.: The R^+-tree: A Dynamic Index for Multi-dimensional Objects. In *Proc. 13rd Int'l Conf. on Very Large Data Bases*, pp. 507–518, Brighton, England, September 1987.
13. Volmer, S.: Tracing Images in Large Databases by Comparison of Wavelet Fingerprints. In *Proc. of the 2nd Int'l Conf. on Visual Information Systems*, pp. 163–172, La Jolla, USA, December 1997.
14. White, D.A., Jain, R.: Similarity Indexing: Algorithms and Performance. In *Storage and Retrieval for Image and Video Databases IV*, vol. 2670, pp. 65–72. SPIE, La Jolla, USA, January 1996.

Non-Conventional Interfaces using Stamp Controllers

Hugh Mallinder, Huw Jones

Lansdown Centre for Electronic Arts,
Middlesex University,
Cat Hill,
Barnet EN4 8HT, UK
<hugh2, huw1>@mdx.ac.uk

Abstract. Artists continue to search for new methods of creation of artworks. The trend to interactive multimedia installation work requires systems that allow participants to interact in subtle ways. The paper describes a number of non-conventional interfaces to computer mediated art works achieved using small Programmable Logic Controllers (PLC) called 'Stamps'. These are programmed in BASIC and can be interfaced to personal computers or used as stand alone devices. They are cheap and extremely versatile in their use for non-conventional interfaces.

1 Introduction

This paper deals with an interface method used in the Lansdown Centre for Electronic Arts (LCEA). Non-conventional interfaces have been developed in LCEA over 12 years to create computer mediated art works. They are popular in a range of artistic and musical works, such as in 'tangible user interfaces' for sound manipulation [1].

It is easier to clarify the concept of a non-conventional interface (NCI) by identifying what it is not. For example, it is not controlled by:

- a conventional device supplied with a computer, such as a keyboard or mouse;
- other devices such as microphones or graphic tablets with interface software.

Hence a non conventional interface involves the custom building of electronic hardware as well as, normally, the writing of interface software.

LCEA [2] has explored new methods in computer mediated art and design from early work in computer animation [3] to later interest in interaction [4] and sonic arts [5]. Recent creations include installations populated by users [6]. These have unobtrusive functionality, 'when a computer is present in the interaction but not noticed' [7, p 397]. The emphasis is to develop innovative methods outside the standard concepts embedded within conventional software and hardware. Users of such systems participate in a puzzle like manner to explore effects created by their physical location, posture or movement. This extends the richness of opportunity for creative artists and designers. It is also necessary in an educational environment to do this cheaply, achieved with ingenuity by the use of low cost commercially available components widely used in other contexts.

2 Component Parts of a Non-Conventional Interface

A non conventional interface is made up of the following three parts:

- Transducers: these convert a physical property into an electrical signal. For example, mechanical motion can turn a switch on or off or the intensity of light falling on a photosensitive cell can produce a corresponding electrical signal.
- Signal conditioning hardware: this conditions the signal by amplification or other modification into a form suitable for feeding into a computer's interface ports, such as USB, printer, modem and microphone ports.
- Driver software: this accesses data from the port into the user program.

This paper describes signal conditioning hardware, particularly a cheap but versatile interface control computer. Modified keyboards [8] and transducer controlled oscillators have also been used as signal conditioning hardware.

3 Signal Conditioning Hardware (SCH)

3.1 Hard Wired Versus Programmable Devices

Installations may require several input transducers with signal conditioning hardware (SCH) inputting these to a computer via few ports. In Macintosh computers used by many artists, serial USB, printer and modem ports are used. Sequencing of the transducer inputs is required, plus generation of the correct protocol serial signal.

Various logic integrated circuits (IC) could be used, but for each new interface, considerable redesign would be needed. These disadvantages can be overcome by using a Programmable Logic Controller (PLC). This is an electronic device that uses programmable memory to store instructions that implement specific functions such as sequencing, timing, counting, logic and arithmetic to control external devices.

Many PLCs are programmed in assembly language, but Stamp devices made by Parallax Inc. use BASIC. Besides having standard language instructions, they allow instructions for common control tasks, such as serial data input/output, debouncing pushbuttons, generating and measuring pulses and sound. This reduces software development time, but the disadvantage is that BASIC is slower than assembly routines. This leads to relatively easy design and construction of NCIs, but imposes limitations on the tasks performed in relatively 'real time'. This has not proved to be over constrictive in the wide range of interfaces created in LCEA.

3.2 Stamp Interface Control Computers

Parallax Inc. makes two types of interface control computers [9, 10], Stamp I with a variant known as a School Stamp and Stamp II with a high speed variant. BASIC programs are created from a PC or Macintosh. The program is stored in EEPROM and is retained when power is disconnected. Stamps have 8 or 16 serial input/output (I/O) lines. Stamps are small (postage stamp size), unobtrusive, and cheap.

Table 1. Comparison of essential features of Stamps

Name	Stamp I (BS1-IC or School Stamp	Stamp II (BS2-IC)	Stamp II (BS2SX)
Programming	PC via parallel port	PC/Mac(Soft PC) via serial port	PC/Mac(Soft PC) via serial port
Prog retained on switch off	yes EEPROM, 256 byte	yes EEPROM, 2 Kbyte	yes EEPROM, 16 Kbyte
Programming language	BASIC approx. 80 lines	BASIC approx. 500 lines	BASIC approx. 4000 lines
Program speed (instr's/sec)	2000	4000	10,000
Internal registers	16 byte	32 byte	32 byte
I/O channels (unconfigured)	8	16	16
Size and physical format	10 mm by 35 mm, 14 pin SIP (BS1-IC) 38 mm by 20 mm 14 pin DIP (Sch'l St.)	31 mm by 26 mm 24 pin DIP	31 mm by 26 mm 24 pin DIP
UK Cost (exc. taxes)	£25 (BS1-IC) £16 (School Stamp)	£39	£49

3.3 Comparison of the Four Stamp Variants

The Stamp I comes in two functionally similar but physically different forms. The School Stamp is more robust than the BS1-IC, using discrete replaceable components. The Stamp II has two functionally different but physically similar forms, BS2-IC and BS2SX. Table 1 compares features of the three functionally distinct versions.

All 4 variants can be used either freestanding or via a serial port to a Macintosh or PC, have a voltage regulator on board and can be powered from PP3 (9 volt) batteries or DC power supplies of 5 to 15 volt. The BS1-IC, BS2-IC and BS2SX can be mounted on very cheap 105 mm by 38 mm Project Boards containing a programming header (3 pin for BS1-IC, 9 way D type socket for others), PP3 battery clips and a prototyping area.

Development kits include programming software, printed manual, programming lead, project board and relevant Stamp. They cost (excluding taxes) £59, £79, & £99 for School Stamp, Stamp I (BS1-IC), and Stamp II BS2-IC respectively.

4 Transducers

Transducers used with Stamps are those that give relatively slow output variations. Stamps are not fast enough to process audio or video waveforms needing typical sampling frequencies of 10K per second. For installations, several input channels need to be read often enough to give a sense of continuous control without delay. Stamps are suitable where sampling is needed at up to 20 per second per channel.

4.1 Input Transducers

Transducers used with Stamps in LCEA work include

- Switches: microswitches, vibration and tilt switches and pressure mats [8].
- Resistors: potentiometers, thermistors, light dependent resistors, conductive foam, body resistance.
- Variable capacitors.
- Infra red receiver photodiodes and ICs.

4.2 Output Transducer Systems

To give the output power required for the transducer, extra signal conditioning hardware is needed, for example current amplification, to drive systems such as:

- Light emitting diodes (LED).
- DC, Servo and Stepper motors and heating elements.
- Shape memory alloys (muscle wires).

4.3 On/Off Switches

Commercial pressure mats are often used for security, being laid on a floor under a carpet, acting as on/off switches when depressed underfoot. Mats frequently used in LCEA have dimensions of about 0.7 by 0.4 metres, with thickness of 0.3 mm, and cost no more than £5 each. They consist of 2 pieces of aluminised thick paper connected to output wires, with aluminised sides facing inwards. They are separated by a 2 mm layer of plastic foam with holes of 10 mm diameter on a 40 mm hexagonal lattice. These parts are contained in an envelope of thin plastic, which holds them in place and keeps out contaminants such as dirt, grit and liquids. An adult's foot standing on a mat will compress the foam sufficiently for the two aluminised surfaces to contact through the holes, so a mat acts electrically as a normally open switch.

5 Use of NCIs in LCEA Student Projects

Students in two postgraduate and one undergraduate course have used NCIs in their project work. The one year MA Digital Arts and MA Design for Interactive Media courses have a Fine Art and a Design bias respectively. Each course involves major projects; a three month individual or group project is the final assessment. Students use scripting or programming languages such as Lingo, C and Java. Projects are displayed in annual London shows and have been described in papers [2, 3, 4]. In order to be effective and usable in such projects, an interface should be:

a) non intrusive, so users should not have to wear or carry special devices to enable the system to work;
b) not apparent to the users in the sense that they should be unaware of the devices that make the system work;

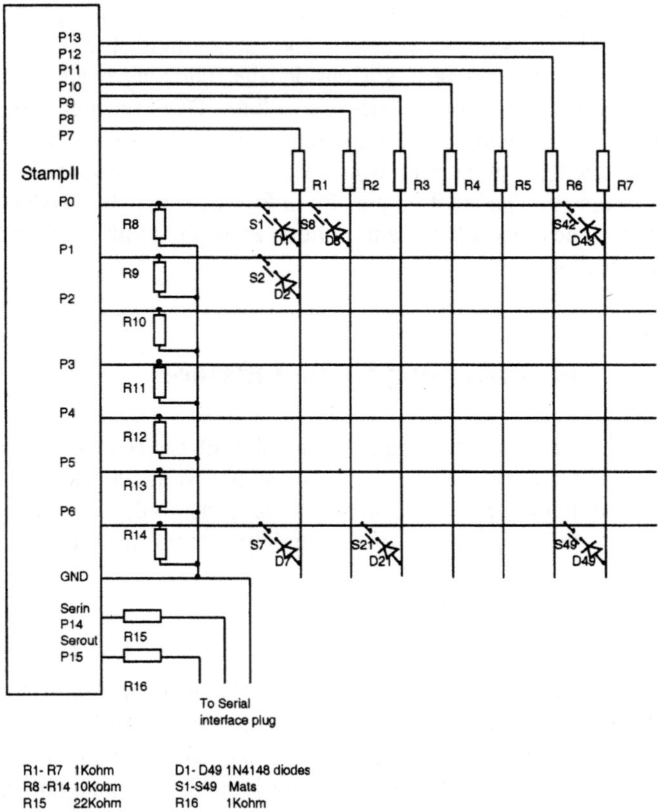

Fig. 1. The circuit diagram for a 49 mat interface using a Stamp II. Only a few mat connections at junctions are shown for simplicity

c) cheap, costing no more than a few hundred pounds — students may want to develop their projects or show them again after completion of the course, so they will have to rebuild or pay for necessary components of the interface;
d) gallery independent, so that they can easily be set up in different spaces.
e) simple, as students need to spend more time on developing conceptual issues of their art works rather than on complex interfaces;
f) sufficiently precise to accomplish the required work.

As an example, a large installations used 49 pressure mats, with inputs arranged on a lattice of seven rows by seven columns as shown in fig. 1. Each mat in this circuit diagram is connected to a 'row on' and 'column on' wire, so occupancy of a single mat can be identified from the row and column for which a switch is closed.

This achieves identification using only fourteen input wires to the stamp rather than the 49 required by connection to each individual mat. The stamp program is very simple. Each column P7 to P13 is set high, the others being low; the state of pins P0 to P6 (high/low) caused by mats being on or off is read and stored in an array; the 7 bytes of data (1 bit per map) is sent to a Macintosh computer in serial form.

Diodes shown in the circuit diagram (fig. 1) allow current to flow only from column to row. This prevent mats that are 'on' in columns other than the 'high set' column from giving spurious results. Consider the following example: mats S1, S8, and S13 are on, all others are off; left-most column P7 is set high, others low. The input on pins P0 to P6 should be 0000001 binary. If there were no diodes, column P8 would also be set high as current would flow through S1 and S8, and hence on through S13 to pin P5. The input on pins P0 to P6 would then be 0100001 binary, not what is required. The diode D8 prevents column P8 from 'going high' and so prevents pin P5 from going high.

6 Examples of Work using Stamp Interfaces.

This section describes uses of Stamps in a number of projects developed in LCEA. Case studies are listed chronologically within a number of main categories. Due to the complexity of some of the interfaces, several projects could have fallen into more than one category, but they are identified according to major features.

6.1 Resistance Detection

Michael Flaherty, MA Digital Arts (1994-5). This was the first LCEA project to use a Stamp, a BS1-IC. A sound space was controlled by a 6 channel input responding to the strength of gripping solid metal objects mounted on a table. If a person, or a ring of people touching each other, simultaneously held more than one of these, they closed an electrical circuit. Changes of contact resistance as these objects were gripped more or less tightly were identified using the charging time of a Resistive Capacitance (RC) circuit. This time was measured, and saved in a register using a Stamp routine. The register value was thus related to the resistance value, which was used to control sound sources via a Macintosh computer.

Anya Langmead, MA Digital Arts (1995-6). This used a Stamp II. A wooden egg the size of a chicken's egg was held in the hand [11]. It contained three types of detector, conductive foam for hand pressure detection, thermistors for hand heat and copper foil for skin resistance. The three worked by changing their resistances, and were combined with suitably valued capacitors to make RC circuits as above. The Stamp measured charging time and enabled the sensors partly to control an abstract swirling image displayed on a monitor at eye level.

Emma Posey, MA Digital Arts (1995-6). This work used two Stamp IIs, as more than 16 channels were required. Stamps of any type can be linked via any of their I/O pins using serial communications with an 'Open Drain' serial output mode. Sensors were stuck to a rounded sculpture shaped like a small seal [12]. A wire frame image of its surface was projected on a screen (fig 2). As a particular sensor was pressed the image rotated to be viewed from where it was pressed. On continuation of pressure, the image enlarged to show abstract shapes, zoom in and out controlled by varying

Fig. 2. Posey's sculpted shape was covered with sensors

finger pressure. 29 conductive foam pads of 5 mm thickness were stuck between square copper plates of 2.5 cm edge length. They were combined with suitable value capacitors to give an RC circuit as above. Again, the Stamp measured the charging times for transmission to an image generating Macintosh computer.

Martin Robinson, Staff Member in Sonic Arts (1996). An input device like the handlebars and front shaft of a motor scooter was developed using a Stamp II by Robinson and Mallinder. This controlled sonic outputs, with different forms of motion controlling timbre, pitch and repetitive percussive sounds [5]. The handle bars and front shaft each had 3 degrees of freedom. Switches, brake-like and twist grip controls lay on the handlebars. Nine potentiometers were used in RC circuits. Output was of 31250 Baud MIDI. Robinson's dance like movements controlled the improvised sounds created, a reverse of cause and effect from the normal dancer/music scenario.

6.2 Light Detection

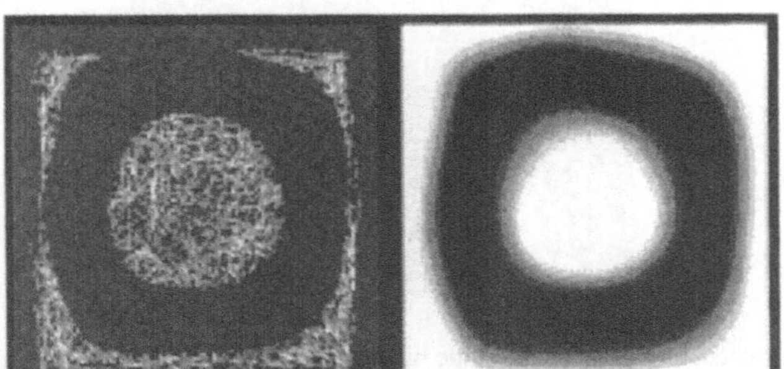

Fig. 3. The left image shows tracks of Warman's robots with bulldozers down, moving earth away from the lighter areas of the index image on the right

Fiddian Warman, MA Digital Arts (1995-6). Hardware infra-red (IR) area transmission of serial control information from a Macintosh computer controlled six small earth moving robots [13]. A School Stamp on each robot received input from the IR receiver/demodulator integrated circuit and from microswitches on the robot plough mechanism. Stamps controlled the on/off switches and direction control of two DC motors driving caterpillar tracks, the plough actuating servo, and small 'grain of wheat' (gow) light. A video camera detected this light to determine the robot's position, giving a closed loop robot positional control system, intended to create a pre-planned terrain layout in the controlled environment by moving earth from high intensity regions of a mapped image towards low intensity regions (fig 3).

Melissa Bliss, MA Digital Arts (1997-8). Entry or exit to or from a small room were identified by sequential breaking of two infra-red (IR) beams, modulated with 30 kHZ and 300 Hz square waves [14]. The receiver integrated circuit (IC) demodulated the 30 kHz signal to give a 300 Hz square wave if the beam was clear or logic high when it was obstructed. This 30 kHz modulation made the system insensitive to other lights. Outputs from the IR receiver ICs were input to the School Stamp, where custom software processed the two inputs. This software discriminated between a person's body passing completely or only partly through the door in either direction, and also could identify a hand waved in the beams. The output to a Macintosh serial port was a single byte which showed if the room had been entered or exited. In the room, two plastic basins representing heads, each containing a loudspeaker, were mounted on vertical axes 50 cm apart. Sounds emanated from the basins, whose motions were controlled by small servo motors from the Stamp, so it appeared that they were in conversation. Entry to the room triggered other interactive actions not described here.

A similar set up was used by Matt Grey, another student in the same group, to identify entrance and exit from a small room [15]. Also in this piece, LEDs were controlled to flash red to signify entrance, green for exit.

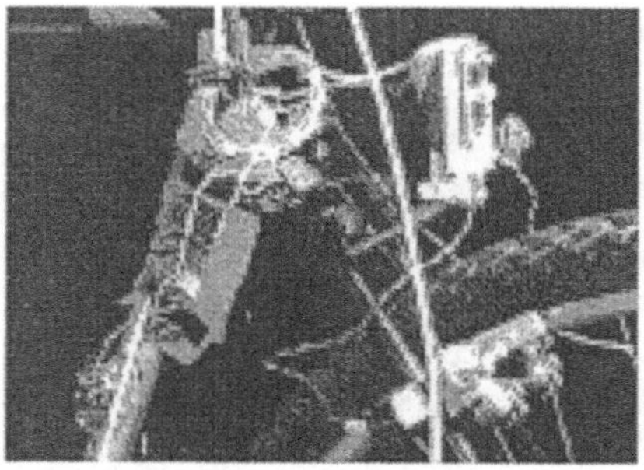

Fig. 4. The rear wheel mounting of the static bicycle shows brake sensors

Suzete Herrmann, MA Digital Arts (1997-8). A static mounted bicycle gave users control of backprojected Quicktime™ movies which they faced as they pedalled [16]. Speed of pedalling was determined by counting the rear wheel spokes to pass through an IR beam. Handlebar direction was sensed by a potentiometer in an RC circuit. Brake actuation was identified by microswitches near the brake pads (fig 4). This information was fed to a Macintosh computer via a Stamp II to control images, enabling participants to navigate through a labyrinthine landscape.

6.3 Capacitance Detection

Chris Rule, MA Digital Arts (1998-9). Rule's project [17] was concerned with perception of an invisible 3D sculpture, made manifest by changes of aural stimulus. A single user wearing cordless headphones entered a nearly dark cube of side 3m, painted black on the inside. Sound changes were caused by the position of the user relative to a large metal plate sensor in the cube's roof. This operated on the principle of one of the earliest electronic instruments, the 1917 designed Theremin [18]. The sensor's capacitance, changed by the presence of a body nearby, with a fixed resistance formed the elements of an RC oscillator, realised using a commercially bought 7555 oscillator IC. The variable frequency square wave output was input to a Stamp II, and the number of cycles in a given time was measured using a 'count' Stamp instruction. The numbers recorded varied as the user moved relative to the sensor. These values were sent by a MIDI interface to the SuperCollider program on a Macintosh 7600 to generate sound output. Each user could be observed through two small windows, making the installation intriguing both for participants and observers.

6.4 Motion Control

Lucy Kimbell, Soda group show at the London Electronic Arts Gallery, Jan-Feb 1998. Soda is a group comprised mainly of LCEA alumni. Lucy Kimbell's piece comprised a wall of 72 Musical Greetings Cards [19]. Cards were opened (to play their tunes) and closed by a low cost sculptural construction of levers, wires and weights on pulleys. Motive force was supplied by a thin wire of shape memory alloy, known as muscle wire. This contracts by 5% of its length with considerable force when subjected to a low voltage. Current, and hence the opening and closing of cards, was controlled by a Stamp II.

David Muth, MA Digital Arts (1998-9) Distorting Mirrors. Two aluminised perspex mirrors of one metre square were mounted vertically in wooden frames to face each other about 1.5 metres apart. The mirrors were mounted so their vertical left and right edges could be moved up to 10 centimetres forwards or backwards from the normal planar position [20]. This was achieved by four vertical axis geared DC motors, two for each mirror. Motors were driven at eight different speeds using a pulse width modulated waveform. Data was input from a Macintosh serial port to a Stamp II. This was conditioned for output to four sets of custom designed driver hardware. These included current limiting to avoid damaging driver ICs. At the limits of motion, a greater torque was required to turn the mirror and the current drawn by the motor increased. Current limits were controlled by microswitches mounted on the mirror frame switched on by the frame's position at the limits of motion. These were connected to the Stamp II, which was programmed to reverse the motor direction on receiving the switch signal. Four floor mats were also used to trigger the motors into action when a participant entered the mirror space, giving interesting distorted views of multiple reflections in the two mirrors.

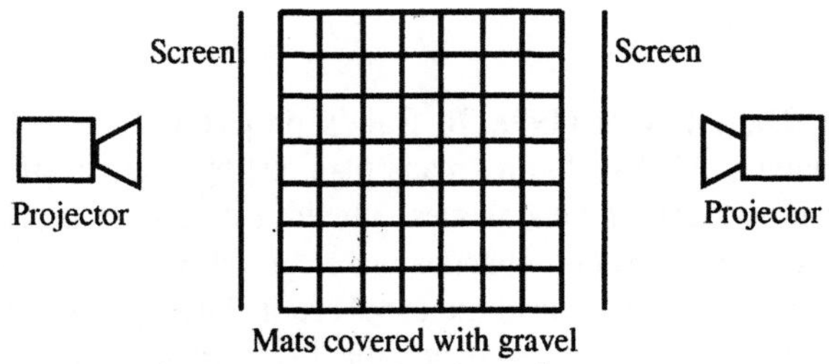

Fig. 5. The layout of the 'Pause for Breath' installation

6.5 Multiple Position Detection within an Area

Pause for Breath, MA Digital Arts (1997-8). This collaboration by 12 students with staff tutors Andrew Deakin and Hugh Mallinder, was presented at the Lovebytes Festival in Sheffield, UK, April 1998. The installation was located in a large darkened studio with a high ceiling. Two projection screens faced each other at a distance of 10 metres (fig 5). The forty nine-mat layout of section 5 above was covered by a layer of grit to evoke an outdoor environment. Conceptually, this represented a spring loaded platform which responded to the centre of mass of those on it by tilting and oscillating. Although the 'platform' was static, screen images gave a sense of motion. By sensing location and motion of users through mat occupancy, rotation and other distortions of star field images were triggered. Slowing down and standing still reduced motion, inducing a meditative mood and clustering the visible stars into patterns such as the shape of a hand. Location identification and control of images using a Macintosh computer was enabled by custom built software on a Stamp II.

Phoebe Jenkins, Jackie Heron & Orit Zetouni, MA Design for Interactive Media and MA Digital Arts (1998-9). 'Double up' comprised a series of two player physical games [21]. Sixteen mats were placed in a 4 by 4 square below a paddling pool filled by a custom made mattress containing plastic beads (fig. 6). This was sufficiently wobbly to make it difficult to keep one's balance. Jumping on the bag triggered image display and sound generation. One game was based on 'Pelmanism'; users had to seek a pair of sounds played in the correct sequence. After 'Houston', 'we have a problem' should follow. The game was engaging with users bouncing vigorously to play a variety of sounds and then closing in on identifiable pairs. Visual and sonic devices used, like the bright pink mattress, specially composed jingles and game show style on-screen flashes, were deliberately trashy, evoking American cable tv game shows.

This project used the same mats and Stamp as the Lovebytes project, showing how the interface is robust and can be readily adapted. Modifications were simple as the mat set was constructed in a modular manner. Mats were connected by multiway plugs and sockets, one plug for each row, the terminals on the sockets being removable. Modifications for this project consisted of using just 4 rows of 4 mats, and reprogramming the Stamp accordingly.

Fig. 6. Orit Zetouni and Pheobe Jenkins are watched as they demonstrate 'Double Up'

7 Summary

This paper describes a number of artist created installations using Stamp interface controllers as components of non-conventional interfaces. These genuine multimedia objects allow a variety of ways of interacting with image, sound and touch in real-time, with responses appearing immediate to participants. As artists devise more interesting installation concepts, the interface designer's technical ingenuity is tested. By extending the normally limited range of interface devices, relatively cheap but conceptually rich solutions to these design problems have been found. Various forms of Stamp have enabled a series of innovative projects in a reliable, low cost and adaptable way.

These were presented in 'one-off' exhibitions, with installations specially built and dismantled. To this extent, normal methods of assessment of interactive systems are inappropriate, as these usually relate to systems used repetitively by many regular users. Interfaces proved robust enough to survive complete shows, usually lasting about one week, and components were reused for subsequent projects.

There are lessons from these examples for more mainstream forms of multimedia, dominated by point-and-click and button pressing interfaces. The work illustrated shows how forms of interface that are natural and transparent to the user can be achieved at relatively low cost. There is considerable interest in such natural human interactions, for example the work of the Gesture and Narrative Language Group at MIT Media Lab [22]. Innovative methods for interacting with sound production for the Sonic Arts are sought in LCEA [5] and elsewhere [1]. The use of low cost non-conventional interfaces could make such advances more reasonably affordable.

8 Acknowledgements

The authors are grateful to the students of the Lansdown Centre for Electronic Arts for the stimulating and innovative ideas that have taxed their ingenuity. Present and past staff of the Centre have also provided interesting ideas; the Centre is an intellectually lively environment that supports creativity. The referees for this paper are also thanked for their perceptive and constructive suggestions.

References

1. Singer, A., Hindus, D., Stifelman, L., White, S.: Tangible Progress: Less is More in Somewire Audio Spaces. Proc. ACM CHI'99 (1999) 104-111 & 625
2. Jones, H.: Trends in Computer Mediated Art and Design: Examples from the Centre for Electronic Arts. Jnl Computer Networks and ISDN Systems, **30** (20-21) (1998) 1951-1960
3. Jones, H., Siffert, H. deA.: Animation Control Using Scalar Fields: a Case Study. Proc. Eurographics UK Conference, Loughborough University (1995) 207-214
4. Poletti, H., Jones-Morris, J., Mallinder, H., Jones, H.: A Three Dimensional Sketching Tool. Proc. Eurographics UK Conference, Loughborough University (1995) 39-48
5. Robinson, M.: Multi Dimensional Manipulation of Timbre and Control. Research Network in Art & Design Conference, Middlesex University (1996)
6. Elliott, T.: Interaction Arising from Installations. Proc ISEA'95, Montreal (1995) 77-78
7. Tannenbaum, R.S.: Theoretical Foundations of Multimedia. Computer Science Press, New York (1998)
8. Mallinder, H., Jones, H.: The Mat as a Non Conventional Interface, Proc. Eurographics UK Conference, University of Wales Swansea (1999) 103-110
9. Parallax Inc.: BASIC Stamp Handbook. (1995)
10. Parallax Inc.: BASIC Stamp II Handbook. (1995)
11. Langmead, A.: Biomonitors in Art and the Body as Interface. MA Digital Arts dissertation, Lansdown Centre for Electronic Arts, Middlesex University (1996)
12. Posey, E.: Siting Virtual Structures. MA Digital Arts dissertation, Lansdown Centre for Electronic Arts, Middlesex University (1996)
13. Warman, F.: Art Practice on the Boundaries of Digital Communication and Control. MA Digital Arts dissertation, Lansdown Centre for Electronic Arts, Middlesex University (1996)
14. Bliss, M.: Are Computers Tools or Collaborators in Digital Art?. MA Digital Arts dissertation, Lansdown Centre for Electronic Arts, Middlesex University (1998)
15. Grey, M.: CreateCell. MA Digital Arts dissertation, Lansdown Centre for Electronic Arts, Middlesex University (1998)
16. Herrmann, S.: under_ground. MA Digital Arts dissertation, Lansdown Centre for Electronic Arts, Middlesex University (1998)
17. Rule, C.: Conveniently Public. MA Digital Arts dissertation, Lansdown Centre for Electronic Arts, Middlesex University (1999)
18. Theremin: http://www.obsolete.com/120_years/machines/theremin/index.html (2001)
19. Kimbell, L.: Soda Show. London Electronic Arts Gallery, Hoxton Square, London. (15 Jan-8 Feb 1998)
20. Muth, D.: Distortion: Mirrors and Interactivity. MA Digital Arts dissertation, Lansdown Centre for Electronic Arts, Middlesex University (1999)
21. Jenkins, P.: Double Up!. MA Digital Arts dissertation, Lansdown Centre for Electronic Arts, Middlesex University (1999)
22. Cassell, J., Bickmore, T., Campbell, L., Chang, K., Vilhjálmsson, H., Yan, H.: Requirements for an Architecture for Embodied Conversational Characters. In: Thalmann, D., Magnenat Thalmann, N. (eds.): Computer Animation and Simulation '99 (Eurographics Series). Springer Verlag, Vienna (1999) 109-120

Interactive, Evolutionary Textured Sound Composition

Sidney Fels[1] and Jonatas Manzolli[2]

[1] Dept. of Electrical and Computer Engineering,University of British Columbia, Vancouver, BC, Canada, ssfels@ece.ubc.ca
[2] Interdisciplinary Nucleus for Studies on Sound Communication (NICS), University of Campinas (UNICAMP), Campinas, SP, Brazil, jonatas@nics.unicamp.br

Abstract. We describe a system that maps the interaction between two people to control a genetic process for generating music. We start with a population of melodies encoded genetically. This population is allowed to breed every biological cycle creating new members of the population based upon the semantics of the spatial relationship between two people moving in a large, physical space. A pre-specified hidden melody is used to select a melody from the population to play every musical cycle. The overlapping of selected melodies provides an intriguing textured musical space.

1 Introduction

Algorithmic composition systems suggest intriguing possibilities for the production of music. They offer the potential to explore unique musical spaces with the aid of computational processes. However, they often suffer from being overly algorithmic and thus too deterministic in the types of music produced. This determinism often leads to a sense of the music lacking expression. To address this problem, our strategy adds three main interactive components to the algorithmic system: first, support for significant human interaction with the system to adjust, in real-time, expressive components; second, the addition of a constrained amount of stochasticity to the process to add complexity; and third, a method of providing control of the system at the process level rather than direct control of musical production to maintain the advantages of algorithmic composition. Our strategy is achieved by using an interactive, evolutionary approach to music composition. Rowe [14] pointed to the concept of interactive musical systems as a composition by refinement. He commented

> because the program reacts immediately to changes in configuration and input, a user can develop compositional applications by continually refining initial ideas and sketches.

In our system, a genetic algorithm underlies the musical process similar to works by Biles[1], Horowitz [5] and our recent system VoxPopuli [12]. In the research presented here, the evolutionary algorithm has control parameters for altering the degree of stochasticity used as well as adjusting the texture of the music. The semantics of the control parameters provide a basis for creating the music interface. Specifically, the performer/composer has access to the process parameters through a semantically relevant mapping of the relationship between two objects. However, the performer does not have direct control over the specific attributes of the melody structure since these are controlled by the evolutionary procedure. The underlying structure of the process is described in section 3. Since the performer controls a process rather than the details of the music, we have also developed techniques for visualizing the process itself to assist the performer in guiding the melodic structure. Thus far, we have been able to generate interesting and rich melodies through experimentation.

2 Related Work

In recent years, Evolutionary Computation has been developed to mirror biological evolution. It is useful to create algorithms and structures of higher levels of complexity. Both biological and simulated evolutions involve the basic concepts of a genotype and a phenotype, and the processes of expression, selection, and reproduction with mutation. Miranda [11] suggested:

> a plausible approach to alife-like musical models and simulation is to consider music as an adaptative system of sounds used by a number of individuals in a certain community, engaged in a collective music making experience.

In the research presented here we use an evolutionary paradigm to control an interactive compositional process in which the genotype is described by a melodic line represented by MIDI parameters. The phenotype is the resultant sound produced by the computer in real time. In biological terms, expression is the process by which a phenotype is generated from a genotype. The selection process developed here selects melodies from the population closest to a hidden melody and plays them. The hidden melody does not affect the evolution of the population, instead, it is only used to determine which melody is heard. The idea of using hidden melody to guide an evolutionary musical process was inspired by a quotation from the XIII century written by Guido d'Arezzo[17] (p. 123):

> to find an unknown melody, most blessed brother, the first and common procedure is this: You sound on the monochord the letters belonging to each neume, and by listening you will be able to learn the melody as if from hearing it sung by a teacher.

Our approach mimics this old musical procedure using a relation between two objects as the paradigm for a monochord and letters of a Gregorian Chant.

One of the first applications of genetic algorithms (GAs) to sound design can be found in the work of Roads [13] in which evolutionary strategies are used to regulate parameters of a granular synthesis process. In this process, thousands of parameters are combined in a complex way to produce a desired sound result.

Following this original work, a series of articles related to the production of sound synthesis using GAs to deal with the complexity of an automated synthesis process were created [7][8][2].

In recent literature, GAs have also been applied to produce evolving trajectories of musical material [6]. Biles [1] presented a genetic algorithm-based model that mimics a student learning to improvise jazz solos under the guidance of a human mentor. In Horowitz's [5] development, an interactive system uses GAs to develop a criterion for distinguishing rhythmic patterns, producing a large number of variations. We have also studied applications of GAs to interactive composition [9] [10]. Evolutionary Computation is also increasingly employed in Computer Graphics to create scenes and animations Sims [16]. In these applications the rules are learned by the system through its interaction with the user, as described by Fogel [4].

3 Composition Process and Melody Representation

The overall system is shown in figure 1. There are three distinct sub-systems: the Music Cycle, the Biological Cycle and the Visualization sub-systems described below. The Music Cycle sub-system is responsible for selecting which melody will be played and when. The Biological Cycle sub-system is responsible for updating the population melodies. The Visualization sub-system is responsible for providing the performer with a sensible view of the evolutionary process and the musical output. Each of these sub-systems is described below.

Each sub-system operates on the melody population shown in figure 1. The melody population is composed of genetically encoded melodies. The notes are the genes in our genetic algorithm. A note's genetic structure consists of these components:

1. MIDI note number;
2. velocity of the note;
3. duration of the note;

The genome for a given melody can be of any length but we currently limit it to 12 notes. Likewise, the population can be of an arbitrary size; we currently use 20 members. Thus our population consists of 20 members, each of which is 12 notes long. Note that other components can be included to the genetic structure for a melody. As we are using only MIDI based music synthesis, other note parameters could be MIDI note controls such as the program change, channel number and panning parameters.

In addition to the melody population, we also encode a special, single melody we call the "hidden melody". Normally, it is not reconfigurable during the composition process and is established *a priori*. The hidden melody is used by the Musical Cycle Sub-system for selecting which melody to play from the melody population as described in 3.1.

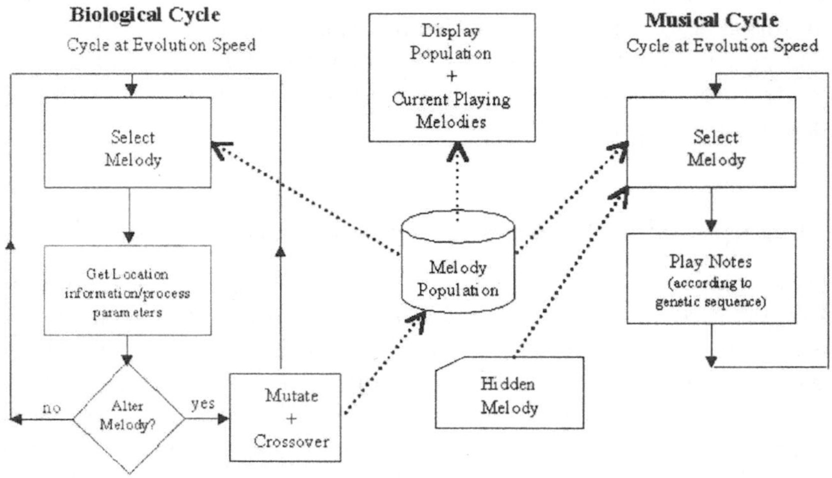

Fig. 1. Three processes run concurrently to control the musical process. The first is the Musical Cycle process which continuously selects melodies from the population closest to the hidden melody and plays them. Depending upon the cycle time, the melodies may overlap. The second is the Genetic Cycle process which continuously updates members of the population using mutation and cross-over. The third process provides visualization of the current melodies.

3.1 Musical Cycle Sub-system

The Musical Cycle Sub-system is responsible for selecting which member of the current population to play and when. A Musical Cycle consists of the following two steps:

1. Select the melody to play.
   The selection of the melody is done by choosing the melody closest to the hidden melody. We determine distance by calculating the mean square difference between gene sequences of two melodies. Mathematically, this is expressed:

$$D = \sum_{i=1:all\_notes} \sum_{j=1:all\_note\_structures} (g_{ij}^a - g_{ij}^b)^2 \tag{1}$$

   where g_{ij}^a is the note structure j of note i for the one gene and g_{ij}^b is for the other. Remember that a gene has MIDI information substructures which are combined to form the melody genome.
2. Play the melody.
   All the notes are scheduled by the system to play according to their duration parameter as specified in the genes. Duration is specified relative to each note's previous note as a power of 2 ± 1 delay units of a fixed tempo. As the duration of each note is a function of the genes, the overall duration of each melody in the population is different. Once scheduled, melodies play autonomously and the musical cycle continues without waiting.

The Musical Cycle repeats at a parameterized frequency called the music cycle time allowing melodies to be overlapped or spread out. When overlapped the music acquires complex texturing whereas when they are spread out a minimalist feel occurs.

By using the distance from the hidden melody as a selection criterion, the melodies have some gravity towards an a priori melodic structure providing some root to the sound produced. However, the biological process, described in section 3.2, provides stochastic variation from the hidden melody to give interesting deviations. Furthermore, the amount of variation is controlled by the performer to provide expressive possibilities. Remember, the hidden melody does not affect the evolution of the population; rather, it determines which member of the current population is heard.

3.2 Biological Cycle Sub-system

Each cycle of the Biological Cycle Sub-system determines a new member of the population based on a currently selected member using a round-robin strategy. The two processes implemented thus far are mutation and crossover applied to MIDI note number, duration and velocity. We chose these as they are the most typical genetic processes for modeling. Additional processes are left for future work.

In mutation, each gene in each genome in the melody has a random chance of being changed to a new value according to the *Mutation Probability.* The performer's interaction with the system sets this parameter dynamically, as discussed in section 4. Mutation provides a degree of randomness in the melody population. This allows the population to wander freely in melody space facilitating freshness in the melodic structures. The amount of wandering in the melody space (genotype variation) is controlled by the Mutation probability. The deviation that is actually heard (phenotype) is mediated by the hidden melody, thus any extreme mutations from the hidden melody are unlikely to be heard. To prevent large variations and maintain note alignment, we constrain note number mutations to a circular two-octave scale and durations to powers of 2 (± 1). Mutations can cause large variations in a gene's value. We constrain the genetic variations to moderate this. When mutation causes a note to move outside a two-octave scale, it is reassigned a value inside the restricted two octaves. This is accomplished by considering the scale as circular; thus, any note number higher than that of the top of the two octaves is circled around to the bottom of the scale (and vice versa).

For crossover, two additional melodies from the population are selected as mother and father melodies. For each gene, with a given *Crossover probability*, crossover will occur. Crossover is performed by replacing the genes (notes) with one from the mother or father melody stochastically. If a gene is not selected for crossover the original is left untouched. Thus, after crossover, depending upon the Crossover Probability, the new melody is a mixture of original notes plus some notes selected randomly from either the other or father melodies. The Crossover Probability is determined from performer interaction with the system, as discussed in section 4. Crossover causes mixing of the current population to produce offspring that are related (at least in genotype) and thus sound similar when played. Like mutation, genotype variation is controlled by the Crossover Probability but the phenotype is still mediated by the hidden melody, so large variations from the hidden melody are likely not to be heard.

4 Interaction Framework

In our current direction we attempt to map performer interaction semantics to the evolutionary semantics provided by the process control parameters. Mapping semantically related control parameters reduces cognitive load, increases intimacy, and is the basis for direct manipulation interfaces[15]. We do this by mapping the distance between two objects to the mutation probability and the angular deviation formed by the vector joining the two objects with a reference angle to the Crossover Probability. This mapping is important since it makes the manipulation of melodic variation more predictable, easier to learn and enhances intimacy with the system.

We have experimented with two different ways of interaction. The first technique is to use two cubes as the objects. These cubes are actually the receivers of a 6 degree-of-freedom tracker (Polhemus Fastrak). The position and orientation of the receivers are measured and used to compute the distance between them and the angle relative to a horizontal line. Figure 2 shows a person using the Fastrak sensors with the system.

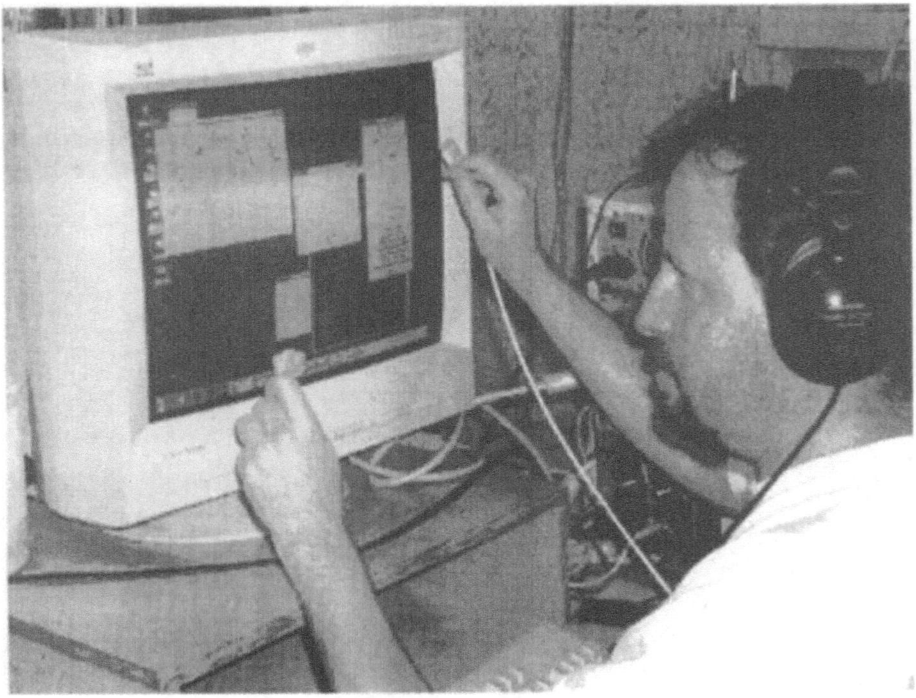

Fig. 2. Photo of person playing with the system using the Fastrak.

In the second technique the two objects are people. The positions of the people are tracked using a local positioning system (LPS) developed in-house at the University of British Columbia. The LPS system uses infrared-based active badges and camera modules for tracking the position of moving objects. The idea behind using the interaction of two people to manipulate the genetic algorithm comes from thinking about the semantics of how two people interact with each other and their environment. We take the physical proximity of two people and map this to the mutation probability; thus, if they are close together the population becomes relatively stable with little mutation to explore the melody space. However, if the two people move farther apart, the mutation probability increases which in turn introduces new genetic information into the population.

The relative angle between the two people and the wall sized visual representation of the population (see section 5) is related to the crossover probability. Thus, the more two people interfere with each other's view of the screen the more likely it is that the offspring of the current crossover mixture will contain genes from the mother and the father melodies. Thus, the two performers can interact with each other while the underlying evolutionary process controlling the melody will relate to their relationship.

The additional parameters, such as tick frequency, biological, and musical cycle times, are adjustable in real-time using a graphical user interface (GUI) (see figure 3). We plan to map object manipulation semantics to these parameters as well in a future version of the system.

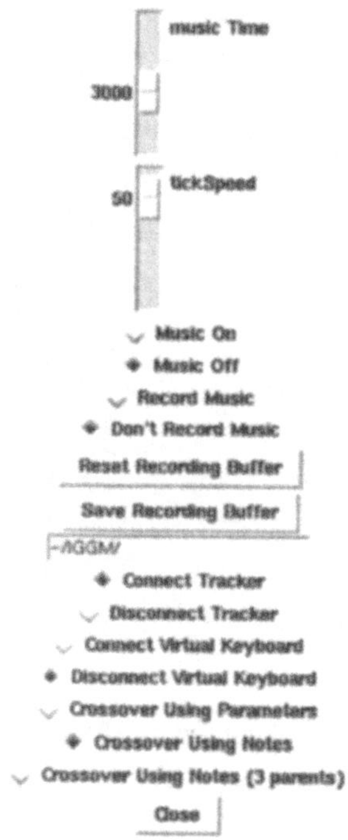

Fig. 3. Graphical User Interface for the system.

In initial experimentation we discovered that the system provides a reasonable amount of controllable melody space. The use of the hidden melody always keeps the navigation reasonably well constrained so that melodies playing concurrently work well together. Further, the ability to adjust the musical cycle time enables flexibility in the texture of the music. The ability to control the biological time allows the performer(s) to adjust how fast the population can explore the different melody spaces possible. The overall effect is that music with interesting texture as well as interesting stochastic variation focused around a predefined hidden melody is produced. Examples of some of the music that is produced are available at: **http://www.ece.ubc.ca/~hct/IGGM**.

5 Visualization

Finally, we have implemented a mechanism for visualizing both the current melodies that play concurrently as well as the overall population. We use the same concept used by [3] for visually representing a gene sequence. We represent each note by a line segment. The length of the line is dictated by the duration of the note. The angle of the vector relative to its neighboring note is related to the two note numbers of adjacent notes. Finally, the velocity of the note is mapped to the thickness of the line. Specifically, the following formulae are used:

$$length = log_{10}(duration) + 1) * 6 \tag{2}$$

$$angle = (((noteNumber2 - noteNumber1) * 10) + 180)/(2.0 * \pi) \tag{3}$$

$$width = ((loudness/127.0) * 4.0 + 1) \tag{4}$$

Where *duration* is the number of ticks the note is sustained, $noteNumber(n)$ is the MIDI note number of adjacent notes, *angle* is in radians, *loudness* is the velocity of the note being played and *width* is in pixels.

The visualization can be displayed either on a typical computer monitor or on a large projection screen. The large projection is useful when two people play music with the system. This is because the dynamics of the two people's interactions map to the control parameters, requiring them to have a large amount of space in which to move. Currently, the space we use is about 5m X 4m. Screen shots of some the melodies in a population are shown in figure 4. The hidden melody is shown in figure 5. Remember, the member of the population selected to play each musical cycle is the melody from the population that is closest to the hidden melody. We are currently investigating other possible visual representations.

6 Summary and Future Work

In summary, we have developed a system that allows a performer(s) to control an underlying evolutionary process which in turn creates music. We have encoded melodic structure as a genome and have defined a number of genetic operations that can be applied to a population of melodies. We have mapped some of the relationship semantics between two objects to control semantically related operations in the evolutionary cycle. This allows performers to manipulate the musical space by adjusting the process parameters, rather than directly controlling the musical output. This process occurs in real-time and is suitable for performances. At each cycle of the musical loop, the melody closest to a predefined hidden melody is selected. This melody is played concurrently with other melodies in play. The music produced has stochastic variations related to the distance between two objects; the mixing of the population is related to the perceived interference of two objects. The music also has interesting textures and structure.

Here are our future plans:

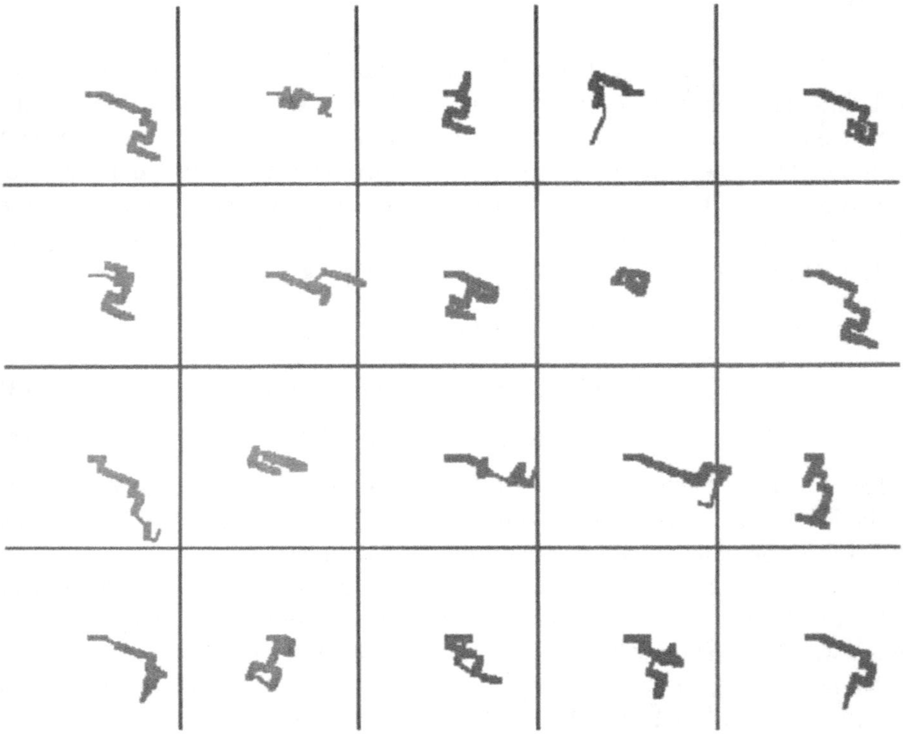

Fig. 4. Screen shots of the stick visualization of various melodies. These melodies were the result of a small amount of mutation (10%) away from the hidden melody for illustration.

Fig. 5. Screen shots of the stick visualization of a hidden melody that we have used. The closest melody from the melody population in figure 4 would be chosen to play every cycle time.

1. to experiment with alternative visualizations;
2. to allow additional control of MIDI parameters to evolve in the genome, such as program change, MIDI panning, etc.
3. to use a MIDI controller or a keyboard to change the Hidden Melody in real-time;
4. to increase the complexity of a melody by including multiple notes and improve the rhythmic representation allowing irregular subdivision;
5. to increase the types of evolutionary processes available, and
6. to further experiment with the mapping of two and three object relationship semantics to the semantics of evolutionary control.
7. to evaluate the various mappings between the interaction space

Evaluation of the system is complicated by the fact that there are no well defined objective criteria for performance. However, one technique we are developing is to use distraction tasks while people are controlling the music. The more distraction that people can tolerate while controlling the system suggests that the interface may support automatic behavior. In this mode of operation, it should be easier to express oneself. Of course, user surveys may be used in conjunction with this method.

Evolutionary processes are excellent candidates for automatic composition as well as real-time exploration of melodic variation. Further, since a process model underlies the creation of the music the performer only indirectly controls the music. The advantage is that process semantics can be mapped to performer semantics. This facilitates creating consistent cognitive maps between manipulation and navigation in the musical space, thus decreasing cognitive load and enhancing intimacy with the interface.

References

1. J. A. Biles. A genetic algorithm for generating jazz solos. In *Proceedings of the 1994 International Computer Music Conference, (ICMC94)*, pages 131–137, 1994.
2. N. M. Cheung and A. Horner. Group synthesis with genetic algorithms. *Journal of the Audio Engineering Society*, 44(3):pp. 130–147, 1996.
3. Palle Dahlstedt. A mutasynth in parameter space: Controlling sound synthesis by interactive evolution. personal communication, 2001.
4. B. Fogel. Evolutionary computation - toward a new philosophy of machine intelligence. *IEEE Press*, pages 46–47, 1995.
5. D. Horowitz. Generating rhythms with genetic algorithms. In *Proceedings of the 1994 International Computer Music Conference, (ICMC94)*, pages 142–143, 1994.
6. B. L. Jacob. Composing with genetic algorithms. In *Proceedings of the 1994 International Computer Music Conference*, pages pp. 452–455, 1995.
7. G. Johnson. Exploring the sound-space of synthesis algorithms using interactive genetic algorithms in g. a. In *Proceedings of the AISB Workshop on Articial Intelligence and Musical Creativity*, 1999.
8. J. R. Koza, F. H. Bennet III, D. Andre, M. A. Keane, and F. Dunap. Automated synthesis of analog electrical circuits by means of genetic programming. *IEEE Transactions on Evolutionary Computation*, 1(2), 1997.

9. J. Manzolli, A. Moroni, F. Von Zuben, and R. Gudwin. A evolutionary approach applied to algorithmic composition. In *Proceedings of the VI Brazilian Symposium on Computer Music (Rio de Janerio, Brazil)*, pages 201–210, 1999.
10. J. Manzolli, A. Moroni, F. Von Zuben, and R. Gudwin. An evolutionary approach applied to algorithmic composition. In *Proceedings of the VI Brazilian Symposium on Computer Music*, pages 201–210, 1999.
11. E. R. Miranda. *Composing Music with Computers.* Oxford (UK): Focal Press, 2001.
12. A. Moroni, J. Manzolli, F. Von Zuben, and R. Gudwin. Vox populi: An interactive evolutionary system for algorithmic music composition. *Leonardo Music Journal*, 10:pp. 49–54, 2000.
13. C. Roads. Genetic algorithms as a method for granular synthesis regulation. In *Proceedings of the 1993 International Computer Music Conference*, 1994.
14. R. Rowe. *Interactive Musical Systems.* Cambridge, Massachussetts(USA): The MIT Press, 1993.
15. Ben Schneiderman. *Designing the User Interface: Strategies for Effective Human-Computer Interaction (Second Edition).* Addison-Wesley, 1992.
16. K. Sims. Interactive evolution of equations for procedural models. *The Visual Computer*, 9(9):466–476, 1993.
17. O. Strunk. *Source Readings in Music History.* Vail-Ballou Press, 1950.

Screen Space: Depiction and the Space of Interactive Media

Stephen Boyd Davis, Huw Jones

Lansdown Centre for Electronic Arts, Middlesex University,
Cat Hill, Barnet, Herts, EN4 8HT
{s.boyd-davis, d.h.jones}@mdx.ac.uk

Abstract. The spatial properties of digital interactive multimedia are analysed and contrasted with those of pictures, and of narrative feature films and factual television. These media have developed distinctive spatial methods and questions arise concerning the transferability of such methods to other, interactive, forms. A taxonomy is proposed which reflects existing practice in digital interactive media and indicates promising lines of enquiry for the future.

1. Introduction

We propose a taxonomy of types of pictorial representation relevant to interactive multimedia. There have been many classifications of static graphics [noted in 17, 23, 9]. Many are focused on visualisation, whereas our aim is to categorise interfaces which are pictorial.

It is rightly assumed when discussing visualisation that the task objectives are the principal influence on the design. We extend this assumption to pictorial systems. This might appear controversial, since it may seem that the purpose of picturing is simply to *resemble*. However, Benford *et al* [4] consider the *degree of resemblance* to real space to be subject to the requirements of the task, and it will become apparent here that the objectives to which imagery is put and the context in which it is used are as decisive for pictorial as for non-pictorial graphics.

The spatial practices of film and pictures have extensive literature, but the spaces of interactive media (and indeed factual television) have been neglected. Boyd Davis [6] has identified some significant differences between spatial representation in media. These call into question the transferability of spatial practices from one medium to another, such as from narrative film or television to interactive media. The demands of interactivity have a strong effect on spatial appearance, and we predict that new genres will appear, incorporating as yet unknown spatial practices.

Before proceeding, it should be noted that here we treat alike those pictures which depict a real scene and those in which the scene is imaginary. We describe a number of projects of which some are unpublished: these tend to take a more adventurous approach to spatial articulation than commercial counterparts, using spatial innovations in part to overcome the technological limitations of standard computer platforms.

2. Characteristics of spatial practice in interactive multimedia

Interactive digital media comprise technological support systems for diverse emergent genres. Spatial practices within interactive systems diverge greatly and are, we argue, immature: form fails to articulate meaning. We illustrate the taxonomy to show how the spaces of interactive media have not as yet acquired the expressivity of their more mature predecessors. This is partly because there is insufficient shared understanding between makers and users (which only time can produce), but partly because insufficient attention is paid to the special problems of interaction.

Two important influences on the spatiality of multimedia are: the desire to offer multiple representations, leading to a variety of composite displays [25, 24]; and the need to provide access to more information than can be displayed on screen at once, necessitating some kind of selection. The distortion-oriented presentation techniques intended to solve problems of detail and overview for visualisation [17] are more difficult to apply where the mode of representation is pictorial.

The book metaphor common in early interactive computing has been largely superseded by spaces derived from more fluid, image-rich technologies like film and television. Makers of interactive multimedia artefacts imitate apparent strengths of these other media. This may be counter-productive, taking insufficient account of differences in objectives and modes of use. The more freedom given to the user, the greater the difficulty of using the practices of spatial articulation exploited in film, since these are outcomes of authorial control. Boyd Davis and Athoussaki [6] and Persson [20] discuss ways in which spatial techniques of cinema could be repurposed for interactive systems through greater use of the variables of viewing such as selective focussing, but such borrowings lead to problems. For example, Hindmarsh *et al* [14] note the problems in making spaces coherent without the authorial control which narrative provides. The difficulties of such transfers are discussed in relation to particular examples below.

We read of media 'convergence' [18, 10], but integration of different spatial forms is elusive. Macromedia *Director* in conjunction with image manipulation tools such as Adobe *Photoshop* has given recent developers more ways of integrating media technologies, but this is not trivial even with such tools. Nevertheless, the combining of pictorial and other segments in single displays is now often taken further in interactive media than in film or television. Segments can be combined into seamless surfaces, often with multiple viewpoints, scales and modes of representation. Such amalgams go beyond mere configuration of parts and approach the status of pictures in their own right, pictures whose spatiality is designed in response to the demands of interaction.

3. The importance of interactivity

Interactivity is not just an additional layer imposed on existing forms of spatial articulation, but fundamentally influences deployment of those forms. The user must be provided with objects with which to interact by pointing. The tools of interaction such as joysticks, joypads, mice and keyboards, have been described as 'curiously alienating devices' [21], and pointer-based interaction significantly constrains spatiality, since pointing requires the presence of an object whenever the user may wish to interact with it, a requirement quite unlike that of film or television where objects previously seen are assumed by the viewer to remain 'present' when no longer on screen. This can also be seen as a major difference between graphical user interfaces and the command line interfaces that preceded them which had no need to display a representation of objects. Multimodal interaction, allowing the user to interact using a mode such as speech [8, 19], could radically affect this spatial characteristic of interactive multimedia since users could then address items not currently visible. Grasso *et al* [11] list comparisons between graphical and multimodal user interfaces, but omit this important fact that graphical interfaces need to visually represent all available objects. This will be seen to be a fundamental problem for most of the artefacts under discussion.

4. Towards a taxonomy

We make a distinction between pre-pictorial and pictorial spaces, borrowing from the approach of synthetic computer graphics in which it is normal to conceptualise two sets of decisions in the design of a picture: one involving the geometry and attributes of the model—that which is to be depicted—while the other relates to the visualisation of the model necessary to its display, including such factors as projection system, mode of rendering, point of view, framing and so forth. It is instructive to consider this framework in relation to other pictorial forms. In the case of a photograph, there may or may not be opportunities to manipulate the pre-pictorial or model space, but there will certainly be opportunities to control many aspects of the picture (above all, point of view and framing). In the case of painting, the pictorial freedoms are far greater, even involving the use of inconsistent projective geometries and of course the depiction of scenes which have never existed. A range of pictorial means has evolved (over centuries in the case of painting) which enable the picture-maker or film-maker to produce certain effects in the viewer [3, 12]. In both cases, the author is sovereign since the user of the picture never sees any more than the author permits. These are essentially pictorial media.

Film might be thought analogous to a virtual environment, since in film there is a scene to be depicted and a depiction. However, this is not a useful characterisation, since it overlooks the fact that the filmmaker decides what should be seen in every shot at every moment. This pictorial character is highlighted by two factors. In fiction film, many 'scenes' are in fact sets, which are designed entirely in the light of how they will be seen by the camera. And scenes often comprise footage from different places and times [5,15] so that the apparently unitary pre-pictorial space does not in fact exist. This contrasts with the space of a virtual environment, in which to a large extent the user may look anywhere. Most current virtual environments are thus—by our definition—far less strongly pictorial than film, though, as we indicate below, the user's freedom of viewing is not complete.

We use the proposed taxonomy to argue that the displays of interactive digital media can productively be considered as a form of picture-making.

5. A spatial classification of pictorial interactive media

We divide the uses of space in interactive multimedia into seven categories:
1. simple assembly
2. two-dimensional pre-pictorial space
3. three-dimensional pre-pictorial space
4. pseudofilmic space
5. hybrid space
6. integrated spaces combining pre-pictorial and pictorial space
7. pictorially dominated space

These range from simple assembly of pictorial components in the plane and in (shallow) depth, through to new pictorial forms designed to support the demands of interaction within the limitations of the technology. Not surprisingly, these new forms are largely derived from inherited practices reinterpreted to meet new objectives. The categories proposed bring out different relations between the design of pre-pictorial models and the pictorial views by which they are presented to the user. These are related to modes of interactivity. We discuss examples illustrating the seven categories.

5.1 Spatial configuration: simple assembly

There is a need to place multiple elements in a single space to make them accessible to vision and interaction. This can lead to segmented spaces like those of the television news broadcast, using juxtaposition and layering of related elements. The spatial organisation of software applications tools such as Adobe Photoshop offers interface objects in discrete areas. The relationship between them is not articulated, so it is not generally apparent which objects control which until the user becomes accustomed to each application.

Fig. 1. Maltez, Bennett and Cova 1997: Interactive Documentary 'Contact'. The user chooses between the main video narrative sequence and supplementary narratives which appears when appropriate in the space. Choosing is done by simply pointing at the item of interest.

A typical device in interactive systems is the opaque overlay which occludes underlying material. Lack of visual semantic relations between windows in the pile, and the fact that windows the user needs to access may be obscured by others, reportedly lead to poor user performance compared with configurations which preserve the visibility of every item [16].

Another approach based on juxtaposition is adopted in *Contact* (Maltez, Bennett and Cova 1997), a prototype interactive documentary, which more resembles factual television (Fig. 1). The user may advance or step back in separate narratives by interacting at any time; ancillary information is offered at predetermined points in narratives, and the user can interrogate individual components of the interface, though authorial control is strongly maintained within each narrative strand.

There is clearly work to be done in considering how simple assembly styles may be more fully articulated to assist the user in understanding the relations between segments.

5.2 Two-dimensional pre-pictorial spaces

We define as pre-pictorial those spaces which can usefully be considered to exist independently of any particular view. In the simplest cases such spaces are two-dimensional but extend beyond the boundaries of any single view. For example *Britain in Brief* (Foreign and Commonwealth Office 1997) offers a six-by-five array of iconic pictures based on photographs. Clicking one of the pictures leads to other screens. The user is never permitted to see all thirty pictures at once since only about four fit the display (Fig. 2.) and there is no facility to zoom-out for a broader view (nor, as a Web-user might expect, to alter the frame of the window). This is clearly deliberate, since there would be sufficient space to exhibit thirty such images at a usable size in a single screen.

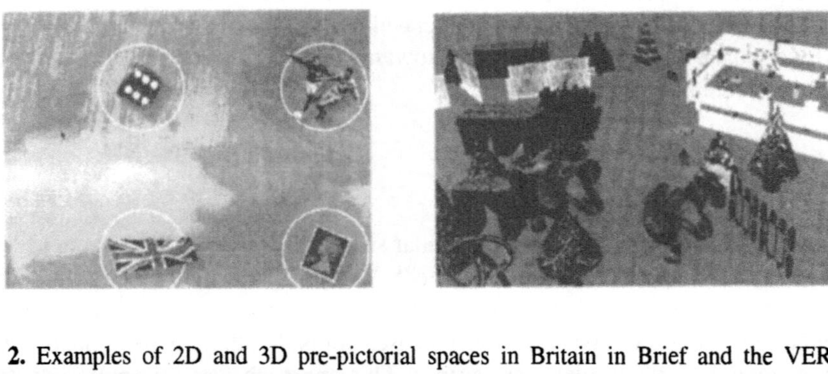

Fig. 2. Examples of 2D and 3D pre-pictorial spaces in Britain in Brief and the VERTEX environment built by young school children Bailey and Moar (2001) in ActiveWorlds.

The character of the space used in this particular product is indicative of some special issues associated with digital media. The user might expect the boundary of the scrolling model-space to be reached, as when scrolling in a word-processor or Web browser, but attempts to scroll horizontally or vertically reach no boundary: the space wraps back on itself. This topography could be conceived as drawn on a torus, but there is no visual evidence of curvature; the graphic suggests the model lies in a plane surface. As with film, it is experience of the visuals over time which constructs this 'space', as much as any single view of it, but in this case the single view and the aggregation of views offer contradictory evidence. Such indeterminate or contradictory spaces are particularly facilitated by digital media.

The window renders in unmediated fashion the view of the 'model' beyond. No aspect of the view is altered in response to what is viewed, unlike in painting for example where it is normal for a picture to *re*-present the observed scene—to create a space—rather than simply to open a frame upon it. Here by contrast the window really is just a window.

5.3 Three-dimensional pre-pictorial space

Many three-dimensional digital spaces are also essentially pre-pictorial; users can look where they wish in the space and no accommodation is made in the view. For example, most *virtual worlds*, such as ActiveWorlds (Fig. 2) allow the user largely unconstrained and unarticulated views of the model. The geometry and other attributes of this world exist independently of any particular view, and there are none of the opportunities to engineer a particular pictorial outcome in order to fulfil particular objectives which are inherent in authored picture-making. Nevertheless there are limitations on viewing. The focal length of the virtual lens is fixed and certain viewing angles are forbidden; the viewpoint may not pass in an arc through the vertical. In addition, since the user is by definition an inhabitant of such shared spaces, the viewpoint is always either through the user's eyes or over the avatar's shoulder (a clear borrowing from film).

The viewpoint typically does not respond to the kinds of scenes or action depicted as it would do in film. However, work by He *at al* [13] and by Tan *et al* [22] begins to apply cinematic approaches to depicting virtual worlds, as does the design of some computer games, in which for example crashing one's car triggers the display of an aerial view of the scene. This is a move towards considering the presentation of such worlds as a depictive process.

5.4 Pseudofilmic space

Pseudofilmic spaces are pictorial in a similar sense to film since, though the user may move about the space to a certain extent, every view is chosen by the maker. Exploration games in which a user's chosen trajectory is responded to by pre-rendered views fall into this category. The user infers that there is one consistent pre-pictorial model of which views are scenes. This approach was originally adopted to cope with performance limitations in the delivery of 3D scenes, but some of its benefits may not be abandoned even when this is not a consideration.

Many artefacts in this category involve some degree of entertainment, such as CD-ROM 'edutainment' titles, adventure and strategy games. They try to make the space immersive by eliminating counter-cues such as the paraphernalia of the everyday computer screen, or at least to subordinate such items as far as possible. In this they aspire to the apparently unmediated qualities of the fiction film. Unfortunately, given the visual constraints from interaction noted earlier, this immersive quality is often interrupted, for example by dialogs and floating tools which exist in an awkward visual relation to the main scene.

An aid to a sense of continuity is the use of environmental sound which is uninterrupted by changes of view. This technique, noted by Persson [20], is an important means by which film conceals its intermittent visual nature, but is outside the scope of this paper.

5.5 Hybrid space

Hybrid spaces combine some of the characteristics of simple assembly with those of three-dimensional worlds, reflecting the combined demands of presentation and of interaction. Such juxtaposition of spatial methods might be disconcerting, but in practice for involved users these spatial hybrids have become acceptable, partly through the efforts of designers to disguise incongruities. It is possible that this impression of incongruity is itself a temporary phenomenon arising from the relative unfamiliarity of these spatial configurations, and that in future they will come to be seen as transparent and natural.

Fig. 3. Chung et al. 2000: Virtual Office, a project visualising a shared virtual work environment. Translucence is used to integrate components with different spatial modes.

A prototype shared workspace tool is given as an example of hybrid space (Fig. 3). Many computer and console games similarly offer central pictorial views with an accretion of supplementary views and tools in the periphery of the display. In Fig. 3, translucence is exploited (a characteristically digital trait) in an effort to integrate pictorial and other components. The axonometric views also have the effect of allowing the overlaid textual and iconic elements to be seen as more tightly integrated than if convergent perspective were used.

The position and visual integration of the chat window give it the character of a speech bubble in a cartoon (cartoons are a rich area of multimodal representation deserving study as spatial artefacts), so it seems part of the space while still being accessible to the user. Like a head-up display for a pilot it also ensures the user may encompass diverse stimuli within a narrow visual field. Use is made in this project of techniques derived from film to bind together separate spaces which are juxtaposed only in time and not in the display: a user seen leaving the room by the lift is next shown emerging from the lift in another space. No other visual information is needed for users accustomed to film techniques.

5.6 Integrated spaces: combining pre-pictorial and pictorial space

In the pre-pictorial and hybrid spaces discussed above it is possible to separate the model from the view so that a coherent pre-pictorial space can be imagined, but in some artefacts the depiction undermines the distinction between view and model.
An example, *Upholstery Weekend* (Eberle 1996), is an animated narrative and is not interactive, and this indicates important aspects of the relationship between film practice, digital space and interactivity. The artefact draws attention to the process of representation for ironic purposes. This is not a unique characteristic of digital animation: traditional animators have also made media-conscious jokes of this kind (for example, a character climbs out of a hole, then picks up the black oval representing the hole). The pre-pictorial 'space' is defined only by the relationships between a small number of objects which are displayed without backgrounds. As in classical film, optimal views from varying viewpoints are exploited to afford the best possible view of an event or situation as well as to create visual interest and engagement. For example, an armchair threateningly approaches a small toy. Next, the victim appears significantly smaller; the approach of the predatory armchair is more easily assessed. There is a brief cut-away to an extreme close-up point-of-view shot of the front of the armchair before the armchair crushes the toy.

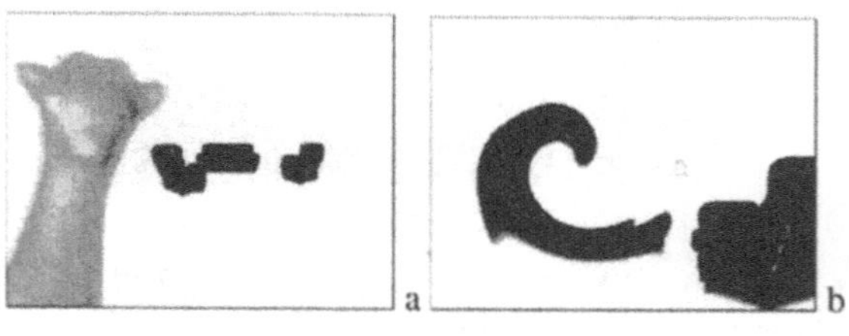

Fig. 4. Eberle 1996: *Upholstery Weekend.* In ***a***, focus is used to create distance and increase the drama of a near object. The evocation of a pre-pictorial space is abandoned in ***b*** by severe distortion of a sofa, forcing the user to 'see' the representation for what it is.

Later defocusing (almost entirely neglected in digital media outside high-budget feature films) gives extreme depth to the 'shot' (Fig. 4). The impression that a second small toy is in the near foreground is a visual joke, since it turns out that this is in fact a giant toy seeking revenge. This seems only a witty exercise in pre-pictorial space, but subsequently the coherence of the pre-pictorial space is subverted when a sofa is transformed in a wholly pictorial way which has nothing to do with the space which it seemed to occupy.

This animated narrative apparently constructs, but then undermines, a pre-pictorial spatial environment. Its strengths arise precisely because it is a wholly authored experience. Far from representing a solution to the difficulties of pictorial interactive media, it confirms them, by underlining the expressivity of authored depictions of space in which the maker decides exactly what shall be seen, from where and when. Every shot is designed in the known context of what precedes and follows it.

Fig. 5. Donald Norman 1994: *Donald A Norman—defending human attributes in the age of the machine*, CD-ROM 1994. Integrated components dissociated from their original photographic contexts, and recombined into a new form of picture.

Similar recombination of photographic and quasi-photographic elements into new 'pictures' has however also been used in interactive media. In a Voyager CD-ROM of 1994 an animate Don Norman is inserted into a new space at a new scale and with shadows which belong to the environment of the virtual page rather than to the real environment in which filming took place (Fig. 5). Such practices are pictorial: the designer *makes space* rather than simply opening a view upon it. Often there is a resemblance to pre-Renaissance forms of picture-making where each component has its own optimal view (and therefore perspective geometry) largely independent of the other components, but all are nevertheless organised into a unitary composition.

5.7 Pictorially dominated space

Differentiated from the previous category not in kind but by the degree of pictorial arbitrariness, the final class of pictorial space takes further the possibilities of recombining dissociated graphical elements into new spaces. Such integrated digital spaces have antecedents in traditional media, such as photomontage which combines fragments taken from their original contexts and assembles them in a unified composition with a conventional underlying pictorial structure; numerous examples are given by Ades [1]. However, we suggest that interaction differentiates the case of digital media from that of static photomontage. Whereas we have previously presented interaction as something of a problem, here we emphasise its beneficial effects on pictorial coherence.

Eclipse (Holley *et al.* 1998) constructs a space from such dissociated graphics, coercing disparate elements into a pictorial ensemble which, when interacted with, operates as an integrated system. This is not simple graphical assembly but neither is it a depiction of apparently pre-pictorial space. For example, an astronomical device is brought into direct connection with the heavens which it surveys, pictorially uniting disparate elements. It facilitates mixed modes of presentation, so it does not seem incongruous to see spatial coordinates presented as text which alters and moves as the space changes. Actions on one part affect the behaviour of the whole display, creating a coherence which exceeds any purely pictorial unity. There is an analogy here with the acceptability of editing in film which is unlike natural vision but is nevertheless perceived as in some sense 'natural' and has through custom become almost invisible to the film viewer.

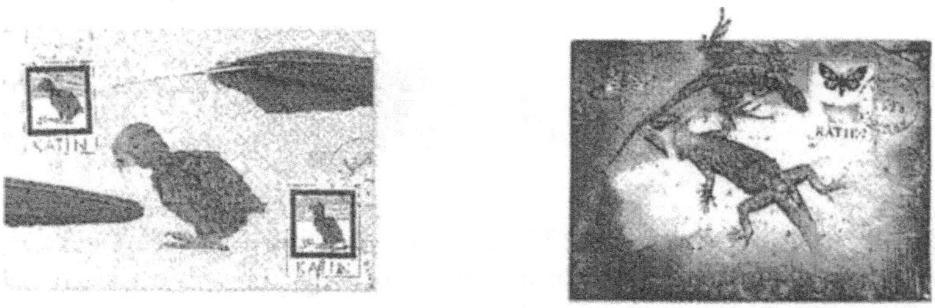

Fig. 6. Mayhew 1997: Ceremony of Innocence. This CD-ROM explores the boundaries between levels of representation.

A final example is *Ceremony of Innocence* (Mayhew 1997), an interactive narrative about a surreal postcard correspondence that makes visual puns on the nature of representation. The narrative suggests that one of the correspondents may have invented the other, so ambiguity and self-reference of representation and of space are appropriate. By representing picture postcards, everything seen is already depictive to at least one degree (Fig. 8). The user interacts with graphic elements in ways which fluctuate between interacting with the scene depicted and with the depiction itself. The bird is also depicted in stamps on the card, confirming its pictorial status, yet it moves, squawks and eats when coaxed by the pointer. The cursor, normally the user's 'property' is often captured by, or becomes part of, the representations with which it interacts.

The point of this paper is to elucidate different spatial forms which have emerged to serve differing requirements. The spatiality of *Ceremony of Innocence* does not offer a paradigm for other kinds of interactive media. Its objectives are relatively simple, to allow the user to progress through a narrative by means of interaction, whereas many of the problems of devising expressive spatial organisation in interactive media arise from the competing demands of widely varying functions.

6. Conclusions

We distinguished seven classes of spatiality in pictorial interactive media. Particularly relevant to interactive media is the situation when the parameters of viewing and picturing are authorially determined, but specific views and pictures are not. While the spatialities of pictures, of film and of television seem to have a high degree of fit with their objectives, the spaces of pictorial interactive multimedia are, with rare exceptions, awkward amalgams of the spatial practices of antecedent media. In general these spaces not only fail individually to serve the functions (both affective and utilitarian) of the artefact but when combined together fail to operate together in a coherent way. We have argued that some of these problems could be solved by a greater consideration of how existing pictorial media work. However, we have shown that it is not a matter of simply transferring existing spatial practices to the newer medium, but of developing new means of achieving similar ends. There is a need to rethink inherited pictorial and spatial practices to suit the demands made on the artefact. It is useful to remember ways in which digital interactive media are unlike their antecedents: they require (at least currently) the display of everything with which the user may interact; the visual experience is only partly authored, reducing the maker's control over viewing and picturing at any moment; for the same reason, there are fewer narrative possibilities for structuring the user's experience over time. These differences affect the spatiality of the medium, and the different genres which the medium supports, fundamentally.

References

1. Ades, D.: Photomontage. Thames and Hudson, London (1986)
2. Bailey, F. and Moar, M.: Children's Creation of Shared 3D Worlds. In: Earnshaw, R. and Vince, J. (eds.): Digital Content Creation, Springer, Berlin (2001)
3. Bann , S. Art. In: Cohn-Sherbok, D. and Irwin, M. (eds.): Exploring Reality. Allen and Unwin, Boston (1987) 83-108
4. Benford, S., Greenhalgh, C., Reynard, G., Brown, C., Koleva, B: Understanding and Constructing Shared Spaces with Mixed Reality Boundaries. ACM Transactions on Computer-Human Interaction, Vol 5 No 3, September 1998. ACM, New York (1998) 185-223
5. Bordwell, D. Space in the Classical Film. In Bordwell, D., Staiger, J., Thompson, K.: The Classical Holywood Cinema. Routledge, London (1985) 50-59
6. Boyd Davis, S. Media Space, Working Paper, Lansdown Centre for Electronic Arts, Middlesex University, London (2001)
7. Boyd Davis, S. and Athoussaki, H.: VRML: a Designer's view. In: Vince, J. and Earnshaw, R.: Virtual Worlds on the Internet. Proceedings of Virtual Environments Conference, Bradford, 15-16 April 1997, IEEE Computer Society (1999) 35-51
8. Cassell, J., Bickmore, T., Billinghurst, M., Campbell, L., Chang, K., Vilhjálmsson, H., Yan, H.: 'Embodiment in conversational interfaces: Rea'. Proceeding of the CHI 99 conference on Human factors in computing systems: the CHI is the limit May 15 - 20, 1999, Pittsburgh, PA USA. ACM, New York (1999) 520-527
9. Card, S., Mackinlay, J., and Shneiderman, B. (eds.). Readings in Information Visualization: Using Vision to Think. Morgan Kaufmann Publishers, San Francisco (1999)
10. Fischetti, M: The Future of Digital Entertainment. Scientific American, November 2000, Vol.283, No.5 (2000) 31-33
11. Grasso, M.A., Ebert, D.S., and Finin, T.W.: The Integrality of Speech in Multimodal Interfaces. ACM Transactions on Computer-Human Interaction, August 1995, Vol.5, No.4, ACM, New York, (1998) 303-325
12. Harrington, J.: The Rhetoric of Film, Holt, Rinehart and Winston, New York 1973
13. He, L., Cohen, M.F. and Salesin, D.H.: The virtual Cinematographer: a paradigm for automatic real-time camera control and directing. Proceedings of the 23rd annual conference on computer graphics August 4 - 9, 1996, New Orleans, LA USA, International Conference on Computer Graphics and Interactive Techniques (1996) 217-224
14. Hindmarsh, J., Fraser, M., Heath, C., Benford, S. and Greenhalgh, C.. Fragmented Interaction: establishing mutual orientation in virtual environments. Proceedings of CSCW98, Seattle Washington, November 14 - 18, 1998. ACM New York (1998) 217-226

15.Hochberg, J.: Perception of Motion Pictures. In: Gregory, RL (ed.) The Oxford Companion to the Mind, Oxford University Press, Oxford (1987) p604-8
16.Kandogan, E. and Shneiderman, B.: Elastic Windows: Evaluation of Multi-Window Operations. Proceedings of ACM SIGCHI 97 Conference on Human Factors in Computing Systems. March 1997. ACM, New York (1997) 250-257
17.Leung, Y.K. and Apperly, M.D.: A Review and Taxonomy of Distortion-Oriented Presentation Techniques. ACM Transactions on Computer-Human Interaction, Vol 1 No 2, June 1994, ACM New York (1994) 126-160
18.Murray, J.H. Hamlet on the Holodeck: the future of narrative in cyberspace. The Free Press (Simon and Schuster), New York (1997)
19.Oviatt, S. and Cohen, P.: Perceptual User Interfaces: multimodal interfaces that process what comes naturally. Communications of the ACM. March 2000. Vol.43, No.3, ACM, New York (2000) 45-53
20.Persson, P.: A Comparative Study of Digital and Cinematic Space with Special Focus on Navigational Issues. Proceedings of Ninth European Conference on Cognitive Ergonomics, University of Limerick, Ireland, August, 1998 (1998) 67-72
21.Poole, S.: Trigger Happy: the inner life of videogames. Fourth Estate, London (2000)
22.Tan, D.S., Robertson, G.G., Czerwinski, M.: Exploring 3D Navigation: combining speed-coupled flying with orbiting. Proceedings of SIGCHI'01, Seattle WA, 31 March-5 April 2001. ACM New York, Vol 3 Issue 1 (2001) 418-425
23.Tweedie, L.: Characterising Interactive Externalisations. Proceedings of CHI97, Atlanta Georgia, 22-27 March 1997. ACM New York (1997)
24.Wang Baldonado, M.Q., Woodruff, A. and Kuchinsky, A.: Guidelines for Using Multiple Views in Information Visualisation. Proceedings of the Working Conference on Advanced Visual Interfaces, Palermo Italy, 24-26 May 2000. ACM New York (2000) 110-119
25.Zeigler, B.P and Oren, T.I.: Multifacetted, Multiparadigm Modelling Perspectives: tools for the 90s. Proceedings of 1986 Winter Simulation Conference. ACM New York (1986) 708-712

Projects and products referred to in the paper

1. Bird, A., Greenhalgh, M., Hamilton, S., Murray, C., Nation, K., Neild, L.: Mobile: a CD-ROM anthology of projects from the Lansdown Centre for Electronic Arts, Middlesex University, UK (1995)
2. Chung, G., Fukner, K., Hoffman, H. and Rousselot, N.: Virtual Office. Masters Project at Lansdown Centre for Electronic Arts, Middlesex University, UK (2000)
3. Eberle, L.: Digital animation: Upholstery Weekend. Postgraduate Project, Lansdown Centre for Electronic Arts, Middlesex University, UK (1996)
4. Foreign and Commonwealth Office, CD-ROM: Britain in Brief. Design and production by Art of Invention and The Central Office of Information, London (1997)
5. Holley, T., Reeves, J., Sauderais, M., Sjaastad, S., Choy, K.K.: Eclipse: a prototype interactive fiction, Masters Project at Lansdown Centre for Electronic Arts, Middlesex University, UK (1998)
6. Maltez D., Bennett, B. and Cova, M. Contact: a prototype interactive documentary, Masters Project at Lansdown Centre for Electronic Arts, Middlesex University, UK (1997)
7. Mayhew, A.: CD-ROM: Ceremony of Innocence, Produced and published by Real World Multimedia Limited, UK (1997)
8. Norman, D.A.: CD-ROM: Donald A Norman—defending human attributes in the age of the machine, Produced and published by Voyager, USA (1994)

SPATIAL VIDEO
Exploring Space Using Multiple Digital Videos

Edmundo M. N. Nobre[1] and Antonio S. Câmara[1]

[1]Environmental Systems Analysis Group, New University of Lisbon,
2825 Monte de Caparica, PORTUGAL
{en, asc}@mail.fct.unl.pt

Abstract. This paper presents and discusses a new approach to collect, organize and explore multiple digital videos on a spatial basis. We present a methodology based on direct video frame indexation to the real space represented in the video images. This approach facilitates the exploration of space through multiple videos. An illustrative application of this technology for multimedia spatial information systems is provided. Future developments related to the three-dimensional explorations of space using digital video are also discussed.

1 Introduction

Digital video captures both the spatial and temporal dimensions of macro-phenomena such as a forest fire or micro-phenomena such as the evolution of biological films.

Video capture is usually a linear process that involves a pointing, rotation or moving operation with a camera. To completely capture on video an open space, a 360 degrees rotation capture operation may be performed with satisfactory results if the area is small. Larger areas with heterogeneous topography will require more than one capture. Those captures may be probably performed with different techniques. As a result, the handling of the different video segments becomes a complex task.

Natural areas are irregular, with rivers, mountains and other natural or artificial obstacles that always occlude some relevant location. How can we see what is behind a hill?

The systematic collection of geo-referenced video segments solves this problem. Land is a mosaic of pieces, like a puzzle, where each piece represents some particular corner, an indoor scene or a large landscape. Each one of them can be documented with a different image or a video. Together they allow a complete visual perception of the space [1, 2].

This paper introduces an approach where pre-defined capture processes and subsequent spatial indexing of video are used to facilitate the exploration of a real world scene. An application to the development of a spatial multimedia information system is provided for illustrative purposes. Future developments related to the use of digital video in the exploration of three-dimensional representations are also discussed.

2 Introducing Spatial Video Systems

Modeling and composing complex synthetic 3D worlds have been explored and applied in fields ranging from scientific interactive visualization to gaming. Most of these techniques typically involve the construction of complex 3D models, which try to reproduce, as closest as possible, the reality they intent to re-create.

Digital video is a more realistic representation of the natural world. Video is less expensive and easier to produce, and incorporates both spatial and temporal dimension. Nevertheless, videos have been looked mainly as rigid data content linear structures with restrictive browsing capabilities (typically, forward or backward). Consequently, the use of video in the development of applications such as the mentioned above is still limited.

Methods to organize, process and visualize video information have been proposed by several authors [7, 8, 9, 10]. In the present approach, we propose an interactive way to explore video, which looks, not only to the video content itself but also to the context of the capture process.

The term "interactive video" is used in the sense that we can compose and travel along different videos and images in a natural way. The interaction is not with the video itself as a simple multimedia object as it is usually done. A real image or a schematic map may be used in the background for geographical reference.

In our system space may be understood as a mosaic of pieces, like in a puzzle, where each peace is represented by a video. These videos are flexible multimedia objects that can be shaped on space to build the needed pieces to fulfill the desirable area (Fig.1).

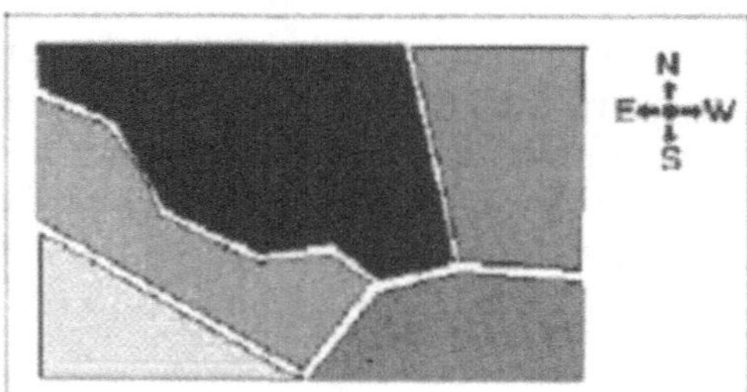

Fig.1. Space as a puzzle where each peace is a spatial video object.

A still image or a video frame collects visual information on a specific geographical area. These images can be naturally indexed to that area in a graphical way by drawing a representation of its spatial distribution (covering area) on a background map or image with a known geographical description.

Once we have enough video captures to cover the surrounding space, it is possible to use the video-space content as the background for several different visual experiments. We can use it as an exploratory tool to search, travel along, or visualize elements present on those videos. We can use it to compose geo-referenced outputs from a spatial simulation process (for example, to visualize a forest fire evolution projected on the video images of the forest). We can also use it to augment reality by superimposing virtual objects, like buildings, dams, or any other 3D structure on the video images.

3 Implementation

There are two main inter-related stages to develop spatial video information systems such as those proposed herein: The *Data Structuring Stage* and the *Exploration Stage*.

3.1 The Data Structuring Stage

The implementation process is based on a basic assumption: an image, whether alone or extracted from a video file, represents spatial data that can be geographically referenced.

The Background Image

A background image (typically a map or an aerial photo) describing the space content is used to facilitate the video spatial indexing process. This background image is also relevant to the *Exploration Stage*.

Composing Spatial Videos

To introduce a new video in the system, a line is drawn on the background surface (Fig. 2). Each drawn line represents an image (if a single image is selected) or a stream of images (when the selected file is a video file). For video files, this line also represents the path along which the video was captured (Fig. 2. (1)), and reproduces the video image stream.

In the implemented prototype, videos and images can be previously picked from a selection box and visualized using a display video window (see Fig. 6).

The Data Structure

Each video-frame image captures a section of a geographical space depending on the camera properties (zoom, lens) and the cameraperson abilities.

Dividing the line in a number of sections equal to the number of frames of the video, each section will represent one frame (Fig. 2. (3)). Selecting one of those sections on the background map will retrieve the corresponding video frame. The content of that frame can then be visualized on the video display window.

In ideal video capture conditions the central axis of each frame will coincide with a different section on the drawn line. These conditions depend on the camera's displacement. The capture should be done in a perpendicular way to the prevailing movement direction.

Automatic capture procedures following principles like the ones present in the moviemaps system [5, 6] would be ideal. Moviemps allows a complete frame flow control once videos are captured along pre-defined routes and filmed with a stop-frame camera triggered by distance rather than by time. With this system, frames become automatically equally distributed over space and quite stables in terms of pointing orientation. A GPS system for automatic video-frame spatial indexation would also improve the data accuracy for spatial distribution.

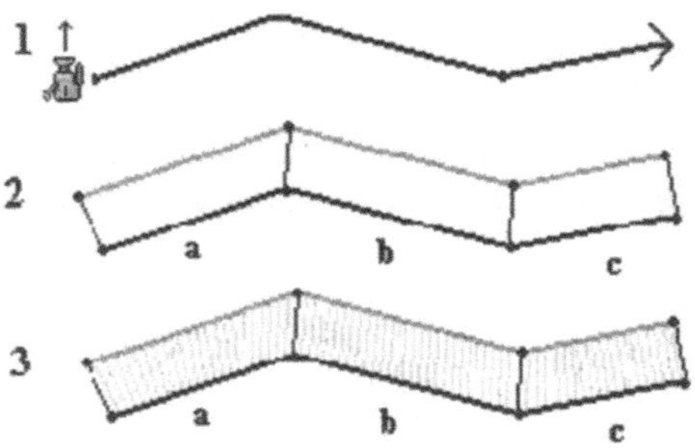

Fig. 2. (1) The video captures Path. (2) The main capture sections. (3) Automatic distribution of the video frames along the space.

Shaping the Video on Space: The Video Covered Area

While the background surface, where video and image-lines are displayed, should represent a top-bottom view, indexed videos usually represent horizontal captures. In a horizontal capture, the area covered by each image goes from the point where the capture camera is until the end line of the landscape or until some obstacle is reached (a mountain or a building). Applying this principle to each frame, we get the covered area for that video.

To define the covered area of a video we use a set of control points. Each point represents a different video-frame (control images). Manipulating those points it is possible to define the extension of the covered area along the video path (Fig.3). The covered area should go straight on from the capture path line until some occluding obstacle is reached (Fig. 4). Occluded areas should be captured in another video from the opposite side of the obstacles, until the entire scenario is covered.

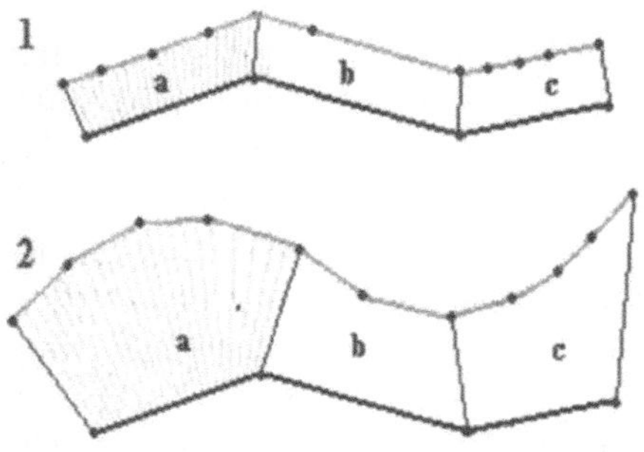

Fig. 3. Using the video line control-points to define the video coverage area.

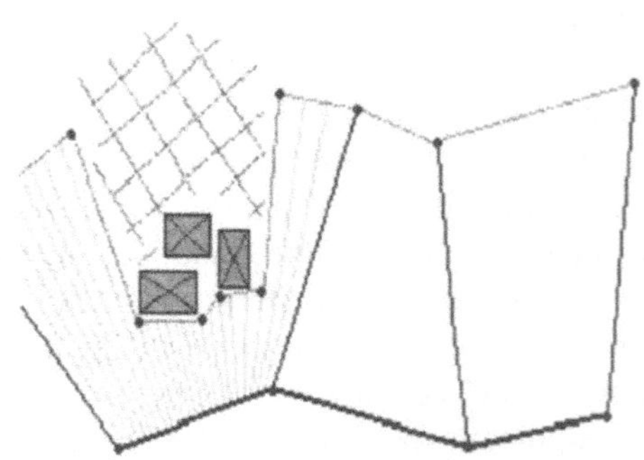

Fig. 4. The image covers exactly the area from the capture point to the existing buildings in front.

Spatial Video-Frame Corrections

Once ideal conditions are difficult to reproduce and sophisticated equipment is not always available, some manual corrections can be performed along the camera path line. These corrections are useful whenever captures are hand-made. In these instances, camera displacements from the perpendicular may occur often.

To perform these corrections, other control points can be introduced and manipulated in order to correct the frame distribution along the line.

When pointing to an object that is referenced in the background map and that is inside some video covered area, the corresponding frame for that point is automatically selected and displayed on the video display window. If the content of any selected video frame reports the same information that is referenced in the background control map, then we reach to the correct video frame distribution along the line (Fig. 5). If not, we have to readjust or introduce some new control points until we get a satisfactory correspondence. This test should be performed on several different points along the camera path until we get a satisfactory video frame distribution with coherent image content correspondence with the content of the background map.

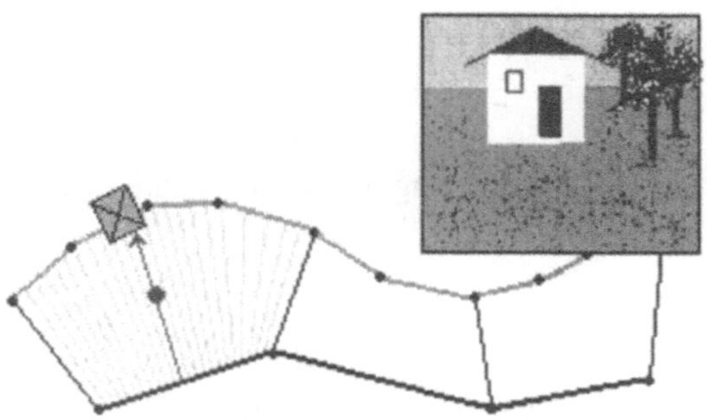

Fig. 5. Achieving the correct correspondence between the selected point in the background and the retrieved video frame for that point.

Automatic Capture Procedures

Ideal capture situations are those where human intervention is minimized, especially if that process allows automatic frame indexation and spatial distribution along the cameras capture path.

The ideal situation can be achieved in a continuo top-view capture from a camera on a plane and connected to a GPS devise. With the GPS data we get the exact position for each frame along the capture path. We can also clearly now the exact image covering range by reading the corresponding height coordinate from the GPS record. Fig.6 shows the projection of the frame distribution diagram resulting from a camera attach to a plane that is flying at different altitudes.

This diagram is slightly different from those represented before. Hear the covered image extends from the central point (the projection of the capture point on the path line) to both sides. Nevertheless, the image axis is still represented by the perpendicular line to the cameras movement along the capture path.

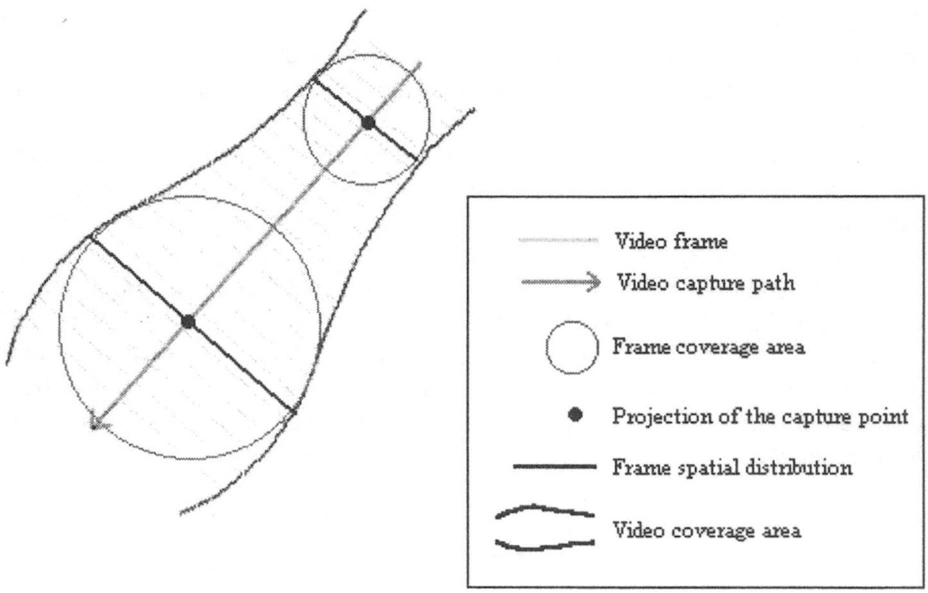

Fig. 6. – The video coverage area along the camera's path in a top-view captures.

3.2 The Exploration Stage

The data exploration stage is where users explore and interact with the visual data. With the presented structure, the data retrieval process is basically a natural consequence of the video spatial organization performed on the first stage.

Exploring Space

Once all videos have been spatially distributed over the background map, we just have to drag the mouse over the map to explore the space. For each selected point, the system will automatically retrieve the image or the video-frame indexed to that point and shows it on the video display window. To do that, the system will first detect to which video belongs the covered area we are pointing to. Once the video is found, the system uses the relative position of each selected point inside the video coverage area to retrieve the frame where those points belong.

If the aim is not a simple exploratory operation but the composition and visualization of some results from a spatial simulation process, the exploratory process is similar to the one described above, except for the point selection process. Now, the selected point is retrieved, not by a mouse 'click' on the map, but, for example, from some selected simulation object which position depends on the simulation evolution.

Overlapping Videos

When traveling on the "information surface" (the background maps with video-lines drawn on it), we may cross over points where several visual records have been introduced – basically, this means that the same point was captured by different videos. The system keeps the reference of which video has been tracked before reaching an area covered by overlapping videos.. If the tracked video is one of the overlapping ones, the system just keeps on it. In this way, it is possible to following a video documented track, even if it is constantly crossed with other existing visual information for the same points. This property allows a smooth traveling experience even in systems with large amounts of overlapping data.

Traveling on Space and Time

It is easy to imagine a collection of pictures or videos from the same place but collected at different hours, days or years. The slider on the Spatial Analysis on Multiple Video System prototype may be used to travel on videos and images that have the same space reference but correspond to different time captures. This capability also allows selecting a time interval and traveling in space only through videos that fit that interval.

4 Browsing on Interactive Digital Video: An Illustrative Example

A computer prototype applying this methodology was implemented and tested on a visual database application as a tool for video and image spatial exploration. Fig.7 reproduces the interface of hat prototype where five main components may be identified. These components are the *video selection box*, the *video display box*, the *drawing toolbox*, the *drawing surface* and the *command bar*.

A background image (for geographical reference) is imported using the *Import image* option from the bottom's *command bar*. Videos are selected, one at a time, from the *video box* and, using the *draw* option from the *toolbox*, the corresponding line is drawn on the *drawing surface* following some specific path on the background image. The area covered by each video can now be adjusted to the background image by moving the control points that are displayed with the drown video-line (see Fig. 8). The stronger lines are the capture paths and the related thin lines are the correspondent control point lines. Each color corresponds to an individual video capture. It is possible to explore the area using the *explore* option. Pressing the left button of the mouse and moving it on the drawing surface does that. As we move the mouse, the image corresponding to each position is calculated and displayed on the *video display box*.

The proposed structure allows navigation facilities through different video files. In this example, if each side of a road is captured on a different video, users can travel directly from the video frame that covers the right side view to the video frame corresponding to the left side view just by crossing the road with the mouse.

For exploratory proposes the actual prototype version supports AVI and MPEG video files as well single BMP image files. For composition procedures of objects or simulation results on video images, AVI video files are required.

A continuous mouse movement on the background map retrieves a sequence of images from several different sources (still images and video images). These images can be composed in a new output video representing the selected exploratory path.

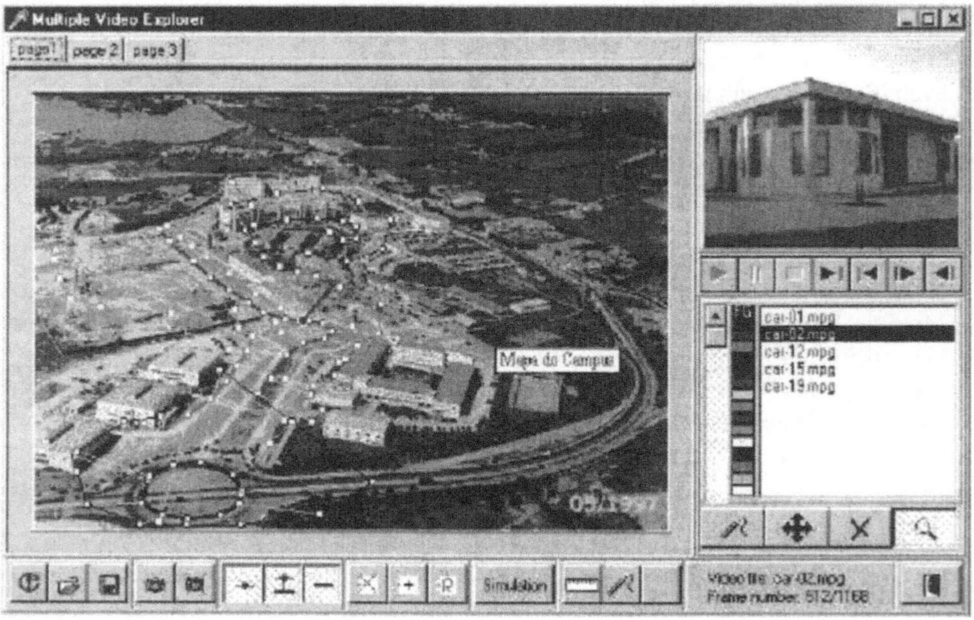

Fig. 7. Example of a spatial multiple video composition covering the College of Sciences and Technology of the New University of Lisbon, Portugal.

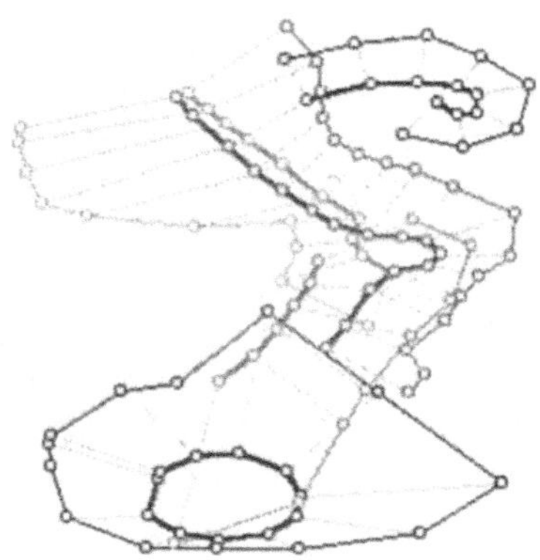

Fig. 8. Detail of the spatial distribution of video lines and their covering area shown on Fig. 7.

5 Guidelines to Future Work: 3D Modeling and Virtual Object Composition

Another application of this methodology is the ability to compose virtual objects on real video images. Having ensured the correct correspondence between the video-frame content and the schematic top-view 2D scenario, any virtual object placed on that scenario can be correctly projected on each video frame. Once we are able to freely travel along the video images trough the 2D representation of the area, we can explore virtual objects that have been placed on that scenario.

Capture-depth: the fourth dimension

Objects are usually geo-referenced using the three main coordinate axes (the X, Y and Z-axis). Time may be introduced as an additional coordinate to introduce temporal variations and allow time evolution. In the present system, to connect synthetic spatial data with real world images captured in a collection of digital videos, a new dimension is introduced. This dimension is the capture-depth of a point. The capture-depth of a point is the distance from the point's geographical position and the camera's position from where the video-frame that covers that area was captured.

This capture-depth information is crucial to perform the correct projection of a synthetic point in the corresponding video image. In the same way, by projecting all points describing any synthetic object in the current image, it is possible to compose complex 3D objects on the video stream to produce the desirable realistic output solution. When exploring the space, the capture-depth of each point has to be recalculated for each new position so we can explore different projections of the same object on images captured from different points of view (different images from the same video or from different videos).

Real environments (captured on the video images), whether they represent natural or humanized landscapes, usually present topographic irregularities that can vary from almost imperceptible variations to ones that are easily noticeable. For most situations, the introduction of height on the cameras capture path is fundamental to achieve the correct projection of virtual data in the video frames. The connection to a GIS or the use of a GPS may provide the additional topographic information required to obtain the correct camera's path.

The Viewing Pyramid: The perspective transformation

Any real world video frame picture is a projection of a 3D world into a 2D plane. Each point of the 2D plane corresponds to the precise mathematical projection of another point from the Real World environment. The formula for this projection depends on the prevailing viewing pyramid. The viewing pyramid defines the portion of eye-coordinate space, which the viewer can actually see [3, 4]. In a video capture situation it defines the portion of the camera-vision-coordinate space captured in a picture that depends mainly on the camera's capture conditions (zoom and lens).

Each set of camera conditions defines a different viewing pyramid. Keeping the same capture conditions, we get the same viewing pyramid for all the captured sequences.

According to Newman&Sproull [3] we can convert world coordinates into dimensionless fractions. As we probably do not know the camera conditions, a manual parameter to control those dimensionless fractions was implemented. The control ratio works as follows: an object is placed in the 2D background in a well known geographical position (for example, placing an object with the shape of a house in the top of the drawing where the house is represented). The system retrieves the image that covers the place and projects the object on it (in the central axis of the image). If the viewing pyramid is correct, the object will fit the house. If not, it will be displayed bigger or smaller than it should be. In this situation, we can move the manual control to up and down until the object fits the image of the house. When it fits, we reach the right value that characterizes this particular viewing pyramid.

Object Composition

If an object is placed in the 2D scenario in a point covered by some spatial video-line, the system will automatically retrieves the corresponding video frame that fits that point. It will also retrieve the distance between that point and the point from where the selected video frame was captured (the capture-depth). Knowing the capture-depth, the viewing pyramid (camera's capture conditions) and the frame related to the objects' position, it is possible to compose the object on the right position of that frame (which means, the right position on a real world picture) (Fig. 9).

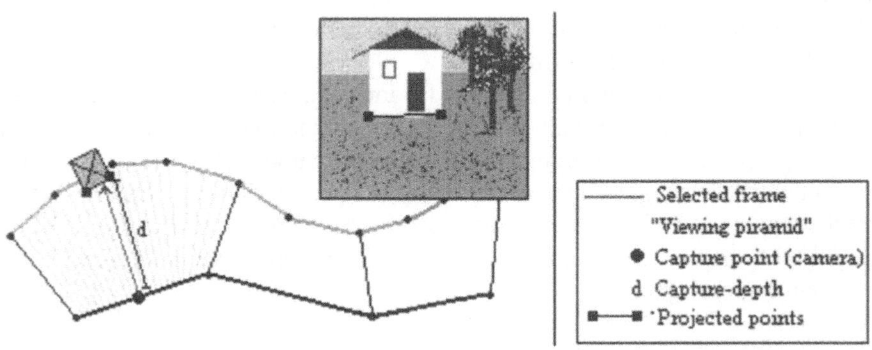

Fig. 9. Composing synthetic points on a video image.

If the object is a 3D model composed by a set of points, each one of them will present a different capture-depth. Applying the viewing pyramid calculated for that video, it is easy to project each object point in the selected image (the wire-frame). Thus, the object points will be projected in the image incorporating the required depth and the perspective corrections.

Once the object's wire-frame is projected on the image, the realistic representation of the object on the video image depends only on a set of operations to apply the correct textures, shading and other image effects procedures. These procedures well known computer graphic applications and will not be discussed here. The composition of different objects placed on the background scenario and projected in the same image is treated as discussed before. When dealing with different objects, knowing the exact position where they have been placed in the background scenario, it is also possible to simulate the occlusion of some objects by other objects and hidden-surface elimination.

Moving the object, or the viewing-point, a new frame will be selected as well as a new capture-depth for the new viewpoint and, consequently, a new perspective of the object will be composed on the selected frame.

6 Main Limitations

The main limitations of this system are related to the techniques involved in the video capture processes, particularly with respect to homogeneity and continuity. These are the most difficult issues, mainly if it is not possible to control the capture process.

The system will assume that all the video has been captured on a single shot and with a uniform movement camera. This means that its possible to access a frame representing some particular spatial position just knowing the corresponding fraction of the drawn line representing the video on that place. With a non-uniform movement of the camera during the capture (i.e. the cameramen moving faster, slower or paused), some delays or advances can occur and the selected image that was supposed to represent a particular point-of-view may correspond to another slightly different one. A possible solution to this problem is to pre-decompose each video into smaller uniform clips. A better solution is to use a stop-frame camera triggered by distance like in the Movimaps system.

Another video capture problem is related to the cameraperson's movements. Even if he or she moves at a constant speed, some rotation movement may be executed (as if it was moving in a car but moving the camera from one side to another). Again, this may result in no coordination between the geographical position and the resulting retrieved image for that point. Nevertheless, this problem can be easily solved using the system tools by compensating the camera's "abnormal" movement with the control points of the video-drowned line. This is a manual process that can be done using the video display to control and confirm the line adjustment.

7 Conclusions

The system proposed herein was developed to organize and display geo-referenced videos that cover an area of interest. Appropriate capture, retrieval and exploration processes are recommended. An illustrative example of a spatial video browser is presented. Future developments related to 3D modeling and composition of objects on spatial video area also discussed.

References

1. E.Nobre A.S.Câmara: Interactive Ecological Movies. (Internal Report), GASA, DCEA, FCT, UNL, Monte de Caparica, Portugal (1997).
2. E.Nobre A.S.Câmara: Programming by Reproduction. (Internal Report), GASA, DCEA, FCT, UNL, Monte de Caparica, Portugal (1998).
3. William M. Newman, Robert F. Sproull: Principles of Interactive Computer Graphics. McGraw-Hill, New York (1979).
4. J. Foley, A. van Dam, S. Feiner, J. Hughes: Computer Graphics: Principles and Practice. Second Edition in C, Addison-Wesley, Reading, MA (1995).
5. Lippman, A.: Movie-Maps: An Application of the Optical Videodisc to Computer Graphics. Proc. ACM SIGGRAPH (1980).
6. Naimark, M.: A 3D Moviemap and a 3D Panorama. SPIE Proceedings, Vol. 3012, San Jose (1997).
7. A.Gupta, R.Jain,: Visual Information Retrieval. Communications of the ACM, vol. 40, N°5 (May 1997) pp.71-79.
8. R.Lienhart, S.Pfeiffer, W.Effelsberg: Video Abstracting. Communications of the ACM, vol. 40, N°12, (December 1997)
9. B.-L. Yeo, M.M. Yeung,: Retrieving and Visualizing Video. Communications of the ACM /vol. 40, N°12 (December 1997)
10. C.H. Chen, L.F. Pau and P.S.P. Wang, (ed.): Video Content Analysis and Retrieval. Hongjiang Zhang Handbook on Pattern Recognition and Computer Vision (1997)

LIVE@WEB.COM – Using CBIR Technology in Interactive Web-TV

Felix Morsdorf and Stephan Volmer

Fraunhofer IGD, Rundeturmstr. 6, Darmstadt, Germany
{felix.morsdorf,stephan.volmer}@igd.fhg.de

Abstract. The increasing amount of internet based television broadcasts has lead to new approachs to interactivity in TV programs. We developed a system which is able to supply the viewer of the program upon interaction with information relating to the program, only based on the low-level visual content of the scene. This aim is achieved by comparing signatures describing the visual content of single frames of the video with a remote database of signatures derived from known videos. The database actually links the visual information contained in the signatures to some second-level information interesting for the user. Two main problems in extending CBIR technology to videos must be overcome, one is the extraction of the visual information out of the highly redundant video material, and the other is reducing the matching time of the system enough to allow for web-based interactivity.

1 Introduction

The steady improvements in performance of the Internet infrastructure and related technologies (e.g. data compression) now give the opportunity to broadcast films, video, live events (such as sports events, shows and conferences) and even TV programs over the Web with rapidly improving quality. Interactive TV over the Web is gradually becoming a reality and advertising over this new media is becoming increasingly attractive. Unfortunately, current approaches to Interactive TV lead to very high production costs, due to the need to create and maintain explicit links for each TV program with the content making the program itself *interactive*. LIVE@WEB.COM is a system that provides interactivity with the user based on *Content-based Image Retrieval* (CBIR) methods. The system is able to supply the user with additional information regarding the program he just watched (e.g. a URL of a product's webpage), only based on the visual content of the scene. In its first prototype version, the system is restricted on the recognition of commercials, as these are small videos and the interest in enhancing those through interactivity is higher than for normal TV-broadcast.

2 Previous Work

In [3], Kreyß et al. have proposed a system for video retrieval, using shot detection to segment the video material, and then constructing so called *mosaic* images containing all the visual information of the shot. On these static mosaiced images they applied traditional CBIR technology in order to retrieve the shots from a database. This approach is not applicable to the LIVE@WEB.COM scenario, as the mosaicing of the shot would have to be done on the client's computer. As this is a time consuming process, it would not allow for realtime interaction. In this paper a different technique is proposed, which is the use of cluster analysis and key frames, which only relies on the extraction of signatures from *single* frames. Other existing video retrieval systems have been established mainly for archiving and browsing in large video databases, but not for an interactive environment over the web, as the LIVE@WEB.COM scenario proposes.

3 System Architecture

The following three modules compose the LIVE@WEB.COM system:

Video Player This module includes the functionality needed to receive TV programs on the Web, accessible by the users via a standard Internet browser, for instance, as a plugin. It also enables the user to interact with the TV program to select frames in the video and to store them for later replay or further examination. The video player is shown in Fig. 1, with the bookmarks set by the user as thumbnails on the right.

Fig. 1. The Video Player

Matching Engine This module leverages mainly upon image analysis technologies that extract significant features from the videos automatically. The main characteristic of this technology is its capability to represent those key features in an

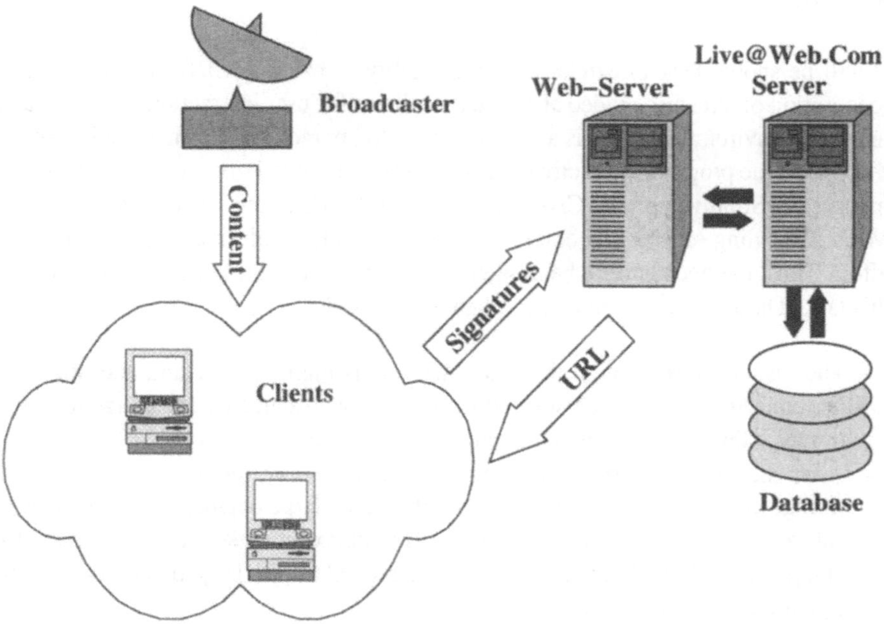

Fig. 2. LIVE@WEB.COM System Architecture

extremely compact signature. The Matching Engine also includes the algorithms which are needed to compare signatures in terms of their similarity concerning those visual features. That way, the video database can be searched by matching the signature of a query image with the signatures of the videos in the database.

Video Database The videos database contains all the videos that are to be linked via the LIVE@WEB.COM system with all the relevant information and links to relevant URLs. Together with each video, there are a number of different signatures stored in the database. Those signatures represent the visual features of the videos and make them distinguishable among all other videos in the database. The videos database comes along with a web-based administration module.

In Fig. 3 a sketch representing the LIVE@WEB.COM server architecture is shown. The Broadcaster provides the client's computers with the streaming video, and is completely independent from the rest of the system. The LIVE@WEB.COM Video Player is installed on the client's computer and provides the interactivity by extracting signatures on user interaction from the video stream and sending those to the LIVE@WEB.COM Server for comparison with the video database and linking of the information. The Video Player parses the information returning from the LIVE@WEB.COM Server, and opens, for instance, a web browser on the client's computer showing a relevant product information page.

4 Innovation

It will be shown how to extend the functionality of existing CBIR technology to the recognition of streaming video at a time that allows for user interaction in an interactive television environment. This is a new approach to interactive TV, since the information that makes the program interactive does not have to be coded manually in the broadcasting stream. Simply applying CBIR technology to the data rich video material (ca. 1-10 MB/s depending on size and colordepth) would surely result in a large computational effort. Thus, methods have to be implemented to minimize the computational effort for this task. These methods can be classified in two fields:

- The visual information in the video material is highly redundant, and thus has to be reduced by some sophisticated means, as for instance by the extraction of key frames, which contain the dominant visual information of a scene.
- After the visual information is extracted, it has to be indexed in some way for storage and retrieval, as a linear search through a large database of the feature signatures would be too time consuming. This indexing makes the comparison time independent of the database size, which is crucial for the large databases of feature signatures we have for videos.

Using both of these methods allows for the implementation of a system that recognises videos in less than 1 second based on a first prototype database containing more than 100 videos. At this speed the system is interactive for an internet based environment.

5 The CBIR Methodology

A variety of visual features can be used for CBIR, based on previous work from [7] two different feature signatures are used in the LIVE@WEB.COM first prototype. One is a colour histogram, which resembles the global colour information, the second is a wavelet fingerprint, which contains the spatial information of the image.

As we need small signature sizes for storing and computation of similarities, the feature signatures for a frame of arbitrary size are restricted to a size less than 512 bytes. The largest advantage of using only small sized signatures for comparison is the ability of having this data transferred over the internet at very short times, even for low bandwidths. The comparison of the signatures of two different frames yields a score, telling how *similar* the particular frames are in respect to this specific visual feature. A detailed description on how the signatures are extracted from the frames, and how their similarity is computed, can be found in detail in [7] and more general in [5],[6].

6 Reducing the Video to Images

On interaction from the user, the LIVE@WEB.COM Video Player extracts feature signatures of n single frames, which were held in a special buffer. These frames need not be consecutive frames, as using a sample interval of approx. 1 second significantly increases the visual information contained in frames, as opposed to using 5 consecutive frames at a sample rate of $1/25$ of a second. The number and sampling of the frames is empirically selected. Thus, the problem of matching videos is reduced to matching $x \times n$ single signatures of the n frames to a database of signatures from the frames of the videos, where x is the number of used feature signatures. In order to keep the computational effort on the client's computer as small as possible (we have no specific information about the hardware on the client's side), no sophisticated method of selecting key frames and/or motion based features is used. The effort in reducing the large amount of data from the videos is solely accomplished on the LIVE@WEB.COM server side, by the means described in the following sections.

6.1 Shot Detection

The approach of recognising video sequences by using CBIR methods on single frames has one big shortcome which must be overcome: the large amount of data that has to be matched if all frames are stored in the reference database. As we pointed out before, the video material is highly redundant, and thus means have to be implemented in order to reduce the large amount of data. The first step is the partitioning of the video in scenes of similar visual content, as for instance via shot detection. This shot-detection is mostly accomplished by tracking the change of one global visual feature. As a comparison of two signatures generates a score determining how close two frames are to each other in the particular feature space, we can track the size of this score (a scalar) in order to detect scene changes. A threshold is used to detect changes in this property, which are candidates for a shot boundary. S_i denotes the signature of the ith frame, and δ is the function for calculating the similarity of two signatures as described in [7]. The similarity value SD_i is zero for identical values and increases with dissimilarity.

$$SD_i = \delta(S_i, S_{i+1}) \text{ with } SD_i \in \mathbb{R}_0^+ \quad (1)$$

A new shot is detected if the difference SD_i is larger than a given threshold. The selection of this threshold is the crucial point in shot detection and has to be optimized empirically. In Fig. 3 an example is given of how these similarity values look for one commercial. In the upper panel, the Color Histogram signature is shown, in the lower the Wavelet Signature. Large peaks indicate abrupt shot changes (*hard cuts*), the numbers mark shot change candidates determined by a threshold with twice the size of the standard deviation. As this method does not take into account any *salient* change in the visual content during the shots and fails to detect shot boundaries if fade effects and transitions are used, we propose the use of unsupervised clustering for key frame extraction, as presented by [10].

6.2 Key Frame Extraction

After the partitioning, so called key frames are extracted from the shot, which are taken as a prototype for the visual content of the scene. Normally one would use for instance the first and the last frame of the scene. This method has the disadvantage of not taking

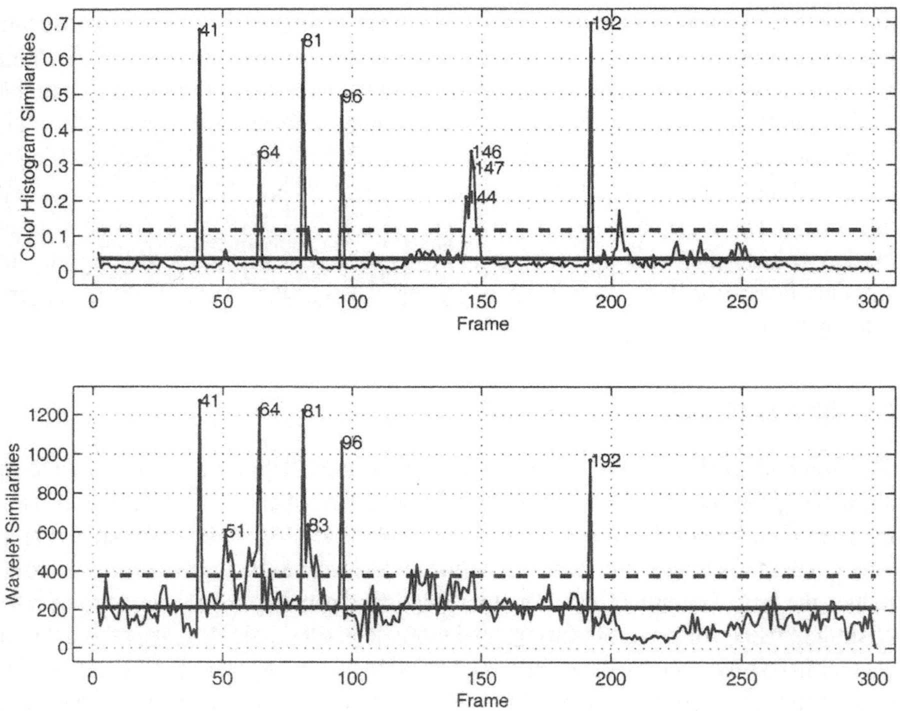

Fig. 3. Thresholding of similarities of consecutive frames for the Color-Histogram (top) and for the Wavelet Signature (bottom). The mean is indicated by the thick solid line, the standard deviation of this mean by the thick dashed line.

into account any changes of the visual content *during* the scene. Furthermore, the first and the last frames of a shot are mostly not stable, and thus not a good representative for the shot. Opposed to key frame extraction for archiving or browsing, where key frames should represent some important *semantic* aspect of the scene [4], the extraction of key frames for content based video retrieval needs to be tuned towards the capturing of the most important low-level visual content, as described by the feature signatures used for the retrieval. This means that the key frames need to cover the area in feature space spanned by *all* frames of teh video as well as possible. Thus, we propose the use of an adaptive key frame extraction using unsupervised clustering, as presented in [10]. In this approach, as many key frames from each shot are selected as needed to describe its visual complexity, for shots with no or a small amount of action this would be only one key frame, but for shots with a lot of action and/or global motion resulting in optical flow, several key frames are selected.

7 Indexing the Database

In [8] a method is proposed of efficiently indexing the database containing the signatures of the key frames, based on the visual features that the signatures represent, using a *k-Medians* clustering algorithm. The indexing yields a matching time of a query frame with the database, which is not dependent on the total database size. The matching time depends only on the size and number of the clusters, that are being used for the signature comparison. This enables the use of this system for arbitrarily large databases of signatures. For very large databases, there will be a trade off between comparison time and retrieval accuracy. This will have to be carefully evaluated as the database population of our first prototype grows.

8 Rejection of Unknown Videos

The concept of similarity yields only the return of the *closest* match on comparing a query frame with the database. Thus, if we want to avoid misleading answers from the LIVE@WEB.COM Server on presentation of an *unknown* video, we need to define a criterion to differ known videos from unknown ones. One way would be the use of the information on *how* close the match was based on the similarity computation. Technically, this can be achieved by using a hardcoded threshold on the similarity values returned from the comparison; if the value is below that certain threshold, the queried frame is match, otherwise it is declared as not known. Unfortunately, the choice of a threshold is crucial and has to be optimized in two opposing directions, as can be seen from Fig. 4.

The recognition reliability for unknown videos (*recognition = classified as unknown*) decreases with increasing threshold size, whereas the recognition reliability for known videos increases. Thus, a compromise in setting the threshold has to be made. If both cases (known video and unknown video) had the same probability, one would choose the intersection of the two curves. But for our scenario, we would in the best case know only 20% of the TV program, the commercials, and hence the threshold has to be pushed to the left to acommodate for the four times higher probability of unknown videos. The selected threshold is indicated by the dashed vertical line. In the first prototype with its relatively small database, this is not a big issue, but as the population of the database will grow, methods have to be implemenented to overcome this shortcome. As we use not one, but n frames for querying, we propose the use of some heuristics, which takes the consecutive order of the frames into account.

9 Results and Conclusion

The first prototype of the system is capable of recognising known videos from a small database of 100 videos in less than a second, and is able to supply the user with the relevant information. The layout of the video player frontend was shown in Fig. 1. During the broadcast, the user is able to click several times in order to set *bookmarks* (thumbnails on the right), and after the broadcast ended (or whenever he desires), he may send the signatures to the LIVE@WEB.COM Server. On correct identification of the query

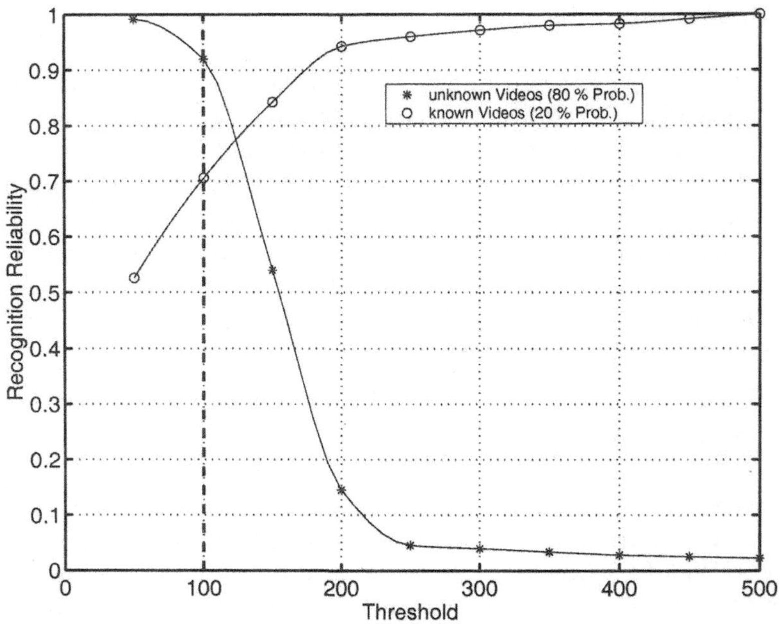

Fig. 4. Recognition Reliability in Respect to Threshold Value

frames, a response containing a URL is sent back to the client's machine, where the LIVE@WEB.COM Video Player opens a web browser window with this specific URL (Fig. 5).

As the database population grows, the above cited methods are becoming more and more important and some fine tuning will be important in order to achieve the projected aims of having a database with more than 5000 videos. We have shown that it is possible to extend CBIR technology to video material without defining special video features, that would for instance include motion based algorithms. The key task in setting up such a system is managing the large amount of data in the video, and this can be achieved by the methods we proposed. First, key frame extraction in the feature domain via clustering guarantees an optimal compromise in reducing the data *and* keeping the relevant visual information. Second, an indexing of the feature signature database allows for fast comparison times applicable for interactive enviroments.

Acknowledgements

This work was supported by the European Commission with the IST Project #12277 LIVE@WEB.COM .

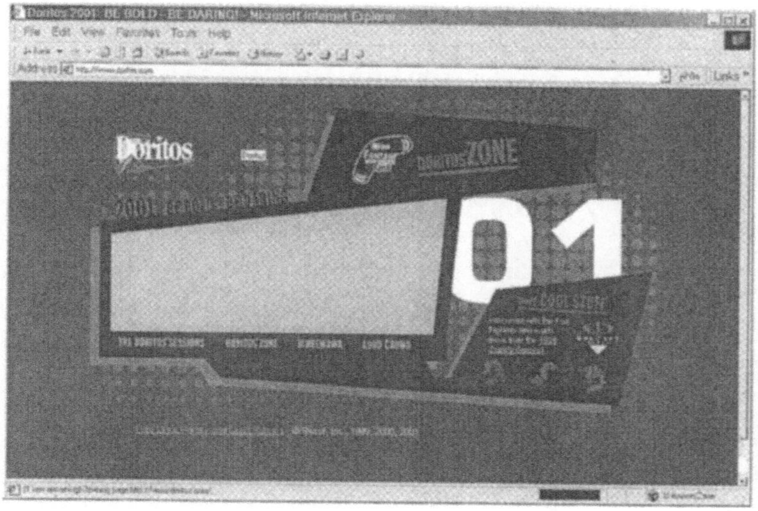

Fig. 5. Web Browser with Product Homepage

References

1. Aigrain, P., Zhang, H.J.,Petkovic, D.: Content-based Representation and Retrieval of Visual Media: A State-of-the-Art Review. *Multimedia Tools and Applications*, 3(3):179–202, July 1996.
2. Herzog, O. , Miene, A. , Hermes, T. , Alshuth, P.: Integrated Information Mining for Texts, Images, and Videos. *Computers & Graphics*, 22(6):675–685, December 1998.
3. Kreyß, J. , Röper, M. , Alshuth, P. , Hermes, Th. , Herzog, O.: Video Retrieval by Still Image Analysis with ImageMiner. In *Storage and Retrieval for Image and Video Databases V*, vol. 3022, pp. 36–44. SPIE, San Jose, USA, February 1997.
4. Macer, P., Thomas, P.: Browsing Video Content. *Proceedings of BCS HCI Group Conference, The Active Web*, Staffordshire University, UK., January 1999
5. Pass, G., Zabih, R.: Comparing Images Using Joint Histograms. *ACM Journal of Multimedia Systems*, 7(3):234–240, May 1999.
6. Swain, M.J., Ballard, D.H.: Colour Indexing. *Int. Journal of Computer Vision*, 7(1): 11-32,1991
7. Volmer, S.: Tracing Images in Large Databases by Comparison of Wavelet Fingerprints. In *Proc. of the 2nd Int'l Conf. on Visual Information Systems*, pp. 163–172, La Jolla, USA, December 1997.
8. Volmer, S.: Buoy Indexing of Metric Feature Spaces for Fast Approximate Image Queries. To appear in *Proc. of the 6th Eurographics Workshop on Multimedia*, Manchester, UK, September 2001.
9. Zhang, H.J., Kankanhalli, A., Smoliar, S.W.: Automatic Partitioning of Full Motion Video. *Multimedia Systems*, 1(1):10–28, June 1993.
10. Zhuang, Y., Rui, Y., Huang, T., Mehrotra, S.: Adaptive Key Frame Extraction Using Unsupervised Clustering. In *Proc. of IEEE Int'l Conf. on Image Processing*, pp. 866–870, Chicago, USA, October 1998.

2BeOn - Interactive Television Supporting Interpersonal Communication

Jorge Abreu, Pedro Almeida, Vasco Branco

Department of Communication and Art, University of Aveiro
3810-193 Aveiro, Portugal
{jfa, almeida, vab}@ca.ua.pt

Abstract. Interpersonal communication mediated by computer services supports the reinforcement and emergence of new communities brought together by leisure or work interests. This paper presents a workbench system that aims to study how the same principle can be applied in interactive television. The main objective is to allow TV users to be online (2BeOn) through the integration of basic and advanced communication services, enabling them to reinforce their interpersonal communication. The 2BeOn system is based on four core components: user tracking, communication services, interface engine and collaboration content/interaction tracing. In addition to the social and behavioural context of the system, its conceptualisation, prototyping and evaluation are addressed.

1. Introduction

The interconnection of networks, on which the Internet was based, had the major objective of linking individuals from separate networks, enabling them to 'talk' with each other and to share information. This last goal was the first to become largely implemented through development of the World Wide Web. Also, through the diversity of supported applications, interpersonal communication services have now established major significance by complementing or even substituting other traditional communication practices. One example of this is the mass adoption of Instant Messaging (IM) services that have probably grown faster than any communication medium in history; AOL claims 100 million registrations [1], ICQ reports an identical number [2] and other providers such as Yahoo and Microsoft also contribute to a huge number of connected users.

The development of network access technologies has enabled a wide use of communication services through a broad range of devices, such as mobile phones, palm tops, handheld PCs and even television in its interactive format. The increasing adoption of online interpersonal communication services, through different access devices, may reflect the user's eagerness to be able to tele-communicate anytime and anywhere.

The 2BeOn name emerges from this context, reflecting the general purpose of the system and expressing the idea of enabling TV users 'To Be Online', communicating through TV mediated communication tools. The aim is to use the system, as a workbench, to study several technological, communicational and social topics related to the use of interpersonal communication processes and services, in interrelation with broadcast TV.

Despite all the hype surrounding Interactive Television (ITV), there is a considerable research gap in this specific area. Jaaskelainem [3] states that the main academic research streams are concerned with technical issues of delivering video-on-demand and with the field of interactive instructional television. Loes de Vos also supports this idea when she refers to ITV research reports [4] '*... those that do have value are hardly made public and not readily shared with other producers of ITV*'.

The system is being developed by a multidisciplinary team with different but intersecting research areas: ITV[1] and telework. However, the purpose of this paper is to highlight and focus on ITV. Nevertheless, section 5 demonstrates how the core conceptualisation of the system, complemented with targeted features, is applied to the telework area.

2. Interactive Television Context

TV users are more and more confronted with a myriad of information sources due to the higher number of digital channels and to the availability of on-line data.

In such a scenario, television is losing its role as a promoter of social ties [6], since users, when absorbed by this overload of information, may neglect their interpersonal relationships. This problem does not seem to be directly related to the surplus of information, but mainly to the absence of a common reference point usually associated with the establishment of a conversation between peers. The lack of this common referential is connected to the information on demand paradigm: when the information on offer is so widely segmented, the probability of seeing what the other person saw permanently decreases [6].

Nevertheless, this issue can be seen from another point of view, where the segmentation of the information, namely in the television arena, may promote a deeper relationship between members of micro communities that share the same interests and, thus, consume the same type of information.

These two perspectives can be understood as a paradoxical situation: from one side the interpersonal relationships could be fragmented and, for the other, intensified [7].

However, it seems there is a valid solution that applies to both approaches, reducing the negative aspects and enhancing the positive ones: the convergence of communication services and television. This blend can offer people the opportunity and the possibility to discuss at any time a common theme, such as a TV program that is being watched.

In this context, a system like 2BeOn is expected to promote communication in existing communities or to create new ones (supported by common references such as TV programs or by sharing specific video contents owned by each user).

---

[1] Although the definition of interactive television is not yet stabilized, our proposal considers the supply of basic and advanced communication services via TV, so it fits one possible format of interactive television [5].

2.1 Research Objectives

In a broad sense, our research in the ITV arena aims to design and integrate online communication services and to understand how users can exploit them when watching TV, engaged in leisure or information activities. The selection of the basic and advanced communication services and their interrelation is oriented towards the promotion of interpersonal communication.

The research also seeks answers to the following questions:

- What is the best approach for integration of communication services in order to cope with the technical limitations of TV as an output terminal?
- What is the role of TV content as a common reference point in the establishment of conversations?
- What is the impact of the proliferation of communication services on TV consumption from the perspective of the user's involvement between these two types of activities?
- How can the availability of mass communication services help to counteract the tendency of TV audiences to fragment and to reinforce socialisation between communities of interest?

2.2 Practical Applications Scenarios

The emerging platforms of ITV are basically oriented towards the supply of information on-demand (video, TV background information, news) and the access to dedicated services (like home shopping or home banking), but not to the promotion of interpersonal communication. Nevertheless, solid discussion centred on real time television viewing, or even on last night's show, can be maintained through these new formats of television, leading to a reinforcement of our sense of community. This principle is even more important in scenarios where tens or even hundreds of TV channels are available, where the paradoxical situation (fragmentation/intensification of interpersonal relationships) tends to be more accentuated.

It is in this context that the 2BeOn system applies to the ITV domain, by integrating adaptable means of transmission of typical forms of communication, enabling people to be in live contact during a TV show (either by IM, chat, voice and video communications) and allowing collaborative TV program recommendations.

The field of application of the system is very wide; nevertheless it seems appropriate to describe two main practical applications:

1. One of the core components of the system (see section 3) is the user tracking module, which enables users to check if other peers are online and if they are watching the same TV program (for example, a talk show). Such information can be an added incentive to establishing personal contacts; it will be more likely that people comment on a TV program as they watch it. Thus, if the user wants to contact a friend, he or she only has to click on that person's name and choose the required service via an opened mini-menu. If the communication service is based on the interchange of text messages, the system can continuously adjust the size of the TV and text areas. This feature can be used to measure the degree of the users' involvement in the dialogue.

2. A user is watching a TV program that he thinks would be interesting for a certain friend, who is not online or is watching a different channel with his or her status configured to 'please do not disturb'. The user can then decide to send a TV Program Recommendation (TVPR): so he or she simply clicks on the friend's name and chooses this option. Automatically, a segment of that program is recorded, sent and attached to a predefined message. In addition, it is also possible to add a text or voice annotation. The addressee is warned (by a clip-email) of that TV program recommendation, either immediately or, if off line, the next time he or she logs in.

The 2BeOn system is not considered by itself as a full ITV platform. The system is being developed as a workbench to test the conceptualisation of solutions that may eventually be applicable to and integrated within an existing ITV system.

3. System Conceptualisation and Prototyping

For the purpose of this research, commercial ITV solutions that could provide platforms for studying the topics referred to above were taken into consideration. However, these did not have the required functionality and flexibility to support the desired integration of communication services into TV. This established a strong need to prototype and develop the 2BeOn system.

For conceptualisation of the system, several contributing factors were taken into consideration:

- The identification and parameterisation of the users' communication mechanisms and the methodology that enables their transmission for such convergent environments;
- The technical limitations of the output devices and the social constraints associated with the home as the primary place for their use;
- The definition of the software agents which allow automatic correspondence between the implemented communication services in order to provide specific answers to the user's needs or requests.

The prototype in development involves interdisciplinary research contributed by complementary work teams: services and systems engineering (set side box prototyping, database and network communication support), interaction design and communications studies.

Some specific features, such as particular information supplied from user tracking (see section 3.1), the TVPR (included in the set of communication services), automatic adaptation of the interface and interaction tracing, underline the differences between 2BeOn's and existing commercial ITV platforms. Another distinction is that 2BeOn can lead us to a new television experience, even without the need to modify the TV content or produce special web sites to enhance it.

From a schematic point of view, the 2BeOn prototype comprises the following main blocks.

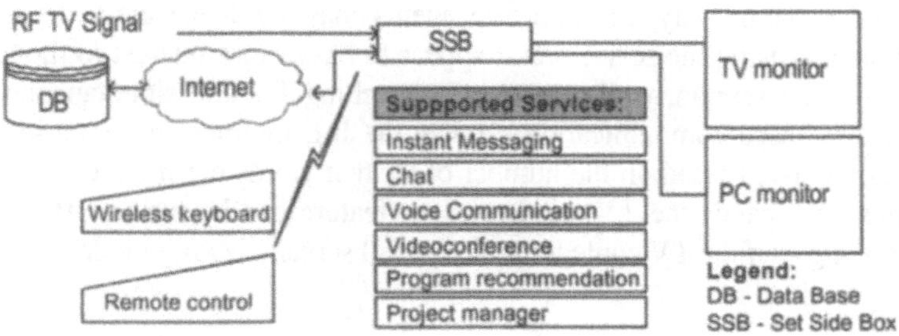

3.1 Core Components

2BeOn integrates general communication and management features that can be applied to different areas. This section describes them from the perspective of ITV.

User tracking. 2BeOn's user tracking module is the main system's core component, dealing with the status of users (who is online, who is in a break, who is watching TV and which channel is tuned – *a user can know what their pals are watching and, if in the mood, start a conversation based on the program they are watching, instead of postponing or even losing that chance*). Because this feature may raise privacy concerns, the system allows users to block all or part of their accessible information. For instance, if users do not want their buddies to know that they are watching a specific channel, they can set up the system to block that information.

Communicational Services. As the main objective of 2BeOn in an ITV scenario is to promote interpersonal communication, synchronous and asynchronous communication services such as voice phone, IM, videoconference, clip-email, e-mail and TVPR are provided. The clip-email feature used in 2BeOn consists of unidirectional or one time bi-directional messages that act as warnings to other users, like SMS in mobile phones, or quick questions with closed answers (yes or no).

The incorporation of synchronous communication services in television is already used by at least two of the main commercial ITV platforms [8, 9]. Nevertheless, they do not supply information about the channels that each buddy is watching. 2BeOn will help to prove if this type of information can be an added value to stimulate the establishment of interpersonal communication. In this context, those services should be considered as having, not only the potential to be used in their traditional way (to put users in contact to discuss whatever they want) [10], but also to start a conversation based on the channel/buddy information supplied by the user tracking module.

Interface engine. The interface engine (InE) aims to enhance the human-computer interaction and deals with automatic features like: prioritisation of icons, based on the frequency of use, organisation of friends/colleagues top lists and tracking of the communication services the user most frequently selects to contact other peers.

In a more dynamic way, the interface agents may influence the communication process by emphasising the services that appear to have more interest to the user. For example, in a chat session, while the user is watching TV and simultaneously is engaged in a text based communication service, the InE monitors the intensity of participation of the user (based on the number of written words per minute) and dynamically shrinks or expands the TV window. This feature can be turned off if the user finds it annoying or if the TV content requires a full screen viewing mode.

Collaboration via content/interaction tracing. The success of a communication-oriented system also depends on the capacity to promote collaboration [11]. The system can contribute to this goal by analysing topics of interest. To identify these topics it uses information from the user's profile and complements it with patterns of interaction with the system: peers contacted, channels viewed or intensity of use of communication services. The user can turn to a search tool to find other users with the same interests or with interests in defined criteria. He or she can also start a conversation based on a query to the system that gives an alert signal when another user with the same interests tunes in to a common TV channel.

3.2 SSB Prototype

The 2BeOn central unit is called Set Side Box (SSB), instead of the traditional concept of Set Top Box (STB), since it is a device that integrates the hardware of a standard Personal Computer (PC), which can still operate in its normal way, and the functions of a typical STB.

The SSB is implemented using off-the-shelf components like a PC, a TV tuner card, a Dual Head Graphic Board (that allows output to TV and also to PC screens) and internal modem, Ethernet card or cable modem to the Internet connection. The client application runs under the Windows Operating System and controls several modules, such as: TV card, user interface (graphic and interaction), wireless input devices, network and database communication, core components and the user's interaction register mechanism.

3.3 Database and network communication

In order to maintain overall access to the system, all users' information and profiles are stored in an online relational database controlled by SQL.

User access is granted by a client application made in Macromedia Director™. This program has considerable multimedia capability, so it is used to implement 2BeOn's interface and interaction front-end. All the interoperability and interrelationships between communication and management services are controlled by this application.

The transmission of information is supported by *Active Server Pages* (ASP) using the POST method (from HTTP Protocol) through Open Database Connectivity. The model *Director<->ASP<->SQL Server* allows communication to be established between the user interface, supported by Director, and the centralised information in the relational database. Alongside this, peer-to-peer communication is implemented to allow direct exchange of messages between users, releasing the server from unnecessary traffic. For a server-client type of communication the system makes use of Macromedia's proprietary multi-user server.

3.4 Interface Design

The interface design process is being undertaken in parallel with the technical implementation phase. Figure 2 shows some drafts of the 2BeOn interface.

Fig. 2. 2BeOn interface draft

Graphic Design. The resolution limitations associated with the TV screen affect the direct use of web design techniques [12]. In this context, special attention must be given to all screen information (text, graphics distortion, colors) that overlap or surround the video content [13].

Interaction Design. The following considerations have influenced the interaction design.

- Navigation – in contrast to other ITV systems, 2BeOn uses a remote control with a pointing device that works like a wireless mouse. In addition, a set of shortcut keys whose colors match those of the active icons can be used.
- Options – in a broad sense, options are displayed as lists, pop-ups and icons. They are mainly activated by means of Direct Manipulation techniques, as defended by Shneiderman [14]. The aim is to give the users the capacity to visually access and interact with information and objects by drag and drop operations.

3.5 Interoperability of Software Agents

The system goes further than simple usage of the communication services discussed here. It aims to take advantage of the interrelation of those services through customised and customisable software agents. By dealing with information from different services and from the online database, these can provide a more complete answer to user needs or requests. For example, when a clip-email is sent, different formats and output devices (PC, TV or mobile) can be used at the destination, depending on the user's status. The system always tries to deliver the message through the communication device that should reach the recipient in a more efficient and direct way. This implies constant interaction with the database in order to get updated information on users' profiles and status.

4. System evaluation

System evaluation made so far been informal was based on personal interviews supported by interactive demos. This has shown that the concept of integration of communication services is pleasing to those users interviewed. The option to allow users to opt for privacy in certain circumstances is seen as a desired/obligatory feature. Users foresee that the ways they will use the system will depend on a variety of factors, namely if they are tired or relaxed and if the friends found online are the ones with whom they want to correspond.

Research topics identified during the article will be evaluated by two main procedures:

- online questionnaires supported by multimedia demonstrations of the system's features;
- qualitative and quantitative testing of the working prototype in domestic environments, followed up by personal interviews.

Two sets of users will be questioned: domestic users, with different levels of technological literacy, and experts on the field.

Register mechanisms built into the system to monitor users' interactions (clicked icons, actions performed and mean time spent) will aid the research team to identify changes needed to the inner structure of the system.

Such system adjustments aim to improve effectiveness of the application taking into account the heuristics proposed by Jakob Nielsen [15] or the interface characteristics identified by Shneiderman: ease of learning, high speed of usage, low user error, user satisfaction and user loyalty [16].

5. Parallel Research - Telework

As referred, the 2BeOn system through its core components is also being applied to the telework research area, where the PC is the main output device, although TV and mobile devices are also addressed. The telematic services and collaborative features of the 2BeOn system also give it the ability to support communication and management activities needed for mobile work.

Remote workers face the challenge of using different communication services to keep in touch with their work team and organisational culture. Despite recent progress in communication technologies and protocols *'the poor convergence towards a user model*' [17] is still noticeable. A strategy of interrelation between services integrated through a common interface can lead to reduction of usage difficulties[2]. Olsen notes that the limitations of human learning force us to aim for a convergence of interactive styles [19]. Such integration is not limited to the interface, it may be exploited by software agents to give users more assistance in situations such as automatic management of messages and tasks or tracking competencies.

Furthermore, users may want to access virtual communities anytime, anywhere and independently of the input/output devices used. For that, a strategy of server centred profiles must be adopted. A unique individual login allows a user to access all his or her updated information (profile, buddy list, messages or tasks) from any device.

Through the development of the 2BeOn system for remote work scenarios, answers to the following research concerns are sought:

- The need for teleworkers to have an equal level of communication with their co-workers as the one they had before teleworking [20]. This requires identification of the best integration metric for communication and management services. The research field of Computer Supported Cooperative Work has mainly focused on the development of independent communication services, without considering their interrelation and integration in a uniform interface [21];
- How the integration of communication and management services within the same system, complemented with automatic support mechanisms, is able to improve communication between co-workers;
- The impact of a tool for dynamic creation of work groups, available in 2BeOn, on the promotion of work communities;
- How the system supports work progress by synchronising processes and helping users to find information, tracking competencies or controlling users' personal or other tasks?

6. Future Research

During the current phase of prototype development, an increasing number of potential applications of the system to entertainment have been identified. Among them, it is planned to try out a TV Interactive contest that makes use of the collaborative features of 2BeOn. The contest, a kind of mystery game, is 'played' by distributed teams represented by a leader at the TV studio. Each leader is faced with local challenges and helped in his mission by the exchange of messages with his team peers, watching the contest at home. Spectators can see the TV broadcast of the contest, monitor the exchange of messages and even play along by participating in a polling system.

In the present scenario of proliferation of TV channels, it is possible to house large affinity groups (such as sailing fans, history lovers, fashion devotees) but it will be difficult to address other more specialist groups which correspond to relatively small TV audiences. Nevertheless, some web procedures that support niche groups, like information sharing and discussion forums, could be translated to the Television arena

[2] The Groove project, www.groove.net, is an example of this effort. However, interface adaptative features still need to be implemented as stated by Herring [18].

using suitable interactive technologies that facilitate peer-to-peer communication. 2BeOn, through some of its proposed features, is already a start-up base to further research in this area.

References

1. http://www.aol.com/aim/home.html (03-06-2001)
2. http://web.icq.com/ (03-06-2001)
3. Jaaskelainem, K.: Strategic Questions in the Development of Interactive Television Programs, Publication series of the University of Art and Design Helsinki UIAH A 31, Ph.D. Thesis, Media Laboratory of University of Arts and Design, Helsinki (2001)
4. Voes, L.: Searching for the Holy Grail - Images of Interactive Television, MSc. Dissertation, University of Utrecht, Department of Media and Communication, Amsterdam (2000)
5. Stewart, J.: Interactive television at home: Television meets the Internet. In: Interactive Television. TV of the Future or the Future of TV?, Aalborg University Press - Media & Cultural Studies 1 (1999) 232-233
6. Wolton, D.: Penser la communication, Paris: Flammarion (1997)
7. Abreu, J., Silva, L.: Televisão Interactiva: do imaginário à realidade – Interactive Television: from the imaginary to the reality. IV Lusocom, S. Vicente, Brasil. In: Eptic online, vol. II nº1, (http://www.eptic.he.com.br/revista/rv2.htm) (2000)
8. http://www.aoltv.com/ (29-07-2001)
9. http://www.opentv.com/interactive/ (29-07-2001)
10. Nardi, B., Whittaker, S. and Bradner, E.: Interaction and Outeraction: Instant Messaging in Action. In: Proceedings CSCW'2000, ACM Press (2000)
11. Hagel, J., Armstrong: Net Gain, Expanding Markets through Virtual Communities. Boston: Harvard Business School Press. ISBN 0-87584-759-5 (1997)
12. Green, M., Senders, J.: The Killer App is TV - Designing the Digital TV Interface; Ergo/Gero - Human Factors Science (1999)
13. Jorgensen, P.: BRAINS - The details of iTV production, in EUROPEMEDIA.NET, http://www.europemedia.net/showfeature.asp?ArticleID=2691 (18-04-2001) (2001)
14. Shneiderman, B. and Maes, P.: Direct Manipulation Vs Interface Agents. In: Interfaces, ACM – 1072-5520/97/1100 (1997)
15. Nielsen, J., and Molich, R.: Heuristic evaluation of user interfaces. In: Proc. ACM CHI'90 Conf. (Seattle, WA, 1-5 April 1990) 249-256
16. Shneiderman, B.: Designing the user interface: strategies for effective human-computer interaction. 3rd edition – Addison-Wesley (1998)
17. Almeida, P., Mealha, Ó.: Conceptualising a telework environment. In: Proceedings from The 5th International Telework Workshop - Telework 2000, Sweden (2000)
18. Herring, Charles Edward: Groove: A Case Study in Adaptive Architecture. In: proceedings of 5th SCI, Orlando, Florida (2001)
19. Olsen, D. R. Jr.: Interacting in Chaos. Computer Science Dep., Brigham Young Univ., USA (1998). In: http://icie.cs.byu.edu/papers/Interactinginchaos (22-03-2000)
20. Nilles, J.: Telework: enabling distributed organisations. In: Information Systems Management 124(4):7-14 (1997)
21. Cartensen, Peter H., Schmidt, Kjeld: Computer Supported Cooperative Work: New Challenges to Systems Design. Handbook of Human Factors, Kenji Itoh (ed.), Tokyo (1999)

Effective Exercise Instruction System Using Virtual Human (Demo)

Yoshikazu Itami, Norimasa Yoshida and Katsuhiro Kitajima

Tokyo University of Agriculture and Technology, Departmentof Computer Science
E-mail: y@itami.com, norimasa@cc.tuat.ac.jp, kitajima@cc.tuat.ac.jp

Abstract
This study aims at developing an aerobics exercise instruction software for personal use by introducing an instruction program best fit to the physical conditions of respective exerciser. The software uses the combination of virtual instructor (virtual human) and *Karvonen* method in order to develop a comprehensive personal aerobics exercise instruction software. Karvonen method is an algorithm of relationship between the movement of the virtual human and exercise intensity. In this study, its effectiveness is verified and confirmed.
The study is mainly focused on the development of synchronization technique between the speed of animation figures' movement for controlling exercise intensity and speed of the sound output, which is the most important technique in the application of the study result into practical use.

GPSR Compliance

The European Union's (EU) General Product Safety Regulation (GPSR) is a set of rules that requires consumer products to be safe and our obligations to ensure this.

If you have any concerns about our products, you can contact us on ProductSafety@springernature.com

In case Publisher is established outside the EU, the EU authorized representative is:

Springer Nature Customer Service Center GmbH
Europaplatz 3
69115 Heidelberg, Germany

Batch number: 10584556

Printed by Printforce, the Netherlands